International Political Economy Series

Series Editor

Timothy M. Shaw
Visiting Professor
University of Massachusetts Boston, USA

Emeritus Professor
University of London, UK

Aim of the Series

The global political economy is in flux as a series of cumulative crises impacts its organization and governance. The IPE series has tracked its development in both analysis and structure over the last three decades. It has always had a concentration on the global South. Now the South increasingly challenges the North as the centre of development, also reflected in a growing number of submissions and publications on indebted Eurozone economies in Southern Europe. An indispensable resource for scholars and researchers, the series examines a variety of capitalisms and connections by focusing on emerging economies, companies and sectors, debates and policies. It informs diverse policy communities as the established trans-Atlantic North declines and 'the rest', especially the BRICS, rise.

More information about this series at
http://www.springer.com/series/13996

Sebastian Krapohl
Editor

Regional Integration in the Global South

External Influence on Economic Cooperation in ASEAN, MERCOSUR and SADC

Editor
Sebastian Krapohl
University of Amsterdam
Amsterdam, The Netherlands

International Political Economy Series
ISBN 978-3-319-81770-5   ISBN 978-3-319-38895-3   (eBook)
DOI 10.1007/978-3-319-38895-3

© The Editor(s) (if applicable) and The Author(s) 2017
Softcover reprint of the hardcover 1st edition 2016
This work is subject to copyright. All rights are solely and exclusively licensed by the Publisher, whether the whole or part of the material is concerned, specifically the rights of translation, reprinting, reuse of illustrations, recitation, broadcasting, reproduction on microfilms or in any other physical way, and transmission or information storage and retrieval, electronic adaptation, computer software, or by similar or dissimilar methodology now known or hereafter developed.
The use of general descriptive names, registered names, trademarks, service marks, etc. in this publication does not imply, even in the absence of a specific statement, that such names are exempt from the relevant protective laws and regulations and therefore free for general use.
The publisher, the authors and the editors are safe to assume that the advice and information in this book are believed to be true and accurate at the date of publication. Neither the publisher nor the authors or the editors give a warranty, express or implied, with respect to the material contained herein or for any errors or omissions that may have been made.

Cover image © Rob Friedman/iStockphoto.com

Printed on acid-free paper

This Palgrave Macmillan imprint is published by Springer Nature
The registered company is Springer International Publishing AG
The registered company address is: Gewerbestrasse 11, 6330 Cham, Switzerland

For Paula and Sarah

Preface

The Genesis of This Book

The starting point for this book was rather unusual for academic work; it came about at Etosha National Park during a holiday trip through Namibia. At the entrance gate, I noticed a sign saying that visitors who were citizens of an SADC member state were allowed to visit the park for a reduced entrance fee. As a student of European politics (I was just about to finish my PhD project on risk regulation in the European Single Market), I had never heard of this mysterious SADC before. Upon returning to Germany, I started to read up on the topic. I found out that SADC is the abbreviation for the 'Southern African Development Community'—an organisation of Southern African states that aim to integrate regionally in order to face the challenges of globalisation and economic development. And SADC is of course not the only regional organisation with such aims; the Association of Southeast Asian Nations (ASEAN) and the Common Market of South America (MERCOSUR) are other prominent examples of regional organisations that imitate the famous European example of regional integration—although with very different regional institutions than the European Union (EU) and with much less success. I noticed very quickly that the classic European integration theories—neofunctionalism, intergovernmentalism and the various forms of institutionalism—can hardly be applied to these regional organisations in the developing world and that they are unable to explain the temporary successes and failures of regional integration in Southeast Asia, South America and Southern Africa. I thus asked myself how the ups and downs of regional integration in developing regions could be explained if the classic integration theories cannot be used. The idea for my next research project was born.

It soon turned out that I alone was not able to manage the task of developing a new theoretical framework and applying it to three different world regions. I knew too little about Southeast Asia, South America and Southern Africa, and too much research needed to be done in order to understand these three regions. Consequently, I tried to get master's and PhD students at the University of Bamberg—where I was Assistant Professor of International Relations—interested in the topic of regional integration in the developing world. This resulted in the Bamberg Cluster of Regional Integration (BaCRI), wherein several master's and PhD students wrote their theses about regional integration in one of these three world regions. We were also able to gain the methodological support of another assistant professor—Dr Simon Fink, Assistant Professor of Comparative Politics—for our project. The authors of this book—Simon Fink, Katharina Meissner, Johannes Muntschick, Daniel Rempe and I—are the inner circle of BaCRI, but other participants of BaCRI—Julia Dinkel, Benjamin Faude and Axel Obermeier—also contributed significantly to our research. I take this opportunity to thank all these colleagues for their cooperation during all these years. Without them, this project would not have been possible.

What followed after constituting BaCRI was the most enjoyable but also most demanding part of academic work; we did field research within the ASEAN, the MERCOSUR and the SADC. We visited Argentina, Botswana, Chile, Indonesia, Uruguay, Singapore and South Africa in order to interview politicians, scholars and stakeholders in the three regional organisations. We thank all our interview partners for their patience with us and for their efforts to explain to us the particularities of their respective regions. I noticed during these interviews that it was difficult to focus on the respective regions alone. Interview partners often deviated to supposedly non-regional topics like the economic interests of Brazil on the world market, South Africa's relations with the EU or the cooperation of the ASEAN with China, Japan and South Korea. Such extra-regional topics were much more prominent than I ever noticed during my studies of European integration. It seemed that regional integration in Southeast Asia, South America and Southern Africa could not be understood without taking extra-regional factors into account. This insight builds the core of this book's argument, which is that despite the economic boom of some emerging markets during the last ten years, developing regions are still rather dependent on investments from and exports to other world regions. Regional integration can improve the standing of developing regions in the competition for investment and export shares, but the influence of extra-regional actors can also be a severe obstacle for regional integration in the developing world if member states' extra-regional interests are in conflict with their regional ones.

Our project had a lot of friends in the academic world who supported us with their comments and encouragement. Prof. Dr Anja Jetschke and Prof. Dr Tobias Lenz from the University of Göttingen, Prof. Dr Dirk Nabers from the University of Kiel, Prof. Dr Berthold Rittberger from the University of Munich, Prof. Dr Jürgen Rüland from the University of Freiburg, Prof. Dr Stefan Schirm from the University of Bochum and Prof. Dr Alexander Warleigh-Lack from the University of Surrey repeatedly discussed parts of our project with us. We always appreciated their challenging comments, which helped us greatly in improving our work. We often met with Dr Laura Carsten-Mahrenbach from Dresden University of Technology, Dr Arie Krampf from Tel Aviv Yaffo Academic College, Dr Frank Mattheis from the University of Leipzig and Dr Jens-Uwe Wunderlich from Aston University in Birmingham at academic conferences, and we had very fruitful discussions with them. Prof. Dr Tanja Börzel and Prof. Dr Thomas Risse, who are directing the research group 'The Transformative Power of Europe' at the Free University of Berlin, invited me several times to very productive and interesting conferences in Berlin. Dr Leo Lay Hwee from the European Union Centre in Singapore hosted Axel Obermeier and myself during our research trips to Southeast Asia. Prof. Dr Trudi Hartzenberg from the Trade Law Centre (tralac) in Cape Town invited me to a conference that brought my knowledge of trade policy in Southern Africa up to date. We thank all of them for their help.

Most important for the success of our project was surely the material and immaterial support we received from the University of Bamberg and most notably from Prof. Dr Thomas Gehring. Thomas not only commented on half-cooked working papers time and again, but also provided necessary financial support for research trips through his Chair for International Relations. We are also highly indebted to the graduate school Markets and Social Systems in Europe at the University of Bamberg, which granted PhD fellowships to Johannes Muntschick and Axel Obermeier. Along with this, the internal research support of the University of Bamberg helped us to finance research trips, as well as student assistants in order to produce our network graphs of regional trade data. I finished my work for this book at my new position as Assistant Professor of International Relations at the University of Amsterdam. I thank my new colleagues, especially Prof. Dr Brian Burgoon and Prof. Dr Geoffrey Underhill, for accompanying me in this journey.

Finally, I thank the editorial team of Palgrave Macmillan, one anonymous reviewer and the series editor Prof. Dr Timothy Shaw for all their support during the final stage of the project.

Sebastian Krapohl
Amsterdam
The Netherlands

Contents

1	Introduction Sebastian Krapohl	1
Part 1	Theory and Methods	31
2	Two Logics of Regional Integration and the Games Regional Actors Play Sebastian Krapohl	33
3	Case Selection and Research Methods for a Comparative Analysis of Developing Regions Sebastian Krapohl	63
Part II	The Economic Structures of Different World Regions	89
4	Trade Network Analyses Simon Fink and Daniel Rempe	91

Part III Cases of Regional Cooperation and Defection in Developing Regions   113

5 ASEAN   115
Sebastian Krapohl

6 MERCOSUR   147
Katharina L. Meissner

7 SADC   179
Johannes Muntschick

Part IV Concluding Remarks   209

8 Conclusion   211
Sebastian Krapohl

Index   237

Abbreviations

ACFTA	ASEAN-China Free Trade Area
ACP countries	African, Caribbean and Pacific countries
AEC	ASEAN Economic Community
AFTA	ASEAN Free Trade Area
AMF	Asian Monetary Fund
APEC	Asia-Pacific Economic Cooperation
APTA	Asia-Pacific Trade Agreement
ASEAN	Association of Southeast Asian Nations
ASEAN+3	Association of Southeast Asian Nations plus China, Japan and South Korea
ASEM	Asia-Europe Meeting
BLNS countries	Botswana, Lesotho, Namibia and Swaziland
CAN	*Comunidad Andina de Naciones* (Andean Community)
CEMAC	Economic and Monetary Community of Central Africa
CEPT scheme	Common Effective Preferential Tariff scheme
CLMV countries	Cambodia, Laos, Myanmar and Vietnam
CMI	Chiang Mai Initiative
CMIM	Chiang Mai Initiative Multilateralization
COMESA	Common Market for Eastern and Southern Africa
EAC	East African Community or East Asian Community
EAS	East Asian Summit
EBA	everything-but-arms
EC	European Community
ECJ	European Court of Justice
ECOWAS	Economic Community of West African States
EDF(s)	European Development Fund(s)
EFTA	European Free Trade Association

EPA(s)	Economic Partnership Agreement(s)
EU	European Union
FDI	foreign direct investment
GATT	General Agreement on Tariffs and Trade
GDP	gross domestic product
IAI	Initiative on ASEAN Integration
ICJ	International Court of Justice
IMF	International Monetary Fund
LDCs	least developed countries
MERCOSUR	*Mercado Común del Sur* (Common Market of South America)
MERCOSUR-CU	customs union of the *Mercado Común del Sur* (Common Market of South America)
PICTA	Pacific Island Countries Trade Agreement
RIKS	Regional Indicators Knowledge System
RISDP	Regional Indicative Strategic Development Plan
SAARC	South Asian Association for Regional Cooperation
SACU	Southern African Customs Union
SADC	Southern African Development Community
SADCC	Southern African Development Cooperation Conference
SADC-CU	customs union of the Southern African Development Community
SADC-FTA	free trade area of the Southern African Development Community
TAC	Treaty of Amity and Cooperation
TDCA	Trade, Development and Cooperation Agreement
TFTA	Tripartite Free Trade Area of the Common Market for Eastern and Southern Africa, the East African Community and the Southern African Development Community
TPP	Trans-Pacific Partnership Agreement
UK	United Kingdom of Great Britain and Northern Ireland
UNASUR	Union of South American Nations
UNU-CRIS	United Nations University Institute on Comparative Regional Integration Studies
US(A)	United States (of America)
WTO	World Trade Organization
ZOPFAN	Zone of Peace, Freedom and Neutrality

List of Figures

Fig. 2.1	Typology of collective goods	37
Fig. 2.2	Prisoner's dilemma and battle of the sexes within the intraregional logic	38
Fig. 2.3	Battle of the sexes and the Rambo situation within the extra-regional logic	47
Fig. 3.1	The causal mechanisms behind regional cooperation and defection	79
Fig. 4.1	Interpretation scheme for network graphs	94
Fig. 4.2	Evolution of the EC trade network from 1965 to 1980	97
Fig. 4.3	Trade interdependence in the EC in 1985	98
Fig. 4.4	Evolution of the ASEAN trade network from 1990 to 2005	100
Fig. 4.5	Trade interdependence in ASEAN in 2010	101
Fig. 4.6	Evolution of the MERCOSUR trade network from 1990 to 2005	103
Fig. 4.7	Trade interdependence in MERCOSUR in 2010	104
Fig. 4.8	Evolution of the SADC trade network from 1990 to 2005	106
Fig. 4.9	Trade interdependence in SADC in 2010	107

List of Tables

Table 3.1	Economic development and intraregional trade of selected regional organisations in 2010	69
Table 3.2	Heterogeneity of the sample in 2010	71
Table 3.3	Observable implications of the causal mechanisms	80
Table 5.1	The three most important export destinations of the ASEAN member states in 1991	119
Table 5.2	The three most important export destinations of the ASEAN member states in 2006	132
Table 6.1	The three most important export destinations of the MERCOSUR member states in 1991	150
Table 6.2	The three most important export destinations of the MERCOSUR member states in 1998	157
Table 6.3	The three most important export destinations of the MERCOSUR member states in 2006	163
Table 7.1	The three most important export destinations of the SADC member states in 1995	183
Table 7.2	The three most important export destinations of the SADC member states in 2008	192

CHAPTER 1

Introduction

Integration Theory and the New Regionalism

Sebastian Krapohl

The latest wave of 'new regionalism' in the 1990s led to the establishment of regional organisations in all regions of the developing worlds. Nearly all developing countries are members of at least one and often more regional organisations in order to escape marginalisation on the global market. Today, 20 years later, one can observe that the development of these regional organisations has been far from uniform; rather, it is distinguished by geographical and temporal variance. Some regional organisations, for example, the Association of Southeast Asian Nations (ASEAN), are much more advanced in their integration efforts than others, for example, the South Asian Association for Regional Cooperation (SAARC). And whereas some developing regions cooperate successfully for certain periods of time, for example, the Common Market of South America (MERCOSUR) in the 1990s, they face huge problems during other periods, for example, the same region at the beginning of the new millennium. This geographical and temporal variance in regional cooperation and defection among developing countries is in need of an explanation (Krapohl et al. 2014).

S. Krapohl (✉)
University of Amsterdam, Amsterdam, The Netherlands
e-mail: s.krapohl@uva.nl

© The Author(s) 2017
S. Krapohl (ed.), *Regional Integration in the Global South*,
International Political Economy Series,
DOI 10.1007/978-3-319-38895-3_1

Regionalism in the developing world is a widespread phenomenon, but our theoretical understanding of it is rather limited. There is widespread agreement in the academic literature that regional integration among developing regions is more difficult to achieve than among well-developed regions (Mattli 1999a),[1] because intraregional economic interdependence is usually much lower within developing regions than within those that are well developed. However, this does not explain why developing regions try to integrate time and again and why they successfully cooperate for at least certain periods of time, and fail to do so for others.

The main argument of this book is that extra-regional factors have a decisive influence on regional integration efforts in the developing world. Regional integration in well-developed regions like the European Union (EU) is based on huge economic interdependence between the member states. Here, the main rationale for regional integration is to liberalise and regulate intraregional trade and investment in order to utilise comparative cost advantages and economies of scale on the regional market (Mattli 1999a). In contrast, developing regions cannot profit as much from intraregional trade and investment, because their most important economic partners are located in other world regions like Europe, North America and Northeast Asia. In course of the new regionalism, developing regions aim to integrate in order to improve their economic competitiveness on the global market and their relations with extra-regional economic partners. Regional integration bears positive size and stability effects, which make well-integrated regions more attractive as trading partners and addressees of investments. But this outward orientation also implies that the reaction of extra-regional actors on regional integration efforts in the developing world has a decisive influence on its success.

The reason why political science has so far failed to provide a convincing explanation of regional integration in the developing world is the often bemoaned divide between EU studies and comparative regionalism literature (Söderbaum and Sbragia 2011; Warleigh-Lack and Rosamond 2010; Warleigh-Lack and Van Langenhove 2011). The various European integration theories provide a well-developed toolbox for analysing European integration, but they do not conceptualise the extra-regional logic of regional integration. The classic integration theories—namely, neofunctionalism (e.g. Haas 1958; Lindberg and Scheingold 1970) and liberal intergovernmentalism (Moravcsik 1993, 1998)—were mainly developed before the background of the famous European example of regional integration. Although the early neofunctionalists tried to apply their theory to other cases of regional integration (Haas 1967; Nye 1968; Schmitter 1970), they soon became frustrated, and EU studies became an independent field of research. Since then, the cultural, economic and political background conditions for integration theories have been hardly discussed in EU studies. Instead, the specific circumstances for regional integration in Europe are taken for granted and are not discussed explicitly. Consequently, European integration theories cannot really explain what is going on in developing regions, where the cultural, economic and political circumstances for regional integration are quite different from the European case.

In contrast, the comparative regionalism literature provides in-depth empirical knowledge about regionalism in the Global South, but it still lacks a well-developed toolbox like the European integration theories. Much of the early comparative regionalism literature developed from the field of area studies and was the domain of specialists in different world regions. Despite belonging to the field of comparative regionalism, the respective analyses are not often comparative themselves, but they concentrate only on single regions (e.g. Acharya 1993; Lee 1989; Schirm 1997). Edited volumes provide first comparisons, but they usually lack a common framework to guide the empirical analyses (e.g. De Melo and Panagariya 1993; Fawcett and Hurrell 1995; Gamble and Payne 1996). The literature became more theoretical during the 1990s when the latest wave of regionalism led to new academic awareness of the topic (Mansfield and Milner 1999). However, the 'new regionalism' literature (e.g. Breslin et al. 2002; Hettne 1999, 2005; Hettne and Söderbaum 2000; Preusse 2004; Shaw et al. 2011) usually stresses the differences of regionalism in other world regions from the famous European example. As a result, this literature states that the European integration theories cannot be applied to other world regions and that different theoretical approaches are needed instead. There are only a few analyses from political economists that explicitly compare European integration with other cases of regional integration (Mattli 1999a; Schirm 2002). This literature gives first insights into the motivation and obstacles for regional integration in the developing world, but they fail to explain under which circumstances developing regions are able to cooperate successfully and under which circumstances regional cooperation is likely to fail.

A gap exists between well-developed European integration theories, which cannot simply be applied to other cases of regional integration, and the study of comparative regionalism, which lacks well-developed integration theories. A comparative analysis that aims to explore under which circumstances regional cooperation among developing countries is likely to proceed or to stagnate falls through this gap within the academic literature. Thus, a theoretical framework is needed to fill this gap by taking care of the special background conditions of regional integration in developing regions while simultaneously including the theoretical insights from EU studies.

1 REGIONAL INTEGRATION: A TERM IN SEARCH OF A DEFINITION

The gap between European integration theories and regional integration in other parts of the world is already visible in the definition of the term 'regional integration' in EU studies. Here, regional integration is often seen as a process in which state sovereignty is further and further delegated to supranational institutions at the regional level (Börzel 2013). The problem with applying such a definition is that only the EU would qualify as an example of regional integration, whereas all other regional organisations around the world would not. Nowhere except in Europe are regional institutions strong enough to claim jurisdiction over their member states. The strength of the European Commission, the European Court of Justice (ECJ) and the European Parliament is unmatched by regional institutions in other world regions. In contrast, most regional organisations outside of Europe are much more intergovernmental in nature and have only weak regional institutions. Consequently, if one aims to compare regional integration in other world regions outside of Europe, a broader definition is needed that is less demanding with respect to supranational institutions.

In contrast to international regimes (Keohane 1984; Krasner 1982), regional organisations cannot be regarded as issue-specific but rather must be seen as region-specific cooperation projects. Whereas issue-specific regimes concentrate on only one policy area and include all states interested in the specific cooperation project, regional organisations operate in different policy areas, but their membership is geographically limited to a certain world region and does not change much between policy areas (although there may be opt-outs for single policies; see Leuffen et al. 2013). Although the different cooperation projects of regional organisations can be aimed at one general goal like market integration, this can nevertheless take place in different issue areas like the creation of transnational infrastructure, the provision of regional security, the abolishment of tariffs, the harmonisation of product regulations and the stabilisation of exchange rates.

Given this character of regional organisations as region-specific but not issue-specific cooperation projects, we define regional integration as a process of iterated cooperation that leads to an ever-increasing web of substantive and procedural institutions at the regional level. Thus, regional integration may—not must—be achieved through the delegation of sovereignty to supranational institutions. And regional integration may—again, not must—take the form of one-dimensional movement from a free-trade area via a customs union, a common market and a currency union towards an economic and political union (Balassa 1961). But regional integration can also be a purely intergovernmental and less predictable process wherein regional cooperation in different policy areas may proceed at different speeds, which in sum leads to an ever-denser web of regional commitments.

Our focus on cooperation or defection of the regional member states implies that regional integration is a political endeavour. Thereby, we distinguish purely economic developments from political projects. This is necessary, because we aim to explore the influence of the former on the latter. If economic actors start to trade and invest more within the region, and if member states' markets grow more and more together in economic terms, we speak of growing economic interdependence, but not of regional integration. Growing economic interdependence may have a positive effect on regional (political) integration, but the economic and political processes are two distinguishable phenomena, and we are interested in the causal relationship between them. We also assume that regional (political) integration may take place in the absence of high economic interdependence, and that it may only lead to growing intraregional trade and investment in the long run.

A broader definition of regional integration not only has the advantage of including integration processes in world regions other than Europe, it also opens the toolbox of cooperation theory. Even if there are important differences between issue-specific regimes and membership-specific regional organisations, the definition of regional integration as a regional cluster of cooperation projects allows us to apply cooperation theory to specific cases of regional cooperation, as has already been done with many rational institutionalist approaches to European integration (e.g. Pollack 1997, 2003). Thus, the focus of analysis shifts from a macro-level comparison of different integration processes in different world regions towards a micro-level analysis of different cases of regional cooperation or defection. The controversial issue of comparability (De Lombaerde et al. 2010) should be much less problematic if cases of regional cooperation or defection instead of entire regional organisations are compared.

2 European Integration Theories

The problem with the classic integration theories is that they were developed to explain the famous European case with its unique background conditions for regional integration. The EU is obviously the most integrated regional organisation in the world, and it serves as a role model for regional integration processes elsewhere.[2] However, Europe differs in many respects from the other world regions to where the model of regional integration is transferred. With respect to economic terms, the most important of these background conditions is the high and ever-increasing degree of economic interdependence within the European Community (EC) and later the EU. Since the very beginning, trade among the EC/EU member states has always been more important than trade with extra-regional partners, and this intraregional interdependence has further increased over the course of European integration (Krapohl and Fink 2013). This economic characteristic of the European region is reflected—usually implicitly rather than explicitly—in all major integration theories.

The importance of intraregional economic interdependence is most evident for neofunctionalism and its concept of spillover (Haas 1958; Lindberg and Scheingold 1970; Schmitter 1970). According to neofunctionalism, once regional integration has been started through a deliberate decision of member states, it becomes a more or less automatic process beyond the control of these states. The reasons behind this are several spillover processes (Tranholm-Mikkelsen 1991). Firstly, a functional spillover occurs when integration in one area leads to functional pressure to integrate other areas as well, so as not to lose the full benefits from integration. Secondly, a political spillover emerges when political actors shift their loyalties and demands towards the new political centre at the European level. Finally, cultivated spillover is the result of the action of supranational actors like the Commission or the ECJ, which use their competencies to push the process of regional integration even further.

At least the recurrence of functional spillovers is dependent on high degrees of intraregional economic interdependence. In order for functional spillovers to occur, integration in one policy area needs to produce negative externalities for other policy areas. These negative externalities then produce functional pressure to cooperate as well in the other policy areas in order to make full use of the benefits of regional integration. However, transnational economic exchange within the regions is necessary in order for such negative externalities to occur. For example, regional market liberalisation may lead to functional needs for harmonised product regulations in order to protect consumers (Krapohl 2008), but only under the precondition that the regional market is utilised by economic actors. The legal creation of a regional market does not endanger the regulatory sovereignty of the member states if no goods are traded across intraregional borders. Without intraregional trade, the member states can still regulate their markets with domestic standards, and further regional cooperation in order to harmonise regulatory standards is not necessary. Thus, without the transmission belt of intraregional economic interdependence, functional spillovers cannot take place, and regional integration does not develop dynamics on its own.

Despite the development of neofunctionalism in the context of European integration, the early neofunctionalists tried to apply this theory to other regional organisations (Nye 1968), especially in South America (Haas 1967; Haas and Schmitter 1964). However, these attempts quickly frustrated these scholars because they were not able to find spillover processes similar to Europe's within other world regions. The political resistance of national governments time and again prevented the self-reinforcing dynamics of regional integration in world regions other than Europe. At the same time, when comparative approaches to regional integration proved unsatisfying, the European integration process entered troubled waters. The French president Charles de Gaulle provoked the so-called empty chair crisis during the 1960s, and the resulting Luxembourg compromise de facto reintroduced unanimity rule in the Council of Ministers. This high threshold for decision-making became an obstacle for further integration and led to a period of Eurosclerosis. As a result, Haas himself declared the 'Obsolescence of Regional Integration Theory' (Haas 1975)—a premature and overly pessimistic step from a present-day point of view.

The importance of intraregional economic interdependence for liberal intergovernmentalism is less obvious than for neofunctionalism, but Moravcsik (1993, 1998) nevertheless sees intraregional economic interests as the main reason for regional integration. Within the first step of Moravcsik's argument, interest groups within the member states of regional organisations (here: the EU) address their national governments with their particular interests. In respect to European integration, economic interests are likely to prevail within the domestic struggle. Within the second step, the asymmetry of member states' interests determine the bargaining outcome at the regional level. Member states with strong interests in regional cooperation have the most to lose and are more likely to make concessions than their counterparts, which may leave the negotiation table more easily. Finally, once an agreement has been found, the member states delegate a limited range of competencies to supranational institutions in order to commit themselves credibly to their agreements. In what follows, these supranational institutions are regarded as too weak to influence the future process of regional integration.

Whereas the intergovernmental mode of decision-making can easily be transferred from the case of European integration to other world regions, liberal intergovernmentalism nevertheless relies on intraregional economic interdependence to explain the more or less constant interests of the EU member states in regional cooperation. In Moravcsik's model, economic interests prevail over security concerns and ideological commitments. And without intraregional interdependence, there would be no need for EU member states to engage time and again in negotiations about treaty reforms. Thus, in its present form, Moravcsik's model proves that the European integration theories take intraregional economic interdependence for granted and do not explicitly discuss the economic background conditions for regional integration. In different economic circumstances, the interests of respective member states in regional cooperation must necessarily be different from those that prevail in well-developed regions like Europe.

In recent years, the academic debate about European integration has not focused as much on the antagonism between neofunctionalism and intergovernmentalism and has rather turned to different institutionalist approaches (Aspinwall and Schneider 2000; Pollack 1996). Here, rational institutionalism (Pollack 1997, 2003) is a further development of Moravcsik's liberal intergovernmentalism. Rational institutionalism takes the supranational institutions of the EU more seriously than liberal intergovernmentalism. Institutionalism asks what functionalist reasons lay behind the establishment of EU institutions and how these institutions influence policymaking once they have been established. However, regional institutions outside of Europe are nowhere near as strong and as independent as the Commission, the ECJ and the European Parliament. According to rational institutionalism, this should indicate that the functional needs for regional commitments are lower in other world regions than in Europe. But so far, rational institutionalism has not explicitly discussed possible explanations for the different degrees of commitment expressed in different regional institutions around the world. As it stands, rational institutionalism takes the strength of the EU's supranational institutions as a rule rather than the exception, and it does not discuss the background conditions for the strength of institutional commitments.

In contrast to rational institutionalism, historical institutionalism and sociological institutionalism stand more in the tradition of neofunctionalism, and they also rely on the background condition of strong intraregional economic interdependence. Stone Sweet and others (Fligstein and Stone Sweet 2002; Stone Sweet and Caporaso 1998) explicitly argue that there is a positive relationship between increasing intraregional trade and regional institution building within the EU. Accordingly, the establishment of a regional market in Europe set in force a virtuous circle of increasing intraregional trade and the establishment of regional norms. Once started, regional market liberalisation leads to more intraregional trade, which in turn leads to more societal demands for regional norms to regulate this trade. When these demands are fulfilled, intraregional trade increases even further, which in turn leads to even more demands for regional norms. This concept of historical and sociological institutionalism concerning a virtuous circle between increasing intraregional interdependence and regional institution building very much resembles the neofunctionalist concept of functional spillovers. Obviously, the virtuous circle cannot emerge if an important link in the circle is missing; in world regions outside of Europe, this missing link is intraregional trade.

The problem with the application of European integration theories to other world regions is that the European theories rely more or less on the background condition of strong intraregional economic interdependence, but this precondition is not a given in developing regions. Despite the economic booms in some emerging markets during the last decade, developing countries and emerging markets still rely heavily on the export of labour-intensive goods, agricultural products and raw materials, and the markets for these goods are not within their own regions but within the well-developed regions of Europe, North America and Northeast Asia. Thus, in the developing world, intraregional economic interdependence is much lower than within Europe (Krapohl and Fink 2013). For example, nowhere in developing regions does the share of intraregional trade exceed about 25 per cent, whereas it is more than 60 per cent in the EU.[3] As a result, spillover processes are less likely to take place in developing regions, their member states have a less-stable economic interest in regional integration and a virtuous circle between increasing intraregional trade and regional institution building is unlikely to emerge. But this leaves the open questions of what motivates developing regions to integrate, and under what circumstances might they be successful with such attempts.

3   THE NEW REGIONALISM

The literature on new regionalism starts with the observation that the latest wave of regional integration, beginning in the early 1990s, is the result of the end of the Cold War and of increasing globalisation (Hettne and Söderbaum 2000). Because the antagonism between the capitalist West and the communist East no longer defined the structure of the international system, many countries were able to reorient their foreign policies at the beginning of the 1990s. At the same time, globalisation has made new alliances necessary in order to survive increasing global economic competition. Under these circumstances, new regional patterns of cooperation and institution building have emerged in the international system. According to this view, globalisation and new regionalism are mutually reinforcing and do not impede each other in their development. The result is a new world order (Gamble and Payne 1996; Hettne 2005), in which regions play a much more important role than during the Cold War, when nation-states had to align with either the East or the West.

Economists and political economists are especially interested in the question of what impact new regionalism has on the global trade regime (Mansfield and Milner 1999). Here, the debated topic is whether the 'spaghetti bowl' (Baldwin 2006) of regional trade agreements is a stumbling stone or a building block for global free trade (Baldwin and Seghezza 2010; Dür 2007). With negotiations stalled in the Doha Round of the World Trade Organization (WTO), countries are relying more on regional or bilateral trade agreements in order to liberalise and regulate international trade. On the one hand, these trade agreements can be obstacles to global free trade if trade diversion effects exceed trade creation effects (for the issue of trade diversion vs. trade creation, see Viner 1950). Moreover, if regional trade agreements reduce the political pressure to come to a conclusion in global trade negotiations, the effects on global free trade may be negative as well. On the other hand, regional or bilateral trade agreements can also be a step towards the liberalisation of international trade, if trade creation effects exceed trade diversion effects. In addition, regional trade agreements can be a first step towards market liberalisation in that they make global agreements at the WTO level more likely at later points in time. The question whether the negative or positive effects on global trade prevail is difficult to answer empirically, because answers necessarily rely on counterfactual reasoning. Currently, the more optimistic view on the relationship between regional trade agreements and global free trade seems to more accepted (Baldwin 2006).

The trade diversion effects of new regionalism are mitigated by the fact that the new regional organisations of the 1990s are not so much inward but rather outward looking (Hettne and Söderbaum 2000; Mansfield and Milner 1999; Schirm 2002). Rather than wall off regional markets from global markets, new regionalism usually implies an opening of the respective regions to global markets—thus, it is sometimes also called 'open regionalism' (Bulmer-Thomas 2001; Frankel and Wei 1998). In developing regions, this goes hand in hand with a turning away in development strategies from import substitution towards export promotion. Developing regions used the 'old regionalism' during the 1950s to 1970s in order to protect their markets against imports from other world regions while simultaneously providing the necessary scale effects for industrialisation within their own regions. After the lost decade of the 1980s demonstrated the failure of this development strategy (Krueger 1997), the new regionalism of the 1990s has followed a (neo-)liberal policy paradigm and aimed to strengthen the position of developing regions in the global market. Here, regional integration may support export-promoting development strategies (Bhagwati 1988) by improving regions' economic competitiveness in two respects: Firstly, it may help regional member states to attract investments from extra-regional actors; and secondly, regional member states as a group may have more leverage in international trade negotiations in order to get access to important extra-regional markets.

With respect to the attraction of extra-regional investments, Schirm (2002) argues that regional integration is a deliberate instrument of member states to improve their competitiveness. His argument has an economic as well as a political dimension. Economically, well-integrated regional markets provide economies of scale and more efficient allocations of resources than smaller national markets, which makes them ceteris paribus more attractive for market-seeking and productivity-seeking investments. And politically, regional cooperation helps governments to commit themselves to liberalising reforms against the resistance of domestic opposition, which again improves the regions' attractiveness as destinations for investments. The attraction of investments from other world regions contributes a lot to export-based development strategies in developing regions, as investments lead to increasing production and economic growth. Even if developing regions cannot profit that much from the benefits of intraregional trade, they may nevertheless profit from increasing extra-regional investment inflows.

Regional integration may also improve access to extra-regional export markets if developing regions manage to speak with one voice in international trade negotiations and if this leads to more favourable trade agreements with other world regions. The effect may occur in global as well as in interregional trade negotiations. Firstly, Mansfield and Reinhardt (2003) provide evidence that countries use bilateral or regional trade agreements in order to increase their bargaining power in WTO negotiations. As negotiation groups that are bound together by trade agreements, such member states become more significant actors in these multilateral negotiations, and thus may be able to achieve more favourable results. And secondly, regional integration allows developing countries to engage in interregional trade negotiations with the EU (Aggarwal and Fogarty 2004; Hänggi et al. 2006). Because the EU actively encourages regional integration in other world regions, it offers to negotiate with regional groups of countries instead of individual countries about preferential market access to the European Single Market. The empirical examples for this phenomenon are manifold and include the Asia-Europe Meeting (ASEM), the trade negotiations between the EU and the MERCOSUR as well as the various negotiations about Economic Partnership Agreements (EPAs) between the EU and African countries. Without cooperating regionally, developing countries could not participate in such negotiations, or at least they would have less bargaining power therein. Thus, they face incentives to integrate regionally in order to improve their standing in interregional negotiations. In the end, this may lead to the phenomenon of 'regionalism through interregionalism', in which interregional negotiations become a trigger for regional integration in the developing world (Hänggi 2003). As in the case of investments, the use of regional integration as an instrument to increase bargaining power in international trade negotiations may lead to economic benefits for developing regions. However, these benefits do not result from intraregional economic interdependence, but rather from improved economic interactions with other world regions.

The discussion of the new regionalism literature demonstrates that developing regions may benefit considerably from regional integration, even if they do not possess the economic preconditions for increasing intraregional trade (Shaw and Fanta 2013). In contrast to well-developed regions, these benefits result more from the interaction of developing regions with other world regions than from the interaction of the member states within developing regions themselves. On the one hand, the problem of European integration theories is that they do not conceptualise such extra-regional effects of regional integration. It remains unclear whether the extra-regional effects may trigger spillover processes, whether they lead to stable interests in regional integration or whether a virtuous circle between extra-regional effects and regional institution building can emerge. On the other hand, the new regionalism literature points our attention to the extra-regional effects of regional integration, though it has not yet developed a theoretical framework that matches European integration theories in coherence and precision. The new regionalism literature provides an explanation as to why developing regions may choose to integrate, but it does not explain the geographical and temporal variance of successful and unsuccessful regional cooperation in the developing world. Thus, a theoretical framework is needed that conceptualises the extra-regional dimension of regional integration and develops testable hypotheses about regional cooperation and defection on this basis.

4 Towards a General Theory of Regional Cooperation and Defection

Our theoretical framework for the analysis of regional cooperation and defection starts from the assumption that there is not only one, but there are in fact two logics of regional integration. We call these the intraregional and the extra-regional logics (Krapohl and Muntschick 2009). The intraregional logic is the one that prevails in European integration theories. Here, the member states of regional organisations cooperate in order to benefit from and to regulate intraregional economic interdependence. The extra-regional logic is the one that can be deduced from the new regionalism literature. Here, the member states of regional organisations cooperate in order to achieve gains in their interactions with extra-regional actors. We argue that the cooperation problems within the extra-regional logic differ from those within the intraregional logic and that this has profound impacts on the course of regional integration.

The intraregional logic of regional economic integration builds on the creation of regional markets, that is, the liberalisation and regulation of intraregional trade. The benefits from regional integration within this logic result from the exploitation of comparative cost advantages and economies of scale through intraregional trade (Mattli 1999a). Thus, benefits are higher the more the regional member states are able to trade with each other. It is important to note that the creation of regional markets does not only include the abolition of tariffs and quotas; it may also address the abolishment of non-tariff trade barriers, the free flow of various production factors within the region, the fixing of exchange rates between the member states and the macroeconomic stabilisation of the region. Regional markets are club goods (Casella 1992; Fratianni and Pattison 2001). There is little rivalry among the member states for the consumption of these goods because intraregional trade of one member state does not reduce the utility of regional markets for other member states, and single countries can be excluded from the consumption of the goods by (re-)establishing trade barriers against them. These characteristics of club goods have positive effects for cooperation among the member states and for the provision of the good 'regional market' because there is little competition between the member states and defecting member states can be sanctioned by excluding them from consumption.

In contrast, the extra-regional logic of regional economic integration is based on improving regions' competitiveness on the global market. The benefits of regional integration within this logic take the form of increasing investment inflows from other world regions (Bende-Nabende 2002; Jaumotte 2004) and of better market access to other world regions. The size and stability effects of regional integration—that is, the larger size of integrated regional markets and the political as well as macroeconomic stability of integrated regions—make regions more attractive as destinations for investments and as negotiation partners in international trade negotiations. It is important to note here that the gains from regional integration in this logic are not generated within the regions themselves but from their interaction with other world regions. Extra-regional investment and export flows are common pool resources (Hardin 1968; Ostrom 2003) for the regions concerned. Firstly, there is some degree of rivalry in their consumption because the countries of such regions not only compete with other world regions for these resources but also compete with their regional neighbours. And secondly, single member states cannot simply be excluded from the consumption of investment and export flows. Although single member states can be excluded from regional organisations, this does not necessarily imply that they are excluded from the common pool resources of extra-regional investments and exports. It is extra-regional actors who decide where to invest and whom to grant access to their markets, and these decisions may partly be independent from regional integration efforts. These characteristics of common pool resources make cooperation between regional member states more difficult because they compete with each other for extra-regional investments and exports and they alone cannot sanction defecting member states by excluding them from the consumption of these resources.

The different characteristics of the collective goods produced in the intraregional and the extra-regional logics imply that regional member states face different cooperation problems when producing these goods. Within the intraregional logic, trade liberalisation and trade regulation can be modelled respectively as a prisoner's dilemma and as a battle of the sexes (Garrett and Weingast 1993; Krapohl 2008). When liberalising trade, each regional member state has to decide either to liberalise its domestic market or to protect its domestic producers against competition from imports from other member states. Here, each member state would prefer to protect its domestic market while simultaneously sharing in the advantages of exporting to other member states. If all member states tried to realise this interest, mutual protectionism would be the result, and the member states could not profit from regional markets. Although the prisoner's dilemma is a problematic situation for regional cooperation, an iteration of the game (Axelrod 1984) and strong regional institutions for monitoring and dispute settlement (Pollack 1997) can help member states to cooperate and to achieve the Pareto-superior outcome of mutual market liberalisation. When regulating the resulting intraregional trade, member states probably agree about the need for common regulatory standards for traded goods, but they are likely to disagree about the concrete form of regulatory standards. Thus, they need to choose between several standards with different distributive effects. Such a battle of the sexes is also problematic because agreeing to particular policies is not a trivial task. However, issue linkages and package deals provide possible solutions, and regional institutions may help to reach agreements by setting the agenda or by allowing majority voting to take place (Pollack 1997).

Within the extra-regional logic, the games that the member states of regional organisations play depend on the behaviour of extra-regional actors. Firstly, extra-regional actors may reward regional integration so that all regional member states benefit from increasing extra-regional investment inflows and improved access to extra-regional markets. This does not necessarily imply that the extra-regional benefits of regional integration are symmetrically distributed across the region, but it does imply that all member states profit in absolute terms from cooperation. In this case, the member states play battles of the sexes. They all have an interest in regional integration, but they may disagree about the concrete form of cooperation. Issue linkages, package deals and regional institutions may help them to reach agreements. However, once agreements are reached, compliance cannot be effectively ensured by the regions themselves, but rather extra-regional actors need to sanction non-implementation with declining investment inflows and restricted access to extra-regional markets. Secondly, it may also be that regional integration leads to absolute losses for one or more member states. This happens if the respective member states are able to achieve or maintain privileges in their extra-regional relations when acting unilaterally. For example, privileged member states may enjoy disproportional extra-regional investment inflows, and regional integration may include the risk that such investments get diverted to other member states of the respective regions. Alternatively, privileged member states may have bilateral trade agreements with extra-regional actors, and these agreements may be at odds with deeper regional integration. In such circumstances, the privileged member states become regional Rambos. A Rambo situation is an asymmetrical game in which one player—unlike the other(s)—lacks any incentive to cooperate, and can only lose out if an agreement is reached. This Rambo's dominant strategy is therefore defection (Holzinger 2003; Zürn 1992, 1993). It is important to note that regional institutions cannot help much to ensure the cooperation of Rambos because these do not defect in order to free ride on the cooperation of others (like in a prisoner's dilemma); they instead do not have any interest in regional cooperation on the respective policy issues at all.

Developing regions profit less from the intraregional effects but more from the extra-regional effects of regional integration. Whereas well-developed regions with their diversified economies are able to profit much from comparative cost advantages and economies of scale within regional markets, developing countries, which usually depend on the export of few primary goods or labour-intensive products, do not profit that much from the liberalisation of intraregional trade (Langhammer 1992; Mattli 1999a; Robson 1993; Venables 2003). In contrast, developing regions rely heavily on extra-regional investment inflows and extra-regional export outflows when following an export-promoting development strategy. As a result, the size and stability effects of regional integration may be a valuable instrument to improve the competitiveness of developing regions on the global market. This does not imply that regional integration has no extra-regional effects for well-developed regions or no intraregional effects for developing regions, but the relative weights of the two logics differ. In fact, the importance of the intra- and extra-regional logics of regional integration correlates with economic development. The more the regional economies develop, the more important the intraregional effects become, and the extra-regional effects of regional integration become less important.

Because the demand for regional integration in developing regions mainly results from the extra-regional logic, regional integration can only be supplied as long as no regional power enjoys extra-regional privileges that are at odds with regional integration. Regional powers, that is, member states that dominate their regions in respect to economic power (Kappel 2010; Nolte 2010; Schirm 2010), profit less from the extra-regional effects of regional integration than their smaller neighbours but are more likely to achieve privileges in their extra-regional relations. Regional powers already constitute large and attractive markets on their own, so the additional effects of regionally integrated markets are comparatively low. Regional powers are already the most attractive partners for extra-regional economic actors, and this may lead to privileged extra-regional relations in comparison with their smaller regional neighbours. In order to protect such extra-regional privileges, regional powers are more likely than their smaller neighbours to become regional Rambos. In contrast to the argument of Mattli (1999a), which states that the existence of regional hegemons is supportive of successful regional integration, our argument points to the fact that regional powers in developing regions do not always behave benevolently, but rather may become regional Rambos with a dominant strategy of regional defection. Despite the fact that they often claim regional leadership for themselves, they may act against their intraregional interest in order to protect their more important extra-regional privileges. Thereby, regional powers become more an obstacle than a backer of regional economic integration.

5 CASE SELECTION AND THE QUESTION OF COMPARABILITY

We apply our theoretical framework to cases of regional cooperation and defection in ASEAN, MERCOSUR and the Southern African Development Community (SADC). We choose these three regional organisations because they are the economically most developed and integrated ones in their respective world regions. Thus, they constitute relatively unlikely cases for our theoretical approach, because intraregional economic interdependence is likely to be more important for these regions than for economically even less-developed ones. Other regional organisations like SAARC, the Andean Community (CAN) and the Economic Community of West African States (ECOWAS) have lower gross domestic products per capita and even lower intraregional trade than the regional organisations chosen by us. Thus, if the extra-regional logic of regional integration prevails in our case studies, we are confident that it would also prevail in even less-developed regions with even lower levels of intraregional economic interdependence.

The usual critique of area specialists of a comparative analysis of regional integration in different world regions is that the respective regions differ too much to be comparable in a meaningful way. This critique of 'comparing apples with oranges' is raised so often that it provoked Haas in 1970 to make the ironic and somewhat resigned statement that everyone knows that 'things are different in Pago Pago' (Haas 1970: 613). And of course, this critique can also be addressed to a comparison of ASEAN, MERCOSUR and SADC. The three regional organisations differ widely in their composition, as well as in cultural and political terms. Whereas MERCOSUR consists of only four member states, ASEAN and SADC include 10 and 15 member states respectively. MERCOSUR and SADC are each dominated by a single regional power, but ASEAN is not. ASEAN and SADC contain authoritarian member states and failed states, whereas MERCOSUR consists only of presidential democracies. The MERCOSUR member states are homogeneous in cultural terms, whereas ASEAN is culturally very heterogeneous and SADC is somewhere in between. However, such diversity between the three regions can also be turned to an advantage if a most different cases design is chosen to guide the comparison (Przeworski and Teune 1970; Ragin 1987). In fact, ASEAN, MERCOSUR and SADC can be understood as dissimilar cases that have little in common despite the fact that they are all developing regions following the (neo-)liberal paradigm of the new regionalism. If we find out that the extra-regional logic of regional integration prevails in all three regions and leads to the same consequences before the background of similar economic but dissimilar political and cultural conditions, this strengthens our confidence in the conclusion that extra-regional influence on regional integration is a general phenomenon in the developing world.

In order to explore the economic structures of ASEAN, MERCOSUR and SADC, we conduct diachronic network analyses of regional trade data. Such network analyses have two advantages in comparison to broad indicators like the share of intraregional trade that are usually applied in comparative analyses (De Lombaerde et al. 2010). Firstly, network analyses are much more detailed and allow us to analyse the importance of extra-regional trade not only for the overall region but also for certain member states. And secondly, network analyses make it possible to observe economic asymmetries within regions, that is, whether regional powers dominate their respective regions or not. This information is necessary for an analysis of whether certain member states face incentives to become regional Rambos in order to protect their extra-regional privileges. We use trade data and not investment data because the former is available in a more comprehensive way. For some regions, investment data is only available sporadically or in highly aggregated terms, which make diachronic network analyses impossible. Moreover, it can be assumed that trade and investment data are positively correlated to a high degree (Kali and Reyes 2010; Van Rijckeghem and Weder 2001). Thus, there are good reasons to assume that trade networks reflect general patterns of economic interdependence within and between world regions.

We rely on case studies and careful process tracing when analysing whether the economic structures within ASEAN, MERCOSUR and SADC, as well as the behaviour of extra-regional actors, have the expected effects on regional cooperation or defection. Here, we choose two or three cases of regional cooperation or defection for each of the three regions, which broadens our empirical basis from three to seven cases (two for ASEAN, three for MERCOSUR and two for SADC). Although it would in principle be possible to follow a quantitative approach in which each occasion of regional cooperation or defection would count as one case, we rely on a qualitative approach because of the complexity of the required information. A detailed dataset—which would have to include information about the economic structures within the regions, the behaviour of extra-regional actors and the cases of regional cooperation or defection—is not available at present. At least at this stage of research, we argue that it makes more sense to test our hypotheses by analysing single cases of cooperation or defection and by carefully following the causal path between economic structures, extra-regional reactions and member states' behaviours, rather than by investing vast resources in the production of a dataset.

6 REGIONAL COOPERATION AND DEFECTION IN ASEAN, MERCOSUR AND SADC

Two unique characteristics distinguish the ASEAN trade network from that of MERCOSUR and SADC: The ASEAN member states trade a lot with neighbouring countries in Northeast Asia, and ASEAN is the only regional organisation analysed in this book that is not dominated by a regional power. The network analysis finds some important intraregional trade links within ASEAN (most of them related to Indonesia, Malaysia, Singapore and Thailand), but extra-regional trade is nevertheless dominant. However, in contrast to MERCOSUR and SADC, ASEAN does not only rely on trade with the EU and the USA; the Northeast Asian countries China and Japan are important trade partners as well. Furthermore, there is no country in Southeast Asia that is able to dominate the whole region in economic terms. Indonesia is the largest country in the region, but its economic development is too low in order to qualify the country as a regional power. And Singapore's economy is much more developed than that of its neighbours, but the country is far too small to act as a regional power. Thus, there exists no regional power that is predestined to enjoy extra-regional privileges. This reduces the likelihood of Rambo situations and increases the chances for successful regional cooperation.

During the last 15 years, ASEAN has been very successful in cooperating with extra-regional actors, and this extra-regional cooperation has reinforced the integration process within the regional organisation. For this reason, ASEAN is the only one of our three regional organisations for which we analyse two cases of successful cooperation and not one case of cooperation and one of defection. The first case is the establishment of the ASEAN Free Trade Area (AFTA) during the 1990s. This integration step was a classic example of new regionalism in the developing world because it not only aimed to improve intraregional trade, but moreover to improve the region's competitiveness and to attract extra-regional investments (Obermeier 2013). Later in the 1990s, ASEAN was shaken by the Asian crisis, and regional liquidity arrangements proved insufficient to bail out the affected countries. While regional solutions were deemed inadequate, ASEAN was able to establish liquidity arrangements with China, Japan and South Korea at the turn of the millennium (Rüland 2000). The so-called Chiang Mai Initiative of the ASEAN+3 (ASEAN plus China, Japan and South Korea) was at first a web of poorly equipped bilateral swap agreements (Dieter 2003), but it was later reformed and increased sixfold in size to become a full regional liquidity fund. Moreover, ASEAN successfully negotiated ASEAN+1 trade agreements with China, Japan and South Korea individually; these grant preferential access to the markets of ASEAN's most important trade partners in Northeast Asia. Because of successful extra-regional cooperation, regional integration within ASEAN gained momentum during the first decade of the new millennium, and this episode constitutes our second case study of regional cooperation in ASEAN. The most prominent result of this new dynamic is the ASEAN Charter, which is a significant step from the informal 'ASEAN way' towards a more formalised and institutionalised regional organisation.

Similar to ASEAN, extra-regional trade flows prevail in the MERCOSUR trade network, but in contrast to ASEAN, MERCOSUR is dominated by a regional power, namely Brazil. Within MERCOSUR, intraregional trade is important for the smaller member states Argentina, Paraguay and Uruguay, but the regional power Brazil trades much more with extra-regional actors than with its regional neighbours. Thus, the smaller member states benefit significantly from getting preferential access to the Brazilian market, but if Brazil's extra-regional interests are at odds with regional integration, the former are likely to prevail. Such an economic structure carries a relatively high risk of Rambo behaviour whenever Brazil is able to achieve privileges in its extra-regional relations by acting unilaterally.

Because of its crucial role within MERCOSUR, Brazil's behaviour has been responsible for progress but also difficulties in regional integration in MERCOSUR during the last 25 years. Firstly, during the 1990s, Brazil provided regional leadership and contributed to the quick success of MERCOSUR. A customs union (although incomplete) was achieved rather quickly, extra-regional investment inflows increased, the EU and MERCOSUR negotiated for an interregional trade agreement (Calfat and Flores 2006) and intraregional trade reached new heights, to the point that MERCOSUR was even called the most successful regional organisation in the developing world (Vaillant 2005). Secondly, however, the MERCOSUR member states entered a period of economic difficulties in the late 1990s. Due to the Asian crisis and the Russian default, investors withdrew their capital from emerging markets and thus the Argentinean peso and the Brazilian real, which were both pegged to the US dollar, came under pressure to be devaluated. In this situation, Brazil floated its currency unilaterally and without consultation with other MERCOSUR member states. Consequently, the Brazilian real immediately lost about one-third of its value, and the Brazilian export industry became competitive again. This was the starting point for an export boom that made Brazil one of the most dynamic emerging markets during the first decade of the new millennium. In contrast, the Argentinean export industry lost competitiveness to the same degree, and the resulting decline in exports was the deathblow for the Argentinean economy, which then entered its crisis (Hausmann and Velasco 2002). In the course of this crisis, Argentina ultimately had to float its currency as well and had one of the biggest defaults in history (Cooper and Momani 2005). Thirdly, Brazil's beggar-thy-neighbour strategy (Kronberger 2002) led not only to a crisis of the Argentinean economy but also to a crisis of regional integration in MERCOSUR. A trade war between Argentina and Brazil emerged in which course both countries reintroduced trade barriers. Despite several attempts to restart the regional integration process, MERCOSUR has so far not returned to its dynamic of the 1990s.

The trade network of SADC shows similar characteristics to that of MERCOSUR. Extra-regional trade dominates the picture, but intraregional trade of the smaller member states with South Africa is also significant. Thus, South Africa is an important destination for exports from the smaller SADC member states, but South Africa itself relies heavily on trade with the EU. Although it is often argued that South Africa needs the regional market in order to sell its manufactured goods, which are not competitive on the world market, intraregional trade accounts for only 10 per cent of South Africa's exports, whereas trade with the EU adds up to 30 per cent (Muntschick 2013a, b). The dominance of extra-regional trade and the privileged position of South Africa carry the risk of Rambo behaviour by the regional power. Whenever regional cooperation is at odds with the extra-regional interests of South Africa, the regional power can be expected to defect regionally in order to protect its extra-regional privileges.

Like in the case of MERCOSUR, the behaviour of the regional power South Africa explains both the success and the failure of regional integration in SADC during the last 25 years. Firstly, South Africa was one of the driving forces behind market integration in Southern Africa until 2008. During the 1990s, SADC developed a plan for economic integration; this plan was to establish a free trade area (SADC-FTA) in 2008, a customs union (SADC-CU) in 2010, a common market in 2015, an economic union in 2016 and a common currency in 2018. The negotiations for the SADC-FTA were dominated by South Africa's interests, and the free trade area was implemented successfully in 2008. Secondly, the planned SADC-CU[4] could not be established, because it was at odds with the extra-regional interests of some SADC member states, most notably those of South Africa. During the 1990s, South Africa had negotiated the Trade, Development and Cooperation Agreement (TDCA) with the EU and gained preferential access to the European Single Market (Frennhoff Larsén 2007). Because the SADC-CU would have required a harmonisation of the member states' extra-regional trade regimes, this would have implied that either the smaller member states would have had to adapt to the terms of the TDCA or South Africa would have had to give up its bilateral trade agreement with the EU. Furthermore, SADC is also currently divided in different negotiation groups for EPAs with the EU (Stevens 2008), and the least developed countries (LDCs) of the region have free access to the European market under the everything-but-arms (EBA) initiative. This fragmentation of the member states' extra-regional trade regimes (Jakobeit et al. 2005) would have to be overcome in order to set up an SADC-CU. Instead of going one step further towards deeper market integration, the SADC member states and the member states of the Common Market for Eastern and Southern Africa (COMESA) and of the East African Community (EAC) plan to establish the so-called Tripartite Free Trade Area (TFTA). However, negotiations about the TFTA will be finished at the earliest in 2018, and it is likely that the TFTA will add just another layer to the already-chaotic web of trade agreements in Africa (Erasmus 2012).

7 THE STRUCTURE OF THE BOOK

In the following, the book is structured in four parts. In the theoretical and methodological part, Sebastian Krapohl develops the theoretical framework for the analysis of regional cooperation and defection in ASEAN, MERCOSUR and SADC, and he explains the research design for the following parts. In the second part of the book, Simon Fink analyses the economic structures of the three regional organisations and of the EU, as a comparative case of a well-developed region, by using diachronic network analysis. In the third part, Sebastian Krapohl, Katharina L. Meissner and Johannes Muntschick provide case studies of regional cooperation and defection in ASEAN, MERCOSUR and SADC, as well as of their consequences for the respective regional integration processes. In the concluding chapter, Sebastian Krapohl compares the findings of the empirical analyses and discusses the implications of our results for regional integration theories.

NOTES

1. Mattli summarised the findings of his book in an academic article (Mattli 1999b). However, the following discussion refers to Mattli's book only.
2. For the diffusion of the EU model to other world regions see: Börzel and Risse (2012), Jetschke and Lenz (2013), Jetschke and Murray (2012) and Lenz (2012).
3. For example, in 2010, the share of intraregional trade was 26.14 per cent in ASEAN, 11.77 per cent in MERCOSUR and 12.15 per cent in SADC, whereas it was 60.84 per cent in the EU (www.cris.unu.edu/riks/web/).
4. The SADC-CU should not be mistaken for the Southern African Customs Union (SACU). The SACU is an old customs union between Botswana, Lesotho, Namibia, South Africa and Swaziland that goes back to colonial times. In contrast, an SADC-CU would comprise all (or almost all) 15 member states of the SADC.

REFERENCES

Acharya, A. (1993). *A New Regional Order in South-East Asia: ASEAN in the Post-Cold War Era*. London: Oxford University Press.

Aggarwal, V. K., & Fogarty, E. A. (Eds.). (2004). *EU Trade Strategies: Between Regionalism and Globalism*. Basingstoke: Palgrave Macmillan.

Aspinwall, M. D., & Schneider, G. (2000). Same Menu, Separate Tables: The Institutionalist Turn in Political Science and the Study of European Integration. *European Journal of Political Research, 38*, 1–36.

Axelrod, R. (1984). *The Evolution of Cooperation*. New York: Basic Books.

Balassa, B. (1961). *The Theory of Economic Integration*. London: George Allen & Unwin.

Baldwin, R. E. (2006). Multilateralising Regionalism: Spaghetti Bowls as Building Blocs on the Path to Global Free Trade. *The World Economy, 29*, 1451–1518.

Baldwin, R. E., & Seghezza, E. (2010). Are Trade Blocs Building or Stumbling Blocs? *Journal of Economic Integration, 25*, 276–297.

Bende-Nabende, A. (2002). *Globalization, FDI, Regional Integration and Sustainable Development*. Aldershot: Ashgate Publishing.

Bhagwati, J. N. (1988). Export-Promoting Trade Strategy. *World Bank Research Observer, 3*, 27–57.

Börzel, T. A. (2013). Comparative Regionalism: European Integration and Beyond. In W. Carlsnaes, T. Risse, & B. A. Simmons (Eds.), *Handbook of International Relations* (pp. 503–530). London: SAGE Publications.

Börzel, T., & Risse, T. (2012). From Europeanisation to Diffusion: An Introduction. *West European Politics, 35*, 1–19.

Breslin, S., Huges, C. W., Phillips, N., & Rosamond, B. (Eds.). (2002). *New Regionalisms in the Global Political Economy: Theories and Cases*. London: Routledge.

Bulmer-Thomas, V. (Ed.). (2001). *Regional Integration in Latin America and the Caribbean: The Political Economy of Open Regionalism*. London: Institute of Latin American Studies.

Calfat, G., & Flores, R. G. (2006). The EU-Mercosol Free Trade Agreement: Quantifying Mutual Gains. *Journal of Common Market Studies, 44*, 921–945.

Casella, A. A. (1992). On Markets and Clubs: Economic and Political Integration of Regions with Unequal Productivity. *American Economic Review, 82*, 115–121.

Cooper, A. F., & Momani, B. (2005). Negotiating Out of Argentina's Financial Crisis: Segmenting the International Creditors. *New Political Economy, 10*, 305–320.

De Lombaerde, P., Söderbaum, F., Van Langenhove, L., & Baert, F. (2010). The Problem of Comparison in Comparative Regionalism. *Review of International Studies, 36*, 731–753.

De Melo, J., & Panagariya, A. (Eds.). (1993). *New Dimension in Regional Integration*. Cambridge: Cambridge University Press.

Dieter, H. (2003). Exploring Alternative Theories of Economic Regionalism: From Trade to Finance in Asian Co-operation? *Review of International Political Economy, 10*, 430–454.

Dür, A. (2007). Regionalism in the World Economy: Building Block or Stumbling Stone for Globalization? In S. Schirm (Ed.), *Globalization: State of the Art and Perspectives* (pp. 183–199). London: Routledge.

Erasmus, G. (2012). Legal and Institutional Aspects of the Tripartite Free Trade Area: The Need for Effective Implementation. In T. Hartzenberg (Ed.), *The Tripartite Free Trade Area: Towards a New African Integration Paradigm?* (pp. 8–37). Stellenbosch: Trade Law Centre for Southern Africa.

Fawcett, L., & Hurrell, A. (Eds.). (1995). *Regionalism in World Politics: Regional Organization and International Order*. Oxford: Oxford University Press.

Fligstein, N., & Stone Sweet, A. (2002). Constructing Polities and Markets: An Institutionalist Account of European Integration. *American Journal of Sociology, 107*, 1206–1243.

Frankel, J. A., & Wei, S.-J. (1998). *Open Regionalism in a World of Continental Trade Blocs* (IMF Working Paper).

Fratianni, M., & Pattison, J. (2001). International Organisations in a World of Regional Trade Agreements: Lessons from Club Theory. *The World Economy, 24*, 333–358.

Frennhoff Larsén, M. (2007). Trade Negotiations between the EU and South Africa: A Three-Level Game. *Journal of Common Market Studies, 45*, 857–881.

Gamble, A., & Payne, A. (Eds.). (1996). *Regionalism and World Order*. Basingstoke: Macmillan.

Garrett, G., & Weingast, B. R. (1993). Ideas, Interests, and Institutions: Constructing the European Community's Internal Market. In J. Goldstein & R. O. Keohane (Eds.), *Ideas and Foreign Policy: Beliefs, Institutions, and Political Change* (pp. 173–206). Ithaca, NY: Cornell University Press.

Haas, E. B. (1958). *The Uniting of Europe: Political, Social and Economic Forces, 1950-1957*. Stanford, CA: Stanford University Press.
Haas, E. B. (1967). The Uniting of Europe and the Uniting of Latin America. *Journal of Common Market Studies, 5*, 315–343.
Haas, E. B. (1970). The Study of Regional Organization: Reflections on the Joy and Anguish of Pretheorizing. *International Organization, 24*, 607–646.
Haas, E. B. (1975). *The Obsolescence of Regional Integration Theory*. Berkeley, CA: Institute of International Studies, University of California.
Haas, E. B., & Schmitter, P. C. (1964). Economics and Differential Patterns of Political Integration: Projections about Unity in Latin America. *International Organization, 18*, 705–737.
Hänggi, H. (2003). Regionalism through Interregionalism: East Asia and ASEM. In F.-K. Liu & P. Regnier (Eds.), *Regionalism in East Asia: Paradigm Shifting?* (pp. 197–219). London: RoutledgeCurzon.
Hänggi, H., Roloff, R., & Rüland, J. (Eds.). (2006). *Interregionalism and International Relations*. London: Routledge.
Hardin, G. (1968). The Tragedy of the Commons. *Science, 162*, 1243–1248.
Hausmann, R., & Velasco, A. (2002). Hard Money's Soft Underbelly: Understanding the Argentine Crisis. *Brookings Reader Forum, 59*–104.
Hettne, B. (1999). Globalization and the New Regionalism: The Second Great Transformation. In B. Hettne, A. Inotai, & O. Sunkel (Eds.), *Globalism and the New Regionalism* (1st ed., pp. 1–24). Basingstoke: Palgrave Macmillan.
Hettne, B. (2005). Beyond the 'New' Regionalism. *New Political Economy, 10*, 543–571.
Hettne, B., & Söderbaum, F. (2000). Theorising the Rise of Regionness. *New Political Economy, 5*, 457–473.
Holzinger, K. (2003). Common Goods, Matrix Games and Institutional Response. *European Journal of International Relations, 9*, 173–212.
Jakobeit, C., Hartzenberg, T., & Charalambides, N. (2005). *Overlapping Membership in COMESA, EAC, SACU and SADC: Trade Policy Options for the Region and for EPA Negotiations*. Eschborn: GIZ.
Jaumotte, F. (2004). *Foreign Direct Investment and Regional Trade Agreements: The Market Size Effect* (International Monetary Fund Working Paper 04/206).
Jetschke, A., & Lenz, T. (2013). Does Regionalism Diffuse? A New Research Agenda for the Study of Regional Organizations. *Journal of European Public Policy, 20*, 626–637.
Jetschke, A., & Murray, P. (2012). Diffusing Regional Integration: The EU and Southeast Asia. *West European Politics, 35*, 174–191.
Kali, R., & Reyes, J. (2010). Financial Contagion on the International Trade Network. *Economic Inquiry, 48*, 1072–1101.
Kappel, R. (2010). *On the Economics of Regional Powers: Comparing China, India, Brazil, and South Africa* (GIGA Working Papers No 145).

Keohane, R. O. (1984). *After Hegemony: Collaboration and Discord in the World Political Economy.* Princeton, NJ: Princeton University Press.
Krapohl, S. (2008). *Risk Regulation in the Single Market: The Governance of Pharmaceuticals and Foodstuffs in the European Union.* Basingstoke: Palgrave Macmillan.
Krapohl, S., & Fink, S. (2013). Different Paths of Regional Integration: Trade Networks and Regional Institution-Building in Europe, Southeast Asia and Southern Africa. *Journal of Common Market Studies, 51,* 472–488.
Krapohl, S., Meißner, K. L., & Muntschick, J. (2014). Regional Powers as Leaders or Rambos of Regional Integration? Unilateral Actions of Brazil and South Africa and Their Negative Effects on MERCOSUR and SADC. *Journal of Common Market Studies, 52,* 879–895.
Krapohl, S., & Muntschick, J. (2009). Two Logics of Regionalism: The Importance of Interdependence and External Support for Regional Integration in Southern Africa. In J. M. Kaunda & F. Zizhou (Eds.), *Proceedings of the 2008 FOPRISA Annual Conference.* Gaborone: Lightbooks.
Krasner, S. D. (1982). Structural Causes and Regime Consequences: Regimes as Intervening Variables. *International Organization, 36,* 185–205.
Kronberger, R. (2002). A Cost-Benefit Analysis of a Monetary Union for MERCOSUR with Particular Emphasis on the Optimum Currency Area Theory. *Integration and Trade, 6,* 29–93.
Krueger, A. O. (1997). Trade Policy and Economic Development: How We Learn. *American Economic Review, 87,* 1–22.
Langhammer, R. J. (1992). The Developing Countries and Regionalism. *Journal of Common Market Studies, 30,* 211–232.
Lee, M. C. (1989). *SADCC: The Political Economy of Development in Southern Africa.* Nashville, TN: Winston-Derek Publishing.
Lenz, T. (2012). Spurred Emulation: The EU and Regional Integration in MERCOSUR and SADC. *West European Politics, 35,* 155–173.
Leuffen, D., Rittberger, B., & Schimmelfennig, F. (2013). *Differentiated Integration: Explaining Variation in the European Union.* Basingstoke: Palgrave Macmillan.
Lindberg, L. N., & Scheingold, S. A. (1970). *Europe's Would-Be Polity: Patterns of Change in the European Community.* Englewood, CO: Prentice-Hall.
Mansfield, E. D., & Milner, H. V. (1999). The New Wave of Regionalism. *International Organization, 53,* 589–627.
Mansfield, E. D., & Reinhardt, E. (2003). Multilateral Determinants of Regionalism: The Effects of GATT/WTO on the Formation of Preferential Trading Arrangements. *International Organization, 57,* 829–862.
Mattli, W. (1999a). *The Logic of Regional Integration: Europe and Beyond.* Cambridge: Cambridge University Press.
Mattli, W. (1999b). Explaining Regional Integration Outcomes. *Journal of European Public Policy, 6,* 1–27.

Moravcsik, A. (1993). Preferences and Power in the European Community: A Liberal Intergovernmentalist Approach. *Journal of Common Market Studies, 31*, 473–524.

Moravcsik, A. (1998). *The Choice for Europe: Social Purpose and State Power from Messina to Maastricht.* Ithaca, NY: Cornell University Press.

Muntschick, J. (2013a). Explaining the Influence of Extra-Regional Actors on Regional Economic Integration in Southern Africa: The EU's Interfering Impact on SADC and SACU. In U. Lorenz-Carl & M. Rempe (Eds.), *Mapping Agency: Comparing Regionalisms in Africa* (pp. 77–95). Farnham: Ashgate.

Muntschick, J. (2013b). Regionalismus und Externer Einfluss: Stört die Europäische Union die Regionale Marktintegration im südlichen Afrika? *Politische Vierteljahresschrift, 54*, 686–713.

Nolte, D. (2010). How to Compare Regional Powers: Analytical Concepts and Research Topics. *Review of International Studies, 36*, 881–901.

Nye, J. S. (Ed.). (1968). *International Regionalism: Readings.* Boston, MA: Little, Brown & Company.

Obermeier, A. (2013). *Mechanismen institutioneller Dynamiken: Eine vergleichende Prozessanalyse der Entwicklung des ASEAN Handelsregimes.* Bamberg: University of Bamberg Press.

Ostrom, E. (2003). How Types of Goods and Property Rights Jointly Affect Collective Action. *Journal of Theoretical Politics, 15*, 239–270.

Pollack, M. A. (1996). The New Institutionalism and EG Governance: The Promise and Limits of Institutional Analysis. *Governance: An International Journal of Policy and Administration, 9*, 429–458.

Pollack, M. A. (1997). Delegation, Agency and Agenda-Setting in the European Community. *International Organization, 51*, 99–134.

Pollack, M. A. (2003). *The Engines of European Integration: Delegation, Agency, and Agenda-Setting in the EU.* Oxford: Oxford University Press.

Preusse, H. G. (2004). *The New American Regionalism.* Cheltenham: Edward Elgar.

Przeworski, A., & Teune, H. (1970). *The Logic of Comparative Social Inquiry.* New York: Krieger Publishing.

Ragin, C. C. (1987). *The Comparative Method: Moving Beyond Qualitative and Quantitative Strategies.* Berkeley, CA: University of California Press.

Robson, P. (1993). The New Regionalism and Developing Countries. *Journal of Common Market Studies, 31*, 329–348.

Rüland, J. (2000). ASEAN and the Asian Crisis: Theoretical Implications and Practical Consequences for Southeast Asian Regionalism. *The Pacific Review, 13*, 421–451.

Schirm, S. A. (1997). *Kooperation in den Amerikas: NAFTA, MERCOSUR und die neue Dynamik regionaler Zusammenarbeit.* Baden-Baden: Nomos Verlagsgesellschaft.

Schirm, S. A. (2002). *Globalization and the New Regionalism: Global Markets, Domestic Politics and Regional Cooperation.* Cambridge: Polity Press.

Schirm, S. A. (2010). Leaders in Need of Followers: Emerging Powers in Global Governance. *European Journal of International Relations, 16,* 197–221.
Schmitter, P. C. (1970). A Revised Theory of Regional Integration. *International Organization, 24,* 836–868.
Shaw, T. M., & Fanta, E. (2013). Introduction: Comparative Regionalism for Development in the 21st Centrury: Insights from the Global South. In E. Fanta, T. M. Shaw, & V. T. Tang (Eds.), *Comparative Regionalism for Development in the 21st Century: Insights from the Global South* (pp. 1–18). Farnham: Ashgate.
Shaw, T. M., Grant, J. A., & Cornelissen, S. (Eds.). (2011). *The Ashgate Research Companion to Regionalism.* Farnham: Ashgate.
Söderbaum, F., & Sbragia, A. (2011). EU Studies and the 'New Regionalism': What can be Gained from Dialogue? *Journal of European Integration, 32,* 563–582.
Stevens, C. (2008). Economic Partnership Agreements: What Can We Learn? *New Political Economy, 13,* 211–223.
Stone Sweet, A., & Caporaso, J. A. (1998). From Free Trade to Supranational Polity: The European Court and Integration. In W. Sandholtz & A. Stone Sweet (Eds.), *European Integration and Supranational Governance* (pp. 92–133). Oxford: Oxford University Press.
Tranholm-Mikkelsen, J. (1991). Neofunctionalism: Obstinate or Obsolete? A Reappraisal in the Light of the New Dynamism of the EC. *Millennium: Journal of International Studies, 20,* 1–22.
Vaillant, M. (2005). MERCOSUR: Southern Integration Under Construction. *Internationale Politik und Gesellschaft, 2,* 52–71.
Van Rijckeghem, C., & Weder, B. (2001). Sources of Contagion: Is It Finance or Trade? *Journal of International Economics, 54,* 293–308.
Venables, A. J. (2003). Winners and Losers from Regional Integration Agreements. *The Economic Journal, 113,* 747–761.
Viner, J. (1950). *The Customs Union Issue.* New York: Carnegie Endowment for International Peace.
Warleigh-Lack, A., & Rosamond, B. (2010). Across the EU-Studies-New Regionalism Frontier: Invitation to a Dialogue. *Journal of Common Market Studies, 48,* 993–1013.
Warleigh-Lack, A., & Van Langenhove, L. (2011). Rethinking EU Studies: The Contribution of Comparative Regionalism. *Journal of European Integration, 32,* 541–562.
Zürn, M. (1992). *Interessen und Institutionen in der internationalen Politik: Grundlegung und Anwendungen des situationsstrukturellen Ansatzes.* Opladen: Leske + Budrich.
Zürn, M. (1993). Problematic Social Situations and International Institutions: On the Use of Game Theory in International Politics. In F. Pfetsch (Ed.), *International Relations and Pan-Europe: Theoretical Approaches and Empirical Findings* (pp. 63–84). Münster: LIT Verlag.

PART I

Theory and Methods

CHAPTER 2

Two Logics of Regional Integration and the Games Regional Actors Play

A Theoretical Framework for the Analysis of Regional Economic Cooperation and Defection

Sebastian Krapohl

Mattli argues in his book *The Logic of Regional Integration* (Mattli 1999) that the success of regional integration depends on the fulfilment of two conditions by the regions in question. Firstly, there needs to be demand for the creation of regional markets. According to Mattli, this demand results from comparative cost advantages and economies of scale that can be exploited by liberalised trade within the regions. Thus, regions with a low potential for intraregional trade face less demands for regional integration. Secondly, the regional member states need to solve prisoner's dilemmas and battles of the sexes in order to supply the collective good that is 'regional integration'. Here, the member states become privileged

---

The phrase 'the games regional actors play' is a reference to Scharpf's book *The Games Real Actors Play* (Scharpf 1997).

S. Krapohl (✉)
University of Amsterdam, Amsterdam, The Netherlands
e-mail: s.krapohl@uva.nl

© The Author(s) 2017
S. Krapohl (ed.), *Regional Integration in the Global South*,
International Political Economy Series,
DOI 10.1007/978-3-319-38895-3_2

groups if one of them is a benevolent hegemon who supplies the 'regional integration' good for the whole group and who acts as a paymaster to compensate single member states for possible losses due to regional integration. According to Mattli, strong regional institutions like in the European Union (EU) can be substitutes for benevolent regional hegemons, but regional integration will be more stable and successful if regional paymasters exist. Thus, according to Mattli, the prospects for regional integration should generally be weak for regions with low intraregional economic interdependence and without regional hegemons.

In contrast to Mattli, we argue that there exist not just one but two ideal-typical logics of regional integration. We call them the intraregional and the extra-regional logics of regional integration. The intraregional logic is the one that Mattli (1999) has in mind and that lays at the heart of European integration theories like neofunctionalism, liberal intergovernmentalism and institutionalism (Haas 1958; Moravcsik 1998; Fligstein and Stone Sweet 2002). According to this logic, the member states of regional organisations integrate in order to liberalise and regulate regional markets and to profit from comparative cost advantages and economies of scale within these markets. In contrast, the extra-regional logic relies on insights from the new regionalism literature (Hettne and Söderbaum 2000; Mansfield and Milner 1999; Schirm 2002) that says that regional integration may also be outwardly oriented in order to improve regions' standings on the global market. Regional states may choose to integrate in order to become economically more attractive for extra-regional investment inflows and to gain leverage in international trade negotiations in order to achieve better market access to other world regions. Thus, there exists another kind of demand for regional integration, and it may also apply to regions with lower potentials for intraregional economic interdependencies.

The intraregional and the extra-regional logics of regional integration do not function in the same way, and this has consequences for the supply of regional integration. The two logics have different goals; they aim to provide different types of collective goods and member states face different cooperation problems within the two logics (Krapohl et al. 2014). The liberalisation and regulation of intraregional trade is a club good, and the regional member states play prisoner's dilemmas or battles of the sexes against each other when seeking this good. Although these games are problematic situations, cooperation can nevertheless be achieved with the support of regional institutions or benevolent regional hegemons.

In contrast, extra-regional investments and exports are common pool resources because the regional member states compete for them and cannot exclude single states from the consumption of these flows. As a result, the ease or difficulty of regional cooperation depends on the behaviour of extra-regional actors. If extra-regional actors reward regional cooperation systematically, the regional member states play battle of the sexes against each other, and cooperation is likely to take place. In contrast, if extra-regional actors grant privileges to specific regional member states and if these privileges are at odds with regional cooperation, the privileged regional states face incentives to protect their extra-regional relations. In such circumstances, the privileged member states become regional Rambos that lose interest in regional cooperation and rather have a dominant strategy of regional defection. Regional powers are the most likely regional states to enjoy privileges in their extra-regional economic relations because they are the most attractive markets within their world regions. If regional powers decide to protect their privileges, they do not act as benevolent hegemons but rather become regional Rambos instead. In such circumstances, regional cooperation is highly unlikely to emerge and the collective good will not be supplied.

1 THE INTRAREGIONAL LOGIC OF REGIONAL INTEGRATION

The European integration theories—namely, neofunctionalism, liberal intergovernmentalism and the institutionalist approaches to European integration—all rely at least implicitly on the intraregional logic of regional integration because they were all developed for the case of the EU, with its high share of intraregional trade and other economic interdependencies. Neofunctionalist spillovers (Haas 1958; Tranholm-Mikkelsen 1991) may only occur if integration in one policy area leads to negative externalities in other areas so that these need to be integrated as well—and such negative externalities cannot emerge without intraregional interdependence. Liberal intergovernmentalism (Moravcsik 1993, 1998) argues that the interests of the EU member states in regional integration are economic in nature and that the negotiation outcomes are determined by asymmetric interdependence between the member states. Finally, Stone Sweet and others (Fligstein and Stone Sweet 2002; Stone Sweet and Caporaso 1998) even explicitly refer to intraregional economic interdependence when they stress the virtuous circle between increasing intraregional trade and regional institution building. Thus, all these theories have in common the fact that they only refer to economic and political developments within the region concerned (here the EU), and they do not take into account the extra-regional effects of regional integration.

1.1 Intraregional Trade as a Club Good

The classic rationale for regional integration is the exploitation of economic gains through liberalising and re-regulating intraregional trade. It is a widely shared piece of wisdom of economic theory that international trade—and this of course includes international trade within respective world regions—is welfare increasing in comparison to closed economies with little economic interaction. This insight goes back to the classic work of Ricardo (1821), who postulated the law of comparative cost advantages. According to it, countries should concentrate on the production of goods for which they have a comparative cost advantage in relation to other countries. This specialisation allows for higher productivity, and international trade then distributes the produced goods. Complementing classic trade theory, new approaches focus on economies of scale, which can be exploited through international trade (Krugman 1980). International trade allows for the selling of goods in larger markets, and the resulting increase in output leads to falling average costs of production. Whereas the law of comparative cost advantages is especially important for trade among states with different factor endowments, the exploitation of scale effects also makes sense for countries with similar factor endowments but diversified production and consumption structures. According to the logics of both comparative cost advantages and economies of scale, global free trade would be the most efficient solution, and regional trade liberalisation can only be the second-best option. Nevertheless, in comparison to closed economies, regional trade liberalisation is welfare increasing and provides a rationale for regional market integration.

Regional integration can be understood as a collective good that has to be supplied by regional groups of states and that includes benefits for these groups. Generally, the theory of collective goods (Cornes and Sandler 1996; Ostrom 2003) distinguishes four different kinds of goods along the two dimensions of excludability and rivalry of consumption (see Fig. 2.1). Firstly, if group members rival for the consumption of certain goods and can be easily excluded from them, the respective goods are private goods.

	Excludability of Consumption	Non-Excludability of Consumption
Rivalry of Consumption	Private Goods	**Common Pool Resources** (Extra-Regional Investments and Exports)
Non-Rivalry of Consumption	**Club Goods** (Regional Market Liberalisation and Regulation)	Public Goods

Fig. 2.1 Typology of collective goods

Secondly, and in direct opposition to private goods, public goods are distinguished by non-excludability and low rivalry of consumption. Thirdly, common pool resources are distinguished by low excludability but high rivalry of consumption. And finally, if group members do not have rivalry for the consumption of certain goods, but can be excluded from them, the respective goods are club goods.

The establishment of regional markets within the intraregional logic of regional integration can be understood as the provision of a club good because intraregional trade is distinguished by excludability and low rivalry of consumption (for the theory of club goods, see Buchanan 1965; Casella 1992; Fratianni and Pattison 2001). In order for intraregional trade to take place, each member state of regional organisations needs to abolish tariffs and non-tariff barriers to trade for all other member states. Such an elimination of trade barriers is a specific measure between each possible pair of member states, and it does not require similar measures of trade liberalisation against third states outside the regional organisation. Therefore, single states can be excluded from intraregional trade if the other member states reintroduce trade barriers specifically for these states. At the same time, the utilisation of regional markets by some member states does not affect the value of the markets for all other member states. If some member states trade with each other, this does not preclude any other member states from trading within the regional market themselves. Thus, the degree of rivalry in the consumption of the club good 'regional market' is low.

The characteristics of the club good intraregional trade have positive consequences for regional cooperation on this issue. Firstly, the fact that there is the possibility of exclusion gives regional groups an instrument for sanctioning single member states who do not shoulder their part of the burden in providing the good. Such free riders can be sanctioned with exclusion from the club, and this possibility should increase the incentives for cooperative behaviour and the chances of supplying the good. Secondly, the non-rivalry in consumption of the club good 'intraregional trade' implies that all member states are able to gain from its provision in absolute terms. Although some member states may be able to gain more from intraregional trade than others, the likelihood that some member states defect, because they fear absolute losses, is low.

1.2 Prisoner's Dilemmas and Battle of the Sexes in the Intraregional Logic

Intraregional trade liberalisation resembles a prisoner's dilemma in which all member states of respective regional organisations share an interest in mutual cooperation but simultaneously face incentives for free riding (Garrett and Weingast 1993; Krapohl 2008). Here, every member state has to decide whether it protects its domestic producers against competition from regional trade or whether it opens its own market for imports from other member states (see the left-hand table in Fig. 2.2). Generally, all member states have an interest in liberalised regional markets because increasing trade within such markets allows them to exploit comparative cost advantages and economies of scale. However, at the same time, each member state also has incentives to protect its own economy against regional competition. The ideal outcome for each member state would be that all other member states open their markets for imports, whereas the respective member state still protects its own market from competition.

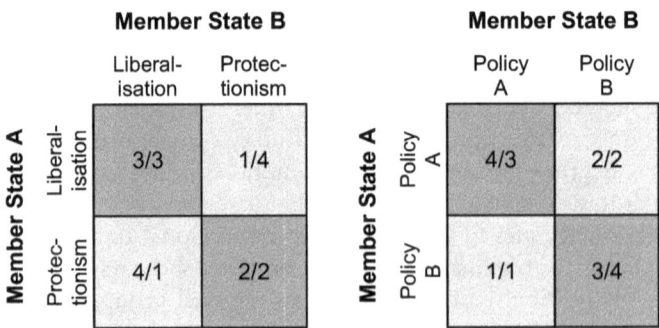

Fig. 2.2 Prisoner's dilemma and battle of the sexes within the intraregional logic

In contrast, the worst possible outcome would be that all other member states protect their markets, and the concerned member state liberalises its own for imports from its regional neighbours. If all member states try to achieve their best possible result and avoid the worst possible one, they protect their domestic markets and intraregional trade cannot be liberalised. Thus, mutual protectionism is a Nash equilibrium, but it is not Pareto efficient because member states lose out on the welfare-increasing effects of liberalised intraregional trade.

Although prisoner's dilemmas lead to Pareto-inefficient results when they are played only once, they can nevertheless be solved by cooperation as soon as they are played repeatedly. Within such iterated games, the players can achieve cooperation by playing tit-for-tat (Axelrod 1984). This means that the players start the game by cooperating in the first round and mirror the behaviour of their counterparts in the following rounds. Thus, cooperation will be honoured by cooperation in the next round, whereas defection is similarly punished by defection. Such punishments of course require that the players are able to respond specifically to the behaviour of their counterparts. In a group of more than two players, punishment is only possible if specific actions against single players can be taken.

Trade liberalisation is not a one-round game but rather a continuous cooperation project in which the member states have to decide every day whether or not to establish trade barriers. Consequently, market liberalisation can be understood as an iterated game in which each member state is able to react today to the behaviour of other member states on the previous day. Moreover, because intraregional trade liberalisation is a club good, member states have a specific measure at hand for punishing single defecting states—namely, exclusion from the club. If one member state tries to free ride and establishes trade barriers, the other member states are able to answer with trade barriers themselves, which means that the defector does not profit from its own behaviour. Thus, even if intraregional trade liberalisation resembles a prisoner's dilemma, and even if such a dilemma is problematic for collective action, the fact that the game is played on a continuous basis and that specific punishment of defecting states is possible allows regional cooperation to emerge.

In iterated prisoner's dilemmas, cooperation can be supported by monitoring bodies, clearly defined rules and dispute settlement mechanisms (Pollack 1997, 2003: 263–322). The crucial factor in prisoner's dilemmas is the prevention of free riding and the stabilisation of tit-for-tat solutions. If players' behaviour is predictable, stable cooperation can emerge because all players have an interest in cooperation in the long run. Such predictability can be improved when the member states of regional organisations set up monitoring bodies that regularly check member states' behaviour. Despite such monitoring bodies, problems may still emerge if it is not sure whether certain behaviour is to be counted as defection or cooperation—this is a result of incomplete contracting. Legalisation (Abbott et al. 2000) may help to solve such problems of incomplete contracting. The establishment of precise and obligatory rules reduces room for arbitrary interpretations of regional agreements. Nevertheless, despite a high level of precision and obligation, incomplete contracting can never be totally ruled out, which means that the member states of regional organisations may still have conflicts about the interpretation of regional agreements. Here, the establishment of formal dispute settlement mechanisms may help the member states to solve conflicts resulting from incomplete contracting. Such dispute settlement leads to legitimate and accepted interpretations of incomplete contracts and can thus reinforce compliance with international commitments (Zangl 2008).

When establishing regional markets, the member states not only need to liberalise trade, they also need to re-regulate regional trade (Duina 2006). As a matter of fact, all markets—including of course regional markets—need some kind of regulation in order to be functional. At least property rights and exchange rules need to be laid down, but it is also widely accepted that modern states need to correct all kinds of market failures in their economies. For example, modern states intensively regulate the safety of foodstuffs and pharmaceuticals in order to protect the health of consumers (Krapohl 2008). However, different regulatory standards may act as non-tariff barriers for trade that prevent the free circulation of goods despite the fact that intraregional tariffs have been abolished. When harmonising such standards, all member states prefer that their own standards become regional norms so that all other states have to take on the adaptation costs, while they themselves can keep their own standards (see the right-hand table in Fig. 2.2). Nevertheless, all member states prefer harmonised policies because failures of coordination would lead to trade barriers and lower levels of welfare-increasing intraregional trade. The resulting game is a battle of the sexes in which all players prefer cooperation, but where they have to choose between different Nash equilibriums with different distributive consequences (Garrett and Weingast 1993; Krapohl 2008). In contrast to prisoner's dilemmas, the crucial issue of such a battle of the sexes is not to reinforce existing agreements, but how to strike such agreements in the first place. Although this is not a trivial task, cooperation can be achieved by negotiating package deals that link different disputed issues with each other.

In battles of the sexes, the decision-making of member states can be disburdened by the introduction of majority vote instead of unanimity rule and by delegating agenda setting or even decision-making competencies to third actors (Pollack 1997, 2003). In order to avoid decision-making deadlocks, the member states may choose to decide by majority vote, which allows the overruling of at least some member states. Furthermore, the member states may also delegate competencies of decision-making to third bodies. These competencies may include the possibility of setting the agenda for regional policymaking. If a third body owns the monopoly of initiative, member states no longer have to decide on all possible options, but only on the approval or rejection of one option. A more far-reaching option could also include the delegating of decision-making itself to third bodies that are not influenced by distributive interests (Majone 2001). Both the introduction of majority rule and the delegation of decision-making competencies require that the member states of regional organisations give up some of their influence on decision-making in the future. The member states will only accept this if their interest in cooperation exceeds potential distributive losses. This is the case in battles of the sexes, wherein the players by definition prefer any coordinated solution over non-coordination.

To sum up, within the intraregional logic, member states face either prisoner's dilemmas or battles of the sexes—depending on whether they liberalise or re-regulate intraregional trade. Both game-theoretical situations are problematic, because either the Nash equilibrium of a one-round game is not Pareto efficient (in prisoner's dilemmas) or the member states have to choose between different Nash equilibriums (in battle of the sexes). Nevertheless, cooperative solutions can be achieved in both games if they are played repeatedly so that tit-for-tat solutions can emerge (in prisoner's dilemmas) or package deals can be negotiated (in battles of the sexes). Regional institutions can stabilise cooperative solutions if they provide means for monitoring and dispute settlement (in prisoner's dilemmas) or if they ease decision-making by allowing majority rule or by delegating tasks to independent bodies (in battle of the sexes).

2 THE EXTRA-REGIONAL LOGIC OF REGIONAL INTEGRATION

In contrast to European integration theories, the new regionalism literature (Hettne and Söderbaum 2000; Mansfield and Milner 1999; Schirm 2002) stresses the outward orientation of regional integration. According to it, the main difference between the 'old regionalism' of the 1950s to 1970s and the 'new regionalism' of the 1990s is that the former aimed to shield regional markets behind tariff walls, whereas the latter aims to open regional markets and to adapt them to the challenges of globalisation. In developing regions, this change goes hand in hand with a turn away from import-substituting development strategies (Krueger 1997) towards those that are export promoting (Bhagwati 1988). Most important to such export-promoting strategies are the attraction of foreign investments and the access to important export markets in order to generate economic activity and growth. However, developing countries and regions compete for their share of investments and exports on the global market, and regional integration is one instrument to improve regions' competitiveness in this global struggle. A stable political environment within the region, a larger regional market and a regional commitment to macroeconomic stability helps regional member states to attract foreign investments and to increase their leverage in international trade negotiations.

2.1 The Common Pool Resources Extra-Regional Investments and Exports

There are at least two ways in which regional economic integration improves regions' competitiveness on the global market. Firstly, size effects result from the fact that economically integrated regions constitute larger markets than do each of their respective member states. Here, the attractiveness of regional markets increases with the number of member states and the size of their economies, as well as with the degree of market integration. The larger and the better integrated regional markets are, the more attractive they are for extra-regional actors, which may profit from scale effects when acting in these markets. Secondly, regional integration is associated with various positive effects on the political and macroeconomic stability of respective regions. For example, the member states of integrated regions are more committed to not fighting wars against each other (Adler and Barnett 1998), strong regional institutions may help to stabilise the commitments of politically unstable member states (Schirm 2002), and macroeconomic coordination within regions reduces the risks of macroeconomic shocks (Dullien et al. 2013). Here, the density of regional institutions—may they be procedural or substantive in character—and the degree of implementation are decisive for the economic attractiveness of world regions. The more regional institutions exist, and the better they are implemented, the more they express a credible commitment of the member states towards political and macroeconomic stabilisation of the respective regions.

Both the size and stability effects of regional integration may have positive influences on extra-regional investment inflows. It is assumed that the stability and size effects of regional integration make well-integrated regions more attractive as targets for investments (Bende-Nabende 2002; Büthe and Milner 2008; Goldstein 2004; Jaumotte 2004). However, at this point, one has to distinguish between three kinds of investments, namely resource-seeking, market-seeking and efficiency-seeking investments (Dunning and Lundan 2008: 63–78). Regional integration is unlikely to have any effect on resource-seeking investments, which are made in order to extract scarce natural resources and to ensure access to these resources. Here, neither the stability nor the size effects of regional integration are likely to influence investors' utility calculation significantly. However, the size effects of regional integration can of course influence market-seeking investments because well-integrated regions allow investors to sell their products with fewer barriers to each of the regions' member states. Thus, regional markets are more attractive than any of the member states' markets alone. In addition, efficiency-seeking investments, that is, investments that seek low labour costs for the global market, are more likely to be influenced by the stability effects of regional integration. In the global struggle for such efficiency-seeking investments, the stability effects of regional integration are a competitive advantage vis-à-vis other world regions because they signal to potential investors that investments are unlikely to be lost due to political or macroeconomic instability.

Regional integration should also help to increase extra-regional export outflows because integrated regions should ceteris paribus have more bargaining power in multilateral (Mansfield and Reinhardt 2003) and interregional trade negotiations (Aggarwal and Fogarty 2004; Gilson 2005; Hänggi 2003; Hänggi et al. 2006). The improved bargaining power of integrated regions results from the increased size and stability of regional markets, which makes them more attractive as economic partners. This, in turn, leads to more concessions from the negotiation partners of these regions. As a result, the member states of integrated regions may receive improved market access to other world regions, which leads to increased extra-regional exports. Thus, although regional integration itself cannot directly influence the regions' exports to other world regions, it may nevertheless support the respective regions in international trade negotiations, which may indirectly lead to increased extra-regional exports.

Of course, regional integration is one but not the only factor in the decisions of extra-regional actors on where to invest and to whom to grant preferential access to their own markets. A variety of additional economic, political and cultural factors may influence extra-regional actors in their decisions as well. As already mentioned, the availability of scarce resources cannot be influenced by regional integration, but it may nevertheless be a decisive factor in investing in and signing bilateral trade agreements with concerned countries. Security concerns may be an important political factor that leads to investments in the form of development aid for key states in order to gain their cooperation or to stabilise their economies (Bearce and Tirone 2010)—even if such key states should not cooperate in regional organisations. Moreover, cultural similarities, which may, for example, result from colonial history, can also influence the decisions of extra-regional actors on where to invest and with whom to trade—independently of the regional integration efforts of the concerned countries. As a result, the positive relationship between regional integration on the one hand and extra-regional investment or export flows on the other hand only holds true under a ceteris paribus assumption, that is, everything else being equal. In real life, the positive effects of regional integration may be overshadowed by the other economic, political or cultural concerns of extra-regional actors. Thus, regions may improve their economic attractiveness through regional integration, but they have no guarantee that this will be systematically rewarded by extra-regional actors.

In contrast to intraregional trade, extra-regional investment inflows and export outflows are common pool resources for the receiving regions because they are distinguished by non-excludability but yet rivalry of consumption (see Fig. 2.1; for the problem of common pool resources, see Hardin 1968; Ostrom 2003). There is rivalry for extra-regional investment and export flows between and within world regions, because the consumption of the common pool resources by one region or state reduces the available amount of these resources for other regions or states. Although it is likely that better investment and trade possibilities in the world lead to growing levels of global investment and trade, there is nevertheless distributional conflict between regions and states for their respective shares of these flows. Furthermore, even if single states can generally be excluded from the consumption of extra-regional investment and export flows, the member states of regional organisations cannot decide independently on such an exclusion; they are dependent on the decisions of extra-regional actors. Although the member states of regional organisations can exclude certain states from their regional club, this does not necessarily imply that they also exclude these states from the common pool resources extra-regional investments and exports. If extra-regional actors decide to invest in or to grant market access to states that are outside of regional organisations, there is nothing that the regional organisations can do to exclude these states from the consumption of these common pool resources. Thus, dependence on extra-regional actors transforms extra-regional investment and export flows into common pool resources for regional organisations.

The rivalry in the consumption of the common pool resources extra-regional investments and exports leads to global competition for these resources (Bjorvatn and Eckel 2006; Goldberg and Knetter 1999; Kind et al. 2000). It is exactly this competition that generates the extra-regional rationale for regional integration. By integrating regionally, regions aim to become economically more attractive and to get bigger shares of the global distribution of these common pool resources. If one region seems to be effective with this instrument, this creates pressure for other regions to integrate economically as well—which explains why new regionalism spread so quickly all over the world during the 1990s (Mansfield and Milner 1999; Mattli 1999). However, competition for the common pool resources extra-regional investments and exports is not only a motivation, but also an obstacle for regional integration. The problem for regional integration is that global competition is mirrored by regional competition between the member states of regional organisations. The rivalry of consumption does not stop at the regional level, but also leads to distributional struggles within regions, because specific extra-regional investment or export flows can only be consumed by one member state at any one time. Thus, whereas global competition is a major motivation for regional integration, intraregional competition may be a significant obstacle for regional cooperation.

The non-excludability from consumption of extra-regional investments and exports prevents regional groups from being able to punish defecting member states effectively. It is not the regional organisations or their member states that decide the distribution of these common pool resources, but rather extra-regional actors that decide where they invest and to whom they grant market access. Thus, only extra-regional actors can sanction defecting member states effectively, whereas sanctions by other regional states alone do not really have bite. If extra-regional actors decide for economic, political or cultural reasons to invest in and to trade with defecting member states, there is nothing the regional organisations can do about it. Thus, the regions alone have no effective means to punish the defection of single member states, and are therefore dependent on the reactions of extra-regional actors.

2.2 Battle of the Sexes Games and Rambo Situations Within the Extra-Regional Logic

Within the extra-regional logic of regional integration, the structure of the games member states play against each other depends on the reactions of extra-regional actors. On the one hand, extra-regional actors may systematically reward regional integration. This means that investments increase only for cooperative member states of regional organisations and that preferential market access is only granted to these member states as well. If single member states did not implement regional rules, they would suffer from declining extra-regional investment inflows and losses of access to extra-regional markets. When extra-regional actors support regional integration in this way, the member states of the respective regional organisations find themselves in battles of the sexes (see the left-hand table in Fig. 2.3). Although collective action in respect to common pool resources is usually associated with prisoner's dilemmas (Hardin 1968), the situation within the extra-regional logic is different because regional member states do not try to avoid an unsustainable exploitation of such resources, but rather aim to improve the access of their region to these resources. Free riding is not a problem for the regional member states as long as regional defection is sanctioned systematically by extra-regional actors through declining investment inflows and a denial of market access. The regional member states may nevertheless have different preferences about common regional rules, because different rules may have different distributive consequences. For example, regional member states may disagree about rules of origin when establishing free trade areas or about common external tariffs when establishing customs unions. Thus, member states need

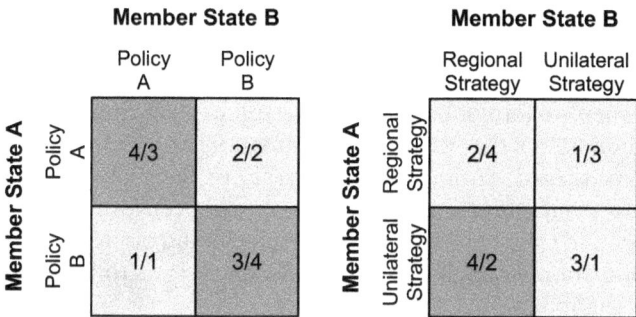

Fig. 2.3 Battle of the sexes and the Rambo situation within the extra-regional logic

to agree to one cooperative solution among many, but once agreements are reached, implementation needs to be enforced by extra-regional actors who sanction regional defection with declining investment flows or the suspension of preferential market access.

On the other hand, the reaction of extra-regional actors may also be less systematic and less in favour of regional integration, which moves the structure of the game from a battle of the sexes towards a Rambo situation.[1] Such Rambo situations are asymmetrical games, wherein one player—unlike the other(s)—lacks any incentive to cooperate, and can only lose out if an agreement is reached. This Rambo's dominant strategy is therefore to defect, while the other player(s) have the dominant strategy to cooperate (see the right-hand table in Fig. 2.3; for Rambo situations in game theory, see Holzinger 2003; Zürn 1992, 1993). In contrast to prisoner's dilemmas, tit-for-tat cannot produce cooperative solutions in Rambo situations because Rambos do not defect in order to free ride from the cooperation of others, but because they have lost any interest in cooperation at all. Thus, the other players of the game cannot effectively punish Rambos by answering with defection themselves.

Rambo situations occur whenever one of the regional member states enjoys privileges in its economic relations to important extra-regional actors. It may well happen that certain member states are more attractive as economic partners for extra-regional actors than are their neighbours within the same region. This may be motivated by various economic, political or cultural reasons. For example, due to market size, investments in some member states may be more attractive than investments in others;

some member states of regional organisations may be more important as part of the security strategies of extra-regional actors; and some regional member states may have more cultural ties to certain extra-regional actors because they are former colonies. The result of such circumstances is that the member states that enjoy special attention from other world regions become privileged within their own regions. Such privileged positions constitute competitive advantages for the respective member states in comparison to their regional neighbours, including disproportionally high shares of extra-regional investment and export flows to the disadvantage of their neighbours.

The extra-regional privileges of certain member states may be at odds with regional integration if regional cooperation requires giving up these privileges. For example, privileged member states need to give up bilateral trade agreements with extra-regional partners when the establishment of customs unions requires the harmonisation of external trade regimes. In such circumstances, the privileged member states have to calculate what counts more: their own share of the intraregional and extra-regional gains of regional integration or the losses of their extra-regional privileges. As long as their shares of the intraregional and extra-regional gains from regional integration exceed the losses of privileges, the games remain battles of the sexes. However, if the losses of privileges weigh more than the gains of regional integration for certain member states, these states become Rambos with a dominant strategy of defection in order to protect their privileges.

If Rambo situations occur before the adoption of certain regional agreements, they lead to deadlocks in decision-making that cannot easily be overcome with the help of regional institutions. In battles of the sexes, regional institutions that offer majority rule, agenda setting or even full delegation of decision-making may help to overcome such deadlocks because all member states prefer any cooperative solution to non-cooperation. Thus, they accept giving up sovereignty in order to not endanger the common project. However, such common interest in cooperation does not exist in Rambo situations, wherein at least one member state has no interest in cooperation at all. Such Rambos cannot accept majority rule or delegation of decision-making because these would lead to cooperative solutions, which reduce the Rambos' pay-offs.

In the case of Rambo situations, deadlocks can only be solved by granting side payments to the defecting member states or by packaging large deals, which combine several cooperation problems with inversed-preference constellations. However, side payments and package deals cannot effectively be facilitated by establishing the usual regional institutions of majority rule or delegation of decision-making competencies; they require high-level intergovernmental negotiations. Side payments always mean the redistribution of wealth from one member state to another, which implies that they need high degrees of political support, and this support can only be provided by the governments of the member states. Package deals require that negotiators overlook a large number of cooperation problems, and are able to package them into one deal. As a result, the specialisation of decision-making into different committees or working groups does not make much sense, because package deals must necessarily transcend the borders of particular issue areas. In contrast, one can expect that summit diplomacy plays a very important role for negotiating side payments and package deals. Only at the top political level are negotiators able to provide the necessary political support for side payments or to combine several issue areas into one package deal. This importance of high-level negotiations for regional integration is grasped under the term 'interpresidentialism' in the academic literature (Malamud 2003, 2005).

If Rambo situations occur after the adoption of certain regional agreements, defection takes the form of non-implementation of regional rules. In such cases, the member states have already agreed to regional rules, but changing circumstances lead to some member states profiting from defection and they become regional Rambos. Due to the inertia of regional institutions (Pierson 2000; Scharpf 1988), it is unlikely that Rambos will be able to turn back the integration process and to renegotiate regional agreements. However, regional Rambos are always able to undermine integration processes by not implementing regional rules that stand against their dominant interests. Thus, regional institutions still exist formally, but their actual effects are limited. If this happens repeatedly, a decoupling of formal institutions and real effects occurs. In the very end, regional integration may even become a Potemkin village with little or no influence on the real economy of the member states.

Legalisation is unlikely to improve implementation in the face of Rambo situations because sanctions by other member states cannot effectively reinforce judicial rulings. Legalisation facilitates cooperation in iterated prisoner's dilemmas because it stabilises the tit-for-tat strategies of the member states. Such tit-for-tat means that defection of one member state is sanctioned by the defection of the other member states in the following round of the game (Axelrod 1984). Here, dispute settlement mechanisms determine which member states are violating regional rules and can thus be sanctioned legitimately by other member states. However, member states can only sanction each other when they are able to hurt single free riders and when all states have an overall interest in regional cooperation. Without the possibility of exclusion, the member states cannot prevent free riders from consuming the collective goods. In addition, if Rambos do not have any interest in cooperation at all, exclusion from the regional group does not harm them. When the competition for the common pool resources extra-regional investments and exports leads to Rambo situations, both the possibility of exclusion and the overall interest in cooperation are not given. Although Rambos can be excluded from regional organisations, they cannot be excluded from extra-regional investment and export flows, because it is extra-regional actors, and not the regional organisations, that decide on the distribution of these goods. Furthermore, Rambos do not try to free ride on the cooperation of others, but instead they have no interest in regional cooperation at all. Thus, judgements of regional dispute settlement mechanisms cannot be effectively reinforced by decentralised sanctions of member states.

To sum up, within the extra-regional logic member states either face battles of the sexes or Rambo situations—depending on whether extra-regional actors reward regional integration systematically or grant extra-regional privileges for some member states. Although battles of the sexes are problematic situations because member states have to agree on one of several coordinated solutions, all member states prefer coordinated to non-coordinated results and the probability of cooperation is high. In contrast, Rambo situations are a severe threat for regional integration; Rambos have no overall interests in cooperation at all, and they will not agree to majority rule or the delegation of decision-making competencies in order to solve deadlocks. Moreover, legalisation is unlikely to ensure the compliance of Rambos because the other member states lack the possibility of enforcing judicial rulings with decentralised sanctions. Only when the pay-off matrix of Rambos is changed by granting side payments or by negotiating large package deals can cooperation take place.

3 HYPOTHESES ABOUT ECONOMIC COOPERATION AND DEFECTION IN DEVELOPING REGIONS

The intraregional logic of regional integration cannot explain the spread of the new regionalism in the Global South or the ups and downs of regional integration in developing regions. Firstly, the level of intraregional trade and economic interdependence is generally much lower in developing regions than in well-developed ones (Krapohl and Fink 2013). Developing countries and emerging markets can usually not utilise large comparative cost advantages and economies of scale when trading with each other. Thus, they do not fulfil Mattli's (1999) demand condition for regional integration. Consequently, the intraregional logic does not provide a convincing rationale as to why developing regions should integrate at all. Secondly, regional integration in developing regions seems to be less stable than regional integration in Europe. European integration has been a steady process over the last 60 years, and even the current Euro crisis, which is seen as path breaking by many contemporary observers, is more likely to lead to more integration of monetary and fiscal matters than to a decline in European integration (Schimmelfennig 2012). Such stable integration processes do not usually take place in the developing world, where optimistic periods of regional integration are often followed by periods of stagnation. The intraregional logic is able to explain the stable integration process in Europe by referring to a self-reinforcing growth of economic interdependence and regional institution building (Stone Sweet and Caporaso 1998), but it does not provide the variance needed to explain the instability of integration processes in the developing world.

In contrast, the extra-regional logic provides a convincing rationale for regional integration among developing countries and emerging markets, and it provides for variance in the dependent variable of regional cooperation in order to explain the ups and downs of regional integration in the developing world. Firstly, even if developing countries and emerging markets may not profit as much from intraregional trade as well-developed regions, demand for regional integration may nevertheless result from its extra-regional effects. The size and stability effects of regional integration may help developing regions to attract more extra-regional investments and to get improved access to extra-regional markets. Secondly, within the extra-regional logic, the supply of regional integration varies, because the reactions of extra-regional actors determine whether the member states play battles of the sexes or find themselves in Rambo situations. Thus, the extra-regional logic generates variance in the supply of regional integration that may explain the patterns of regional cooperation or defection in developing regions.

3.1 *The Demand for Regional Integration in Developing Regions*

It is often stated in the academic literature that the economic gains of intraregional trade correlate positively with economic development, and that they are much smaller for developing regions than for well-developed regions (Langhammer 1992; Robson 1993; Venables 2003). In order for increasing intraregional trade to produce economic gains for the member states, the latter need to be able to utilise comparative cost advantages and economies of scale by trading with each other (Mattli 1999). And yet, such economic advantages can only be exploited if the factor endowments and production structures of the member states are diversified and complementary to each other. The problem is that developing countries and emerging markets rely on the export of labour-intensive goods and on a few primary products like raw materials and agricultural goods. The neighbouring countries in developing regions are usually not able to consume these goods or to process them further. Moreover, regional neighbours may even compete with each other by exporting similar products. Even if tariffs and non-tariff trade barriers were completely abolished in developing regions, intraregional trade would remain low in the short run because the regional economies cannot trade with each other. Only in the long run, when regional economies develop and diversify further, may intraregional trade increase to levels similar to that in well-developed regions. But so far, the main export markets for developing countries are well-developed countries in other world regions. This dependence of developing countries has been stressed by scholars of dependency theory during the 1960s and 1970s (Cardoso and Faletto 1979), and even if the policy advice of this literature is somewhat outdated, their empirical findings are supported by economic analyses (Hout and Meijerink 1996; Smith and White 1992; Van Rossem 1996).

Even if the intraregional gains from regional integration are lower in developing regions than in well-developed regions, developing countries and emerging markets may profit from the extra-regional effects of regional integration. Since import substitution failed to generate economic development during the 1950s to 1970s (Krueger 1997), many developing countries and emerging markets have followed an export-promoting development strategy (Bhagwati 1988) during and since the 1990s. At the core of such a (neo-)liberal strategy are the attraction of investments and the increase of exports in order to create economic activity and growth. Developing countries and emerging markets compete with each other for investment and export shares, and regional integration may be one instrument to improve one's own competitiveness within that struggle. Regional integration has size and stability effects for developing countries and emerging markets. Thus, integrated developing regions should ceteris paribus attract more market- and efficiency-seeking investments from other world regions than the single member states would do on their own. In addition, integrated regions should ceteris paribus gain more leverage in global or interregional trade negotiations than each of their member states would, which may improve the regions' access to important extra-regional export markets.

Because extra-regional economic relations are more important for developing regions than intraregional ones, regional cooperation within such regions is to a large degree motivated by its extra-regional effects. Mattli (1999) argues that regional integration in developing regions is doomed to fail because developing regions cannot exploit significant comparative cost advantages and economies of scale through intraregional trade. Thus, according to Mattli, the demand for regional integration in developing regions is necessarily low. However, this argument neglects the positive extra-regional effects of regional integration. These positive extra-regional effects may lead to demands for regional integration, even if this demand is different from that in well-developed regions. Developing regions do not integrate in order to exploit comparative cost advantages and economies of scale through increasing intraregional trade but do so in order to improve their competitiveness on the global market by generating size and stability effects.

The dominance of the intraregional logic in well-developed regions and of the extra-regional logic in developing regions does not imply that well-developed regions cannot profit from the extra-regional effects of regional integration, or that developing regions cannot profit from the intraregional ones. The intra- and extra-regional logics of regional integration are not mutually exclusive, but the relative weights of the two logics differ between world regions. Well-developed regions like Europe may well attract more extra-regional investments or may achieve advantages in international trade negotiations with other world regions when they constitute large and stable regional markets, but it is unlikely that these effects will weigh more than the gains from liberalised trade and the resulting intraregional economic interdependence. Thus, in cases where the member states have to choose between their intra- and extra-regional interests, the former are likely to prevail. Developing regions may also profit from increasing intraregional trade due to regional integration, but it is unlikely that this intraregional trade will become important enough to trump dependence on extra-regional investments and exports—at least in the short run, as long as the participating economies have not developed and diversified any further. In fact, the more developed that regional economies are, the more important intraregional effects become and the less important are the extra-regional effects of integration.

3.2 The Supply of Regional Integration in Developing Regions

Because the demand for regional integration in developing regions results mainly from the extra-regional effects of regional integration on the global market, the likelihood of cooperation and the supply of regional integration depend on the reactions of extra-regional actors. On the one hand, extra-regional actors may systematically reward regional integration with increasing investment inflows and preferential market access. In such cases, all regional member states profit in absolute terms from regional integration even if these gains may be distributed unevenly across the respective regions. Consequently, the member states play battles of the sexes with each other. They may negotiate the distribution of gains from regional integration, but they all have a general interest in regional cooperation, so that cooperation is likely to take place. Regional institutions may help to achieve cooperation, but they are not mandatory because package deals and issue linkages make negotiated solutions possible as well. Thus, Hypothesis 1 about regional cooperation in developing regions can be formulated as such:

> *Hypothesis 1: As long as regional integration is systematically rewarded by extra-regional actors, the member states of developing regions cooperate within battles of the sexes.*

On the other hand, extra-regional actors may not reward regional cooperation nor punish regional defection systematically. For example, some regional member states may receive disproportionately high shares of extra-regional investments because of their huge market size. Alternatively, some member states may be able to sign bilateral trade agreements with extra-regional partners that grant them privileged access to important extra-regional markets. The more integration proceeds, the more likely it is that such privileges will be in conflict with regional cooperation, because integration necessarily reduces the differences between the regional member states. For example, investment inflows may be redirected to regional neighbour states, or bilateral trade agreements may have to be abolished when customs unions require the harmonisation of external trade regimes.

As soon as such losses of extra-regional privileges exceed member states' gains from regional cooperation, these member states necessarily defect from regional integration and become regional Rambos.

The probability of Rambo situations increases with growing asymmetries in market size between the member states of regional organisations because member states with large markets profit less from regional integration and are more likely to gain extra-regional privileges than smaller member states. The most asymmetric situation within regional organisations exists when regions are dominated by only one regional power,[2] and the other member states are economically relatively unimportant. The large domestic markets of regional powers already provide possibilities for exploiting comparative cost advantages and economies of scale, and the smaller markets of neighbouring countries do not add much to this situation. Thus, whereas the smaller states need the regional powers in order to escape economic marginalisation, the regional powers themselves do not gain much in economic terms. In addition, regional powers are probably able to attract disproportionately high shares of investments and to achieve better market access to other world regions than their smaller neighbours because they represent the most attractive markets in their respective regions. When regional integration endangers such privileges, the regional powers face the risks of losing investment and trade flows to their smaller neighbours, and consequently, the regional powers become regional Rambos with a dominant strategy of defection in order to protect their extra-regional privileges. As a result, Hypothesis 2 about regional defection can be formulated as such:

Hypothesis 2: As soon as regional integration is at odds with important extra-regional privileges, the regional powers of developing regions become regional Rambos with a dominant strategy of defection.

Mattli (1999) applies the general argument of hegemonic stability theory (Gilpin 1981; Kindleberger 1973; Krasner 1982) to regional integration and argues that regional integration is more likely to succeed if benevolent regional hegemons solve cooperation problems by providing regional leadership and by acting as paymasters who compensate the possible losses of smaller member states. However, regional powers in developing regions are less likely to act benevolently towards regional integration than regional powers in well-developed regions. Within well-developed regions, where intraregional trade and economic interdependence are high, regional powers have a constant interest in regional integration. Despite their relatively small size, the economic development of the smaller neighbours makes them—at least in sum—attractive as markets for the exports of the regional powers. As a result, regional powers in well-developed regions are likely to provide constant regional leadership and to supply the good 'regional integration'. In contrast, within developing regions, the regional powers may constitute attractive markets for their smaller neighbours because their sheer size makes up for their relatively low level of economic development, but the opposite does not hold. In developing regions, the smaller member states are unlikely to be important export markets for the regional powers. Thus, the regional powers have to take care of their economic relations with other world regions. If their extra-regional interests are at odds with regional cooperation, the regional powers necessarily defect and become regional Rambos. The above argument implies that it may be more advantageous for regional integration in developing regions if no regional powers exist, because regional powers may do more harm by protecting their privileges than good by supporting integration through providing regional leadership.

4 Conclusion

This chapter argues that there exist not one but two logics of regional integration: the intraregional and the extra-regional logics. Intraregional trade is a club good, and the member states play prisoner's dilemmas and battles of the sexes with each other when liberalising and regulating that trade respectively. Such games are problematic situations, but the creation of regional markets is a long-term project and not a one-round game, so the member states can achieve mutual cooperation by playing tit-for-tat and by negotiating package deals across various issue areas. Furthermore, cooperation can be facilitated if member states credibly commit themselves, with the help of institutions like dispute settlement mechanisms or the delegation of decision-making competencies to regional bodies. Thus, the game of regional market creation comprises the nucleus from which regional integration stems and complex and differentiated regional organisations emerge (Gehring 2002).

In contrast to intraregional trade, extra-regional investment inflows and export outflows are common pool resources. When regional groups of states integrate in order to become more competitive on the global market and to attract these common pool resources, they find themselves either in battles of the sexes or in Rambo situations—depending on the behaviour of extra-regional actors. If extra-regional actors reward regional integration systematically, the member states play battles of the sexes. All member states have common interests in integration in order to increase their share of the common pool resources, and extra-regional actors would punish cheating member states with a decline in extra-regional investment and export flows. However, when extra-regional actors do not reward regional integration systematically, some member states may gain privileges in their extra-regional relations by acting unilaterally. Consequently, such privileged member states become regional Rambos that lose any interest in regional cooperation and opt for regional defection. The results are either decision-making deadlocks or implementation deficits, and due to the characteristics of such Rambo situations, cooperation cannot be achieved with the help of the usual regional institutions but instead only through large side payments and package deals.

The extra-regional logic provides a rationale for regional economic integration even in regions where the potential for intraregional trade and economic interdependence is low. In contrast to Mattli (1999), we argue that demand for regional integration may not only emerge from the utilisation of comparative cost advantages and economies of scale through liberalising intraregional trade, but it may also emerge from size and stability effects that improve the regions' competitiveness on the global market. These extra-regional effects of regional integration are more important for developing regions than for well-developed regions. Developing countries and emerging markets cannot profit as much as well-developed countries when trading with their regional neighbours. However, when following an export-promoting development strategy, developing countries and emerging markets need to attract extra-regional investments and to get access to extra-regional export markets. Because they compete with other world regions for extra-regional investments and export flows, the size and stability effects of regional integration are of particular importance for developing regions in order to be more competitive in this struggle. Consequently, there exists a demand for regional integration in developing regions, although this demand differs from that in well-developed regions.

If the demand for regional integration in developing regions results from the extra-regional logic, the supply of regional integration depends on the reaction of extra-regional actors. As long as extra-regional actors reward regional integration systematically, all regional member states should have an interest in regional cooperation, even if they may disagree about the specific form of regional institutions. However, regional powers in developing regions face incentives to protect privileges in their economic relations with extra-regional actors. Regional powers constitute the largest and most attractive markets of their regions, and this means that they gain less from regional integration than their smaller neighbours, and are more likely to enjoy extra-regional privileges. If such privileges are at odds with regional integration, the regional powers lose interest in regional cooperation and become regional Rambos. Thus, regional powers are not necessarily benevolent in terms of regional integration, which is Mattli's supply condition for successful regional integration; their behaviour towards regional integration is at best volatile. They may provide regional leadership only as long as regional integration is not at odds with important extra-regional interests, but they become regional Rambos as soon as such important extra-regional interests are at stake.

Notes

1. The term 'Rambo' does not refer to the Hollywood movie with Sylvester Stallone, but to a theoretical game with a constellation of actors that was first described and analysed by Zürn (1992, 1993).
2. The problem of the term 'regional power' is that most definitions in the literature include structural (e.g. market size) as well as behavioural (e.g. regional leadership) aspects (see Kappel 2010; Nolte 2010; Schirm 2010). However, we propose a purely structuralist, economic definition of regional powers, because we are interested in the variant behaviour of such states, which precludes the inclusion of behavioural aspects in the definition.

References

Abbott, K. W., Keohane, R. O., Moravcsik, A., Slaughter, A.-M., & Snidal, D. (2000). The Concept of Legalization. *International Organization, 54*, 401–419.
Adler, E., & Barnett, M. (Eds.). (1998). *Security Communities*. Cambridge: Cambridge University Press.
Aggarwal, V. K., & Fogarty, E. A. (Eds.). (2004). *EU Trade Strategies: Between Regionalism and Globalism*. Basingstoke: Palgrave Macmillan.
Axelrod, R. (1984). *The Evolution of Cooperation*. New York: Basic Books.
Bearce, D. H., & Tirone, D. C. (2010). Foreign Aid Effectiveness and the Strategic Goals of Donor Governments. *The Journal of Politics, 72*, 837.

Bende-Nabende, A. (2002). *Globalization, FDI, Regional Integration and Sustainable Development.* Aldershot: Ashgate Publishing.

Bhagwati, J. N. (1988). Export-Promoting Trade Strategy. *World Bank Research Observer, 3,* 27–57.

Bjorvatn, K., & Eckel, C. (2006). Policy Competition for Foreign Direct Investment between Asymmetric Countries. *European Economic Review, 50,* 1891–1907.

Buchanan, J. M. (1965). An Economic Theory of Clubs. *Economica, 32,* 1–14.

Büthe, T., & Milner, H. (2008). The Politics of Foreign Direct Investment into Developing Countries: Increasing FDI through International Trade Agreements? *American Journal of Political Science, 52,* 741–762.

Cardoso, F. H., & Faletto, E. (1979). *Dependency and Development in Latin America.* Berkely, CA: University of California Press.

Casella, A. A. (1992). On Markets and Clubs: Economic and Political Integration of Regions with Unequal Productivity. *American Economic Review, 82,* 115–121.

Cornes, R., & Sandler, T. (1996). *The Theory of Externalities, Public Goods and Club Goods* (2nd ed.). Cambridge: Cambridge University Press.

Duina, F. (2006). *The Social Construction of Free Trade: The European Union, NAFTA, and MERCOSUR.* Princeton, NJ: Princeton University Press.

Dullien, S., Fritz, B., & Mühlich, L. (2013). Regional Monetary Cooperation: Lessons from the Euro Crisis for Developing Areas? *World Economic Review, 2,* 1–23.

Dunning, J. H., & Lundan, S. M. (2008). *Multinational Enterprises and the Global Economy* (2nd ed.). Cheltenham: Edward Elgar Publishing.

Fligstein, N., & Stone Sweet, A. (2002). Constructing Polities and Markets: An Institutionalist Account of European Integration. *American Journal of Sociology, 107,* 1206–1243.

Fratianni, M., & Pattison, J. (2001). International Organisations in a World of Regional Trade Agreements: Lessons from Club Theory. *The World Economy, 24,* 333–358.

Garrett, G., & Weingast, B. R. (1993). Ideas, Interests, and Institutions: Constructing the European Community's Internal Market. In J. Goldstein & R. O. Keohane (Eds.), *Ideas and Foreign Policy: Beliefs, Institutions, and Political Change* (pp. 173–206). Ithaca, NY: Cornell University Press.

Gehring, T. (2002). *Die Europäische Union als komplexe internationale Organisation: Wie durch Kommunikation und Entscheidung soziale Ordnung entsteht.* Baden-Baden: Nomos Verlagsgesellschaft.

Gilpin, R. (1981). *War and Change in World Politics.* Cambridge: Cambridge University Press.

Gilson, J. (2005). New Interregionalism? The EU and East Asia. *European Integration, 27,* 307–326.

Goldberg, P. K., & Knetter, M. M. (1999). Measuring the Intensity of Competition in Export Markets. *Journal of International Economics, 47,* 27–60.

Goldstein, A. (2004). *Regional Integration, FDI and Competitiveness in Southern Africa.* Paris: OECD Publishing.

Haas, E. B. (1958). *The Uniting of Europe: Political, Social and Economic Forces, 1950-1957.* Stanford, CA: Stanford University Press.

Hänggi, H. (2003). Regionalism through Interregionalism: East Asia and ASEM. In F.-K. Liu & P. Regnier (Eds.), *Regionalism in East Asia: Paradigm Shifting?* (pp. 197–219). London: RoutledgeCurzon.

Hänggi, H., Roloff, R., & Rüland, J. (Eds.). (2006). *Interregionalism and International Relations.* London: Routledge.

Hardin, G. (1968). The Tragedy of the Commons. *Science, 162,* 1243–1248.

Hettne, B., & Söderbaum, F. (2000). Theorising the Rise of Regionness. *New Political Economy, 5,* 457–473.

Holzinger, K. (2003). Common Goods, Matrix Games and Institutional Response. *European Journal of International Relations, 9,* 173–212.

Hout, W., & Meijerink, F. (1996). Structures in the International Political Economy: World System Theory and Unequal Development. *European Journal of International Relations, 2,* 47–76.

Jaumotte, F. (2004). *Foreign Direct Investment and Regional Trade Agreements: The Market Size Effect* (International Monetary Fund Working Paper 04/206).

Kappel, R. (2010). *On the Economics of Regional Powers: Comparing China, India, Brazil, and South Africa* (GIGA Working Papers No 145).

Kind, H. J., Midelfart, K. H., & Schjelderup, G. (2000). Competing for Capital in a 'Lumpy' World. *Journal of Public Economics, 78,* 253–274.

Kindleberger, C. P. (1973). *The World in Depression: 1929-1939.* Berkeley, CA: University of California Press.

Krapohl, S. (2008). *Risk Regulation in the Single Market: The Governance of Pharmaceuticals and Foodstuffs in the European Union.* Basingstoke: Palgrave Macmillan.

Krapohl, S., & Fink, S. (2013). Different Paths of Regional Integration: Trade Networks and Regional Institution-Building in Europe, Southeast Asia and Southern Africa. *Journal of Common Market Studies, 51,* 472–488.

Krapohl, S., Meißner, K. L., & Muntschick, J. (2014). Regional Powers as Leaders or Rambos of Regional Integration? Unilateral Actions of Brazil and South Africa and Their Negative Effects on MERCOSUR and SADC. *Journal of Common Market Studies, 52,* 879–895.

Krasner, S. D. (1982). Structural Causes and Regime Consequences: Regimes as Intervening Variables. *International Organization, 36,* 185–205.

Krueger, A. O. (1997). Trade Policy and Economic Development: How We Learn. *American Economic Review, 87,* 1–22.

Krugman, P. R. (1980). Scale Economies, Product Differentiation, and the Pattern of Trade. *The American Economic Review, 70*, 950–959.
Langhammer, R. J. (1992). The Developing Countries and Regionalism. *Journal of Common Market Studies, 30*, 211–232.
Majone, G. (2001). Two Logics of Delegation: Agency and Fiduciary Relations in EU Governance. *European Union Politics, 2*, 103–122.
Malamud, A. (2003). Presidentialism and Mercosur: A Hidden Cause for a Successful Experience. In F. Laursen (Ed.), *Comparative Regional Integration: Theoretical Perspectives* (pp. 53–73). Aldershot: Ashgate.
Malamud, A. (2005). Presidential Diplomacy and the Institutional Underpinnings of Mercosur: An Empirical Examination. *Latin American Research Review, 40*, 138–164.
Mansfield, E. D., & Milner, H. V. (1999). The New Wave of Regionalism. *International Organization, 53*, 589–627.
Mansfield, E. D., & Reinhardt, E. (2003). Multilateral Determinants of Regionalism: The Effects of GATT/WTO on the Formation of Preferential Trading Arrangements. International Organization, 57, 829–862.
Mattli, W. (1999). *The Logic of Regional Integration: Europe and Beyond*. Cambridge: Cambridge University Press.
Moravcsik, A. (1993). Preferences and Power in the European Community: A Liberal Intergovernmentalist Approach. *Journal of Common Market Studies, 31*, 473–524.
Moravcsik, A. (1998). *The Choice for Europe: Social Purpose and State Power from Messina to Maastricht*. Ithaca, NY: Cornell University Press.
Nolte, D. (2010). How to Compare Regional Powers: Analytical Concepts and Research Topics. *Review of International Studies, 36*, 881–901.
Ostrom, E. (2003). How Types of Goods and Property Rights Jointly Affect Collective Action. *Journal of Theoretical Politics, 15*, 239–270.
Pierson, P. (2000). Increasing Returns, Path Dependence, and the Study of Politics. *American Political Science Review, 94*, 251–267.
Pollack, M. A. (1997). Delegation, Agency and Agenda-Setting in the European Community. *International Organization, 51*, 99–134.
Pollack, M. A. (2003). *The Engines of European Integration: Delegation, Agency, and Agenda-Setting in the EU*. Oxford: Oxford University Press.
Ricardo, D. (1821). *On the Principles of Political Economy and Taxation*. London: John Murray.
Robson, P. (1993). The New Regionalism and Developing Countries. *Journal of Common Market Studies, 31*, 329–348.
Scharpf, F. W. (1988). The Joint-Decision Trap: Lessons from German Federalism and European Integration. *Public Administration, 66*, 239–278.
Scharpf, F. W. (1997). *Games Real Actors Play: Actor-Centered Institutionalism in Policy Research*. Boulder, CO: Westview Press.

Schimmelfennig, F. (2012). Zwischen Neo- und Postfunktionalismus: Die Integrationstheorien und die Eurokrise. *Politische Vierteljahresschrift*, 53, 394–413.
Schirm, S. A. (2002). *Globalization and the New Regionalism: Global Markets, Domestic Politics and Regional Cooperation*. Cambridge: Polity Press.
Schirm, S. A. (2010). Leaders in Need of Followers: Emerging Powers in Global Governance. *European Journal of International Relations*, 16, 197–221.
Smith, D. A., & White, D. R. (1992). Structure and Dynamics of the Global Economy: Network Analysis of International Trade 1965-1980. *Social Forces*, 70, 857–893.
Stone Sweet, A., & Caporaso, J. A. (1998). From Free Trade to Supranational Polity: The European Court and Integration. In W. Sandholtz & A. Stone Sweet (Eds.), *European Integration and Supranational Governance* (pp. 92–133). Oxford: Oxford University Press.
Tranholm-Mikkelsen, J. (1991). Neofunctionalism: Obstinate or Obsolete? A Reappraisal in the Light of the New Dynamism of the EC. *Millennium: Journal of International Studies*, 20, 1–22.
Van Rossem, R. (1996). The World System Paradigm as General Theory of Development: A Cross-National Test. *American Sociological Review*, 61, 508–527.
Venables, A. J. (2003). Winners and Losers from Regional Integration Agreements. *The Economic Journal*, 113, 747–761.
Zangl, B. (2008). Judicialisation Matters! A Comparison of Dispute Settlement Under GATT and the WTO. *International Studies Quarterly*, 52, 825–854.
Zürn, M. (1992). *Interessen und Institutionen in der internationalen Politik: Grundlegung und Anwendungen des situationsstrukturellen Ansatzes*. Opladen: Leske + Budrich.
Zürn, M. (1993). Problematic Social Situations and International Institutions: On the Use of Game Theory in International Politics. In F. Pfetsch (Ed.), *International Relations and Pan-Europe: Theoretical Approaches and Empirical Findings* (pp. 63–84). Münster: LIT Verlag.

CHAPTER 3

Case Selection and Research Methods for a Comparative Analysis of Developing Regions

Sebastian Krapohl

Our theoretical argument (see Chap. 2) can be summarised like this: Due to low levels of intraregional economic interdependence, regional economic integration in developing regions is mainly driven by the extra-regional logic of regional integration. Developing countries and emerging markets do not profit much from comparative cost advantages and economies of scale within regional markets (Langhammer 1992; Mattli 1999; Robson 1993; Venables 2003) because their most important export markets are well-developed economies in other world regions. In contrast, when following export-promoting development strategies, developing countries and emerging markets can improve their competitiveness on the global market when integrating regionally (Schirm 2002). The size and stability effects of regional integration help them to attract extra-regional investments and to negotiate access to important extra-regional markets. This extra-regional logic leads to two hypotheses about economic cooperation and defection in developing regions. Firstly, as long as extra-

S. Krapohl (✉)
University of Amsterdam, Amsterdam, The Netherlands
e-mail: s.krapohl@uva.nl

© The Author(s) 2017
S. Krapohl (ed.), *Regional Integration in the Global South*,
International Political Economy Series,
DOI 10.1007/978-3-319-38895-3_3

regional actors reward regional integration systematically, the member states of regional organisations in the developing world cooperate within battles of the sexes. Here, all regional member states have an interest in regional economic cooperation, and they only disagree about the concrete form of regional rules. The solution of such situations is not banal, but issue linkages and package deals should be sufficient to reach negotiated agreements. Secondly, however, as soon as regional integration is at odds with important extra-regional privileges, the regional powers of developing regions become regional Rambos with a dominant strategy of defection. Here, the regional powers do not defect in order to free ride on the cooperation of others, but rather lose all interest in regional integration. In such Rambo situations, cooperation is very difficult because it usually requires huge side payments to the potential Rambos.

We follow a comparative case study design in order to test our two hypotheses about economic cooperation and defection in developing regions. In contrast to quantitative analyses, which rely on probability statements, qualitative comparisons depend on a conscious and careful case selection in order to improve their analytical leverage (Mahoney 2007). Thus, we do not select our cases by chance; they are chosen because they represent specific values for the independent and dependent variables of interest. Our case selection is based on three strategies: Firstly, we choose prominent regional organisations of the developing world because they constitute unlikely cases for our theory. These regional organisations are economically more developed and politically more integrated than other, less-prominent developing regions. If the extra-regional logic of regional integration prevails in our sample, it should be even more dominant in less-developed and less-integrated regions, which profit even less from the intraregional effects of regional integration. Secondly, the three selected regional organisations are dissimilar cases (Przeworski and Teune 1970) in many political and cultural respects but not in their dependence on extra-regional economic exchange. As a result, if our hypotheses are supported in all three case studies, it is very likely that economic structures are indeed the crucial determinants of regional integration in the developing world. Thirdly, in-case comparisons (George and Bennett 2005) of regional cooperation and defection within the three selected regional organisations keep the political and cultural background more or less constant between the different observations. The in-case comparisons provide variance of the dependent variable and allow exploration as to whether this variance can be explained by variance of only one independent variable, namely the presence or absence of extra-regional privileges for the regional powers.

The choice of a comparative case study design means that qualitative research methods need to be applied in order to improve our analytic leverage. Our sample includes three regional organisations and seven cases of economic cooperation or defection within these regions; these numbers are certainly insufficient to improve the confidence in our hypotheses by way of statistical inference. Thus, we apply two different qualitative research methods in our analysis. At the macro-level, diachronic network analyses of trade data are used to explore the economic structures of the three regions. Such network analysis allows a much more detailed view of the economic structures of developing regions than stylised facts like the share of intraregional trade could do (De Lombaerde et al. 2010). At the micro-level, careful process tracing follows the causal paths from regional economic structures and extra-regional privileges to instances of economic cooperation or defection within the respective regions. This process tracing does not only increase the number of empirical observations (as argued by King et al. 1994), but it also demonstrates that these observations are linked in a specific and meaningful way (George and Bennett 2005). To sum up, we are confident that the qualitative analysis of complex trade patterns and the careful analysis of collective and unilateral actions allow us to gain a deeper understanding of our empirical cases and to reach more confidence in our hypotheses than a quantitative analysis would do, because the latter would necessarily have to rely on the relatively low number of regional organisations existing today (Genna and De Lombaerde 2010).

1 CASE SELECTION

Scholars of comparative regionalism are confronted with two major problems whenever they aim to compare different world regions and their integration efforts. Firstly, whereas the universe of more than 190 sovereign states—the usual subject matter of comparative politics—is relatively clear-cut, it remains much more unclear what defines world regions or regional organisations (Genna and De Lombaerde 2010). Regions have no clearly defined borders, and their organisational structures vary between non-existence and almost state-like political systems like that of the European Union (EU). Thus, before selecting regional organisations as cases for comparison, one first needs to define the universe of cases to which the respective theory applies. Secondly, whereas comparing sovereign states is widely accepted as a research method, the comparison of regions and of their integration efforts meets much more criticism (De Lombaerde et al. 2010). Especially the EU is often seen as a sui generis political system that cannot be compared with other international organisations or with sovereign states. To answer such criticism, some thinking needs to be done on the comparability of the selected regional organisations and on the conclusions to be drawn from such a comparison. One answer to the problem of comparability is to compare dissimilar regions in order to draw conclusions in respect to the influence of one common independent variable (Przeworski and Teune 1970). Another answer is to conduct in-case comparisons within the selected regional organisations; this comes as close as possible to controlled comparisons, because only one independent and the dependent variable vary between the different observations (George and Bennett 2005).

1.1 The Selection of Unlikely Cases from the Universe of Regional Organisations in the Developing World

In order to select the cases for the empirical analysis, it is first necessary to define the scope conditions of our theory. The approach of this book represents a classic middle-range theory (George and Bennett 2005; Merton 1957) because it addresses a specific group of cases in a concrete time period. The theory aims to explain economic cooperation or defection in regional organisations of the developing world during the period of the new regionalism (i.e. during and after the 1990s). Here, the terms 'regional organisations', 'developing regions', and 'new regionalism' need further clarification in order to establish the universe of cases for case selection.

A simple way to define 'regional organisations' would be to refer to the list of 379 regional trade agreements that are notified to the World Trade Organisation (WTO).[1] However, this list includes a wide spectrum of agreements including regional organisations like the Southern African Development Community (SADC), but also bilateral trade agreements like that of Chile and Mexico. Thus, the WTO list includes more cases than what can be reasonably called regional organisations. In the following, we define our universe of regional organisations as agreements between more than two neighbouring states that set up at least rudimentary forms of organisational structures (like secretariats or institutionalised meetings of member states' representatives) and grant some kind of preferential market access for each other (like free trade areas or customs unions. As a result, SADC qualifies as a regional organisation, whereas the Chile-Mexico trade agreement does not because it is a bilateral agreement and the participating states are not regional neighbours.

The next term that needs to be defined is 'developing regions'. Although contested, developing countries are relatively straightforward to define. Here, we refer to the classification by the World Bank, which is based on gross domestic product (GDP) per capita, and we put low-income and middle-income economies under the term 'developing countries'.[2] Emerging markets are a subgroup of developing countries, and that term usually refers to large developing countries with rapid economic growth. However, the definition of developing regions is more difficult because it includes a judgement of how many member states need to be developing countries in order for whole regions to count as developing regions. There exist regional organisations like the North American Free Trade Agreement (NAFTA) and the Association of Southeast Asian Nations (ASEAN) that consist of both developing and well-developed countries. At this point, we define developing regions as regions in which the majority of member states are developing countries and whose average GDP per capita is that of developing countries. As a result, NAFTA does not qualify as a developing region because Mexico is the only developing member state and the average GDP per capita of the region is that of a high-income economy. In contrast, ASEAN counts as a developing region because its high-income economies, Brunei and Singapore, are in the minority and the average GDP per capita of the region is that of a lower-middle-income economy.

Finally, we restrict our study to cases of economic integration over the course of the 'new regionalism' because the theoretical framework only addresses developing regions that aim to increase their competitiveness on the global market. The 'old regionalism' of the 1950s to 1970s was mainly an instrument of import substitution in the developing world, wherein each region protected itself with high tariff walls from global competition and tried to generate comparative cost advantages and economies of scale within its own region (Axline 1977). Here, the extra-regional logic of regional integration could not work because member states did not try to attract extra-regional investments or to gain access to extra-regional markets. In contrast, the new regionalism—sometimes also called 'open regionalism' (Bulmer-Thomas 2001; Frankel and Wei 1998)—in the developing world is usually accompanied by export-promoting development strategies (Bhagwati 1988). Here, extra-regional investments and export possibilities are crucial for such export-promoting development strategies and the extra-regional logic of regional integration may work as expected. Restricting the scope of the theory to cases of the new regionalism does not imply that the respective regional organisations have to be established during or after the 1990s—like the Common Market of South America (MERCOSUR). Some regional organisations—like ASEAN and SADC— were established before the 1990s or followed on preceding organisations but set up new goals and developed new dynamics of economic integration over the course of new regionalism. In such cases, where regional organisations were reinvented during or after the 1990s, the theory may explain the new developments over the course of the new regionalism but not the establishment or development of the organisations in earlier periods.

Applying these selection criteria to the list of regional trade agreements notified at the WTO boils down the number of 379 agreements to about 20 regional organisations in Africa, Asia, Central Europe, and South America. These include relatively well-known examples of regional organisations in the developing world as ASEAN, MERCOSUR, and SADC. However, the WTO list also includes regional organisations like the Asia Pacific Trade Agreement (APTA), the Pacific Island Countries Trade Agreement (PICTA), and the Economic and Monetary Community of Central Africa (CEMAG), about which practically no academic literature exists. Arguably, the number of regional organisations in the developing world is much higher than such a rough estimate based on the WTO list indicates because not all regional organisations of the developing world are notified to the WTO. For example, the number of regional organisations included in the Regional Indicators Knowledge System (RIKS)[3] exceeds that of the WTO list by far, but not all of them include preferential trade agreements among their member states.

For the empirical analysis of regional cooperation and defection, we choose ASEAN (Chap. 5), MERCOSUR (Chap. 6), and SADC (Chap. 7) from the universe of regional organisations in the developing world. These three regional organisations are arguably the most successful and thus the most relevant ones on their respective continents. All three organisations have organisational structures, which work day-to-day, and they have reached the levels of free trade areas (ASEAN and SADC) or even a customs union (MERCOSUR). Thus, rather than choosing mere paper tigers, which are rarely discussed in the academic literature and which are unlikely to have real effects on the member states' economies, we pragmatically concentrate on cases that raise the interest of the academic world and that seem to have a real impact on the ground.

ASEAN, MERCOSUR, and SADC constitute unlikely cases (Eckstein 1975; George and Bennett 2005) for our theory. Compared with other prominent regional organisations on their continents, the three selected regional organisations are distinguished by relatively high economic development and intraregional trade (see Table 3.1). In 2010, the GDP per capita and the share of intraregional trade of ASEAN was more than twice as much as that of the South Asian Association for Regional Cooperation (SAARC). The same applies to a comparison of SADC with the Economic Community of West African States (ECOWAS). MERCOSUR's GDP per capita is also twice as much as that of the Andean Community (CAN), but the difference in the share of intraregional trade is not that big because the intraregional trade of MERCOSUR declined sharply after the Argentine crisis at the turn of the millennium. Our theoretical approach assumes that regional integration in developing regions is driven and constrained by the extra-regional interests of the regional member states because the gains from intraregional trade are likely to be low. If this is confirmed by an analysis of relatively well-developed regional organisations of the developing world, it should be even more true for less-developed regional organisations with lower GDPs per capita and less intraregional trade. Thus, if the hypotheses are supported by the analysis of relatively unlikely cases, this strengthens our confidence that the dominance of the extra-regional logic

Table 3.1 Economic development and intraregional trade of selected regional organisations in 2010[a]

	GDP per capita (in US$)	Intraregional trade share (%)
ASEAN	3146	26.14
SAARC	1291	11.85
MERCOSUR	10,267	11.77
CAN	5252	8.84
SADC	2174	12.15
ECOWAS	1027	4.32

[a]The data is taken from the database of the Regional Integration Knowledge System (RIKS) of the United Nations University on Comparative Regional Integration Studies (UNU-CRIS) (www.cris.unu.edu/riks/web/data)

of regional integration is a general phenomenon of the new regionalism in the developing world and that it prevails even in economically less-developed regional organisations.

1.2 A Comparison of Dissimilar Regions

An issue that is discussed repeatedly in the area of comparative regionalism is the comparability of different world regions and their integration efforts (De Lombaerde et al. 2010). Emphasis on the uniqueness of different world regions and scepticism of comparative analyses of their regional integration efforts was already prominent in the early times of regional integration studies of the 1960s and 1970s. The question of comparability is most prominent in the field of EU studies, where scholars often argue that the EU is a 'sui generis' political system (Haas 1976; Von Bogdandy 1993) and that it can be compared neither with other international organisations nor with national political systems. According to this argument, the strength of supranational institutions and the special character of EU law prohibit comparing the EU with other international organisations, and the strong influence of the member states within EU policymaking and the vast array of competencies left at the national level distinguish the EU sharply from federal states. Nevertheless, there also exists a growing academic literature that compares the EU either with other international organisations (Gehring 1996, 2002) or with national political systems (Hix 1998; Hix and Hoyland 2011). Such comparisons provide valuable insights into the functioning of the EU as long as they are carefully undertaken and respect the obvious differences of the compared cases.

Although we generally believe that the EU can and should be carefully compared with other regional organisations, we do not need to address this issue here because our comparison deals exclusively with regional organisations of the developing world. Nevertheless, we need to deal with the question of comparability of ASEAN, MERCOSUR, and SADC to each other, because the three regions differ widely in composition as well as in cultural and political terms (see Table 3.2). As a result of the heterogeneity of our sample, a controlled comparison (George and Bennett 2005), in which only one independent variable is allowed to vary, is not possible. In fact, such a controlled comparison is hardly imaginable in the field of comparative regionalism because the number of potential cases is still relatively low, but the range of possible independent variables and the heterogeneity of possible samples are high (Genna and De Lombaerde 2010). However, the

Table 3.2 Heterogeneity of the sample in 2010

	Member states	Regional power	Democracies[a]		Failed states[b]	Religions[c]
ASEAN	10	None	5		1	4
MERCOSUR	4	Brazil	4		0	1
SADC	15	South Africa	6		3	1

[a]This column counts the number of democracies among the regions' member states. Data is derived from the Democracy Index of the Economist Intelligence Unit in 2010 (graphics.eiu.com/PDF/Democracy_Index_2010_web.pdf). Full and flawed democracies are counted as democracies, whereas hybrid and authoritarian regimes are not

[b]This column counts the number of member states for which the Fund for Peace raised an alert in 2010 (www.fundforpeace.org/global/library/cr-10-99-fs-failedstatesindex2010-1103g.pdf)

[c]This column counts the number of majority religions in the regions' member states. Whereas MERCOSUR and SADC consist only of member states with Christian majorities, ASEAN includes member states with Buddhist, Christian, folk religion, and Muslim majorities (www.pewforum.org)

heterogeneity of our sample can also be turned into an advantage because ASEAN, MERCOSUR, and SADC constitute dissimilar cases (Przeworski and Teune 1970; Ragin 1987). In fact, the three regional organisations have little in common aside from the fact that they are all developing regions. ASEAN, MERCOSUR, and SADC are different in composition and they show different degrees of political and cultural homogeneity. Thus, if the empirical analysis demonstrates that the extra-regional logic of regional integration prevails in all three regions, it is highly unlikely that this is the result of the regions' composition or of political and cultural variables. Instead, if rather dissimilar cases show similar observations at the dependent variable, it is likely that the independent variable, which is common to all cases, is responsible. In this way, it can be demonstrated that alternative explanations for regional integration in the developing world are implausible.

A first alternative hypothesis to our political economy argument could be that the success or failure of regional integration varies with the regions' numbers of member states. It is often argued in the literature on European integration that the latest rounds of enlargement increased cooperation and coordination problems within the EU (Magnet and Nicolaidis 2004). During the first decade of the new millennium, the number of the EU member states increased from 15 to 27, and the heterogeneity of the member states grew as well. This increase in numbers and heterogeneity poses problems for EU policymaking, especially in the Council. In analogue to this argument, one could claim that the likeliness of being a successful region declines with a greater number of member states. Applied to our sample, this would mean that MERCOSUR, with 4 member states (Venezuela became the fifth member state in 2012), should be the most successful; SADC, with 15 member states, should be the least successful; and ASEAN, with 10 member states, should be in between.

Secondly, from a realist perspective, one could propose the hypothesis that the success of regional integration correlates with the existence of regional powers. In accordance with Olson's group theory (Olson 1965), hegemonic stability theory (Gilpin 1981; Kindleberger 1973; Krasner 1982) argues that groups of states face severe cooperation problems when they aim to provide collective goods because all group members face incentives to free ride on the cooperation of the others. The chances for cooperation increase significantly if the existence of benevolent hegemons turns groups of states into privileged groups. Mattli (1999) applied this argument to regional organisations and claims that the supply of the collective good regional integration is ensured if benevolent regional hegemons act as regional paymasters. Within our sample, MERCOSUR and SADC are dominated by the regional powers Brazil and South Africa. These two countries dominate their respective regions in economic terms, and their cooperation is crucial for regional integration. In contrast, ASEAN does not have a real regional power. Although Indonesia is the largest economy of the region, its economic power is balanced by Malaysia, Singapore, and Thailand (see Chap. 4). Thus, realists would argue that regional integration in MERCOSUR and SADC should be more successful than in ASEAN.

A third alternative explanation from a more liberal point of view (Moravcsik 1997; Schirm 2009) would be that regional integration is more successful when more member states are well-functioning democracies. The argument behind this hypothesis is that democracies are more likely to translate societal demands for regional integration into regional policies. Whereas authoritarian states may decide not to cooperate regionally in order to protect their autonomy, influence, and sovereignty, democracies are more likely to behave amicably and cooperatively—which is also one reason for the fact that democracies do usually not fight wars against each other (Doyle 1997). Within our sample, MERCOSUR consists only of presidential democracies, whereas only 50 per cent of the ASEAN and 40 per cent of the SADC member states are well-functioning democracies.

Moreover, one ASEAN and three SADC member states count as failed states, which are even less likely to translate societal demands into domestic or regional policies. As a result, from the perspective of liberalism, regional integration should be more successful in MERCOSUR than in ASEAN or SADC.

Finally, a sociologically inspired hypothesis would build up on cultural variables and would argue that regional integration is more successful when the respective regions are more homogenous in cultural terms. A common regional culture may have two positive effects on regional integration. Firstly, a homogenous culture probably leads to similar politics and policies of the member states so that the need for expensive adaptation and coordination is reduced. And secondly, a regional culture may lead to some form of regional identity and solidarity, which facilitates regional coordination when necessary (McCormick 2010). Taking religion as a proxy (Huntington 1996), ASEAN is by far the most heterogeneous region of our sample in cultural terms. Majority populations of four different religions distinguish the ASEAN member states. Whereas Christianity and Islam dominate the archipelagic states of ASEAN, the mainland is dominated by Buddhism and (in Vietnam) folk religions. In contrast, Christianity is the dominating religion in all member states of MERCOSUR and SADC. Here, SADC is more heterogeneous in cultural terms than MERCOSUR (because of tribal structures in Southern Africa and of a much larger number of colonial powers), but both should be more homogeneous than ASEAN. As a result, from a cultural point of view, one should expect that regional integration is easier to achieve in South America than in Southeast Asia, with Southern Africa falling somewhere in between.

Two of the alternative explanations—the one based on the number of member states and the liberal one based on the number of democracies—would claim that MERCOSUR should be the most successful regional organisation of our sample, whereas SADC should be the least successful one and ASEAN should be in between. The other two alternative hypotheses—the realist and the cultural ones—would even argue that ASEAN is likely to be the least successful regional organisation, and MERCOSUR and SADC should face less problems in integrating. However, these hypotheses do not fit particularly well with the empirical evidence. As the empirical analyses demonstrate (see Chaps. 5–7), economic cooperation in ASEAN has been successful during the last 15 years, whereas economic integration in MERCOSUR and SADC has stagnated. This pattern of regional cooperation and defection cannot be explained by the alternative hypotheses but by diverging extra-regional influences on regional economic integration in the three regions.

1.3 In-Case Comparison of Regional Cooperation and Defection

We do not only compare the three regional organisations ASEAN, MERCOSUR, and SADC with each other, but we also conduct in-case comparisons of regional cooperation and defection within the three regions. In the case of MERCOSUR and SADC, we compare cases of successful economic cooperation with cases of regional defection. The examples for cooperation are the establishment of the MERCOSUR Customs Union (MERCOSUR-CU) during the early 1990s and the setup of the SADC Free Trade Area (SADC-FTA) in 2008. These form a contrast to Brazil's unilateral devaluation in 1999, to the stagnation of MERCOSUR in the 2000s, and to the failure in establishing the SADC Customs Union (SADC-CU) in 2010, respectively. In the ASEAN, we choose two cases of successful regional cooperation, namely the establishment of the ASEAN Free Trade Area (AFTA) during the 1990s and the adoption of the ASEAN Charter in 2007. The fact that we do not choose a case of regional defection for ASEAN results from the current dynamic of economic integration within the region, which is very much driven by the region's economic cooperation with China, Japan, and South Korea in the so-called ASEAN+3 process (Nabers 2003). Successful extra-regional cooperation with the +3 countries pushes regional integration forward within ASEAN, so that contemporary cases of regional economic defection are hard to find.

The in-case comparison of single cases of regional cooperation and defection has three advantages when testing the hypotheses of our theoretical approach. Firstly, the analysis of two or three cases of economic cooperation and defection for each region increases our number of cases and of observable implications, which necessarily improves the validity of our analysis (King et al. 1994). Secondly, the selection of different cases of cooperation and defection produces variance on the dependent variable. We do not start from the observation that regional cooperation is difficult to achieve in developing regions and then look for possible explanations of regional defection, but rather analyse under which conditions regional cooperation in developing regions is possible or not. Thereby, we avoid the mistake of selecting our cases in respect to only one value at the dependent variable, which is regarded as the most severe selection bias in qualitative analyses (King et al. 1994). Thirdly, and most importantly for the research design, such in-case comparisons come as close as possible to controlled comparisons (George and Bennett 2005). When comparing the single instances of regional cooperation and defection, most alternative independent variables remain the same. The number of member states remains constant, the presence or absence of regional powers remains constant, the number of democracies or failed states within the region remains constant, and the cultural homogeneity or heterogeneity remains constant as well. In this way, our confidence that extra-regional privileges are responsible for the occasional defection of regional powers in developing regions is improved.

2 Research Methods

We distinguish between two different levels of analysis in our empirical research, and different research techniques are applied at the respective levels. Firstly, diachronic network analyses of regional trade patterns constitute the macro-level of analysis (see Chap. 4). These trade networks provide a more detailed view of regional economic structures and their development than simple indicators like the share of intraregional trade could do. Secondly, case studies of single instances of regional economic cooperation or defection constitute the micro-level of our analysis (see Chaps. 5–7). At this level, process tracing needs to follow the causal mechanisms that link the regional economic structures and the presence or absence of extra-regional economic privileges with the resulting behaviour of the regional member states. Finally, instances of regional economic cooperation or defection at the micro-level may lead to changes in regional economic structures, which is the reason why diachronic instead of static network analyses are necessary at the macro-level.

2.1 Network Analysis of Regional Trade Patterns

Traditional indicators for intraregional economic interdependence like the share of intraregional trade have been criticised in the academic literature because they provide an overly simplified picture of the complexity of intraregional economic relations (De Lombaerde et al. 2010). Firstly, the share of intraregional trade correlates positively with the size of regional organisations. The more regional states that participate in trade liberalisation, the bigger the regional market becomes, and the higher the potential for intraregional trade (Iapadre 2006). Thus, the share of intraregional trade has little informative value when regions of different sizes are compared—as is the case in our sample, which includes regions with 4, 10, and 15 member states. Secondly, different indicators of intraregional economic interdependence lead to different results in comparisons. For example, whereas the share of intraregional trade is much higher for the EU than for ASEAN, MERCOSUR, and SADC, the intraregional trade intensity index[4] reverses this order with SADC at the top and MERCOSUR, ASEAN, and the EU behind (De Lombaerde et al. 2010). As a result, stylised facts like the share of intraregional trade can at best only be a first indicator for the relative importance of the intra- and extra-regional logics of regional integration in ASEAN, MERCOSUR, and SADC.

Furthermore, indicators like the share of intraregional trade do not help to identify whether the respective regions are dominated by regional powers and what the interests of these regional powers are within their regions. For our hypotheses, it is not only important whether intra- or extra-regional economic interdependence is in total more important for ASEAN, MERCOSUR, and SADC; it is also important whether the respective regions are dominated by single regional powers and whether these regional powers trade more with their regional neighbours or with extra-regional partners. The likelihood of extra-regional privileges declines when regions are not dominated by single regional powers. Moreover, even when such dominant regional powers exist, they may be benevolent towards regional integration when they themselves trade heavily with their regional neighbours despite the fact that the overall level of intraregional interdependence may be low. However, the share of intraregional trade does not provide any information either about the dominance of single member states within their regional organisations or about the economic embeddedness of single member states within their regions. Thus, we need more finely tuned instruments to explore the economic structures of ASEAN, MERCOSUR, and SADC.

Because indicators like the share of intraregional trade provide too little information to explore our independent variables, we provide diachronic network analyses of regional trade data to disaggregate regional trade patterns further and to gain a more complex view of regional interdependence (Brandes et al. 1999, 2006; Scott 2006). Network methods have been mostly used in policy analysis (Kenis and Schneider 1991; Thurner and Binder 2009), but in international relations, the potential of network analysis has not yet been used to its full extent. International relations scholars have only seldom used network methods and reasoning (but see Hafner-Burton et al. 2009; Hafner-Burton and Montgomery 2009; Maoz 2011). This is surprising, as interdependence—a key concept of international relations—is also the cornerstone of network analysis. Thus, chapter 4 is also an attempt to demonstrate the usefulness of network analysis for international relations.

Trade networks produce much more nuanced and detailed pictures of economic interdependence within and between world regions than single indicators could ever do. The centrality of intraregional or extra-regional actors within regional trade networks allows exploring whether intra- or extra-regional trade is more important for their regions. And the relative size of the regional member states within these trade networks can be used as an indicator as to whether the respective regions are dominated by single regional powers or not. Thus, regional trade networks allow us to explore the independent variables at the macro-level that are necessary to test our two hypotheses. Moreover, the dynamic analysis of trade networks gives us first hints as to whether intra- and extra-regional interdependence patterns change in the course of regional integration processes.

The advantages of applying network analysis to regional interdependence are straightforward. Network analysis and visualisation allows us to disaggregate regional interdependence patterns, assess the centrality of actors and the asymmetry of relations conjointly, and present them in an intuitive fashion. In this regard, network visualisations are able to communicate a large amount of data. We could also use tables of relational data to tackle the same research questions, but tables of relational data can easily consume a considerable amount of space, while the interpretation of the data is less than intuitive. This is all the more true if a time dimension is added. For example, trade between five countries may be displayed in a table, but if the number of countries gets larger—or if we want to add a time dimension—the tables get unwieldy (e.g. Mattli 1999: 144). Graphs depicting specific relations (e.g. exports of South Africa to the EU over time) necessarily reduce the information contained in the data and cannot communicate as much information as networks. In contrast, our network approach allows us to communicate and analyse a large amount of disaggregated and theoretically relevant information.

The diachronic network analyses rely on trade data and not on investment data because only trade data is available in relational form for all of the three regional organisations of our sample. In order to draw networks, it is necessary to have relational data for the nodes within the networks, in our case for the regional member states and their most important extra-regional economic partners. Such relational data exists worldwide for international trade in the UN Comtrade database,[5] but it does not exist for investment, which is usually only provided in highly aggregated terms.[6] However, investment and trade data can be expected to correlate (Kali and Reyes 2010; Van Rijckeghem and Weder 2001) because inward investments are often followed by outward trade relations. Market-seeking investments within a regional market should lead to increasing intraregional trade, whereas efficiency and resource-seeking investments should lead to increasing extra-regional trade. Because of this positive correlation between investments and trade, we are confident that the trade networks represent general patterns of intra- and extra-regional economic interdependence.

2.2 Causal Mechanisms and Process Tracing

The two hypotheses about regional cooperation and defection in developing regions are based on two causal mechanisms (see Fig. 3.1). The first causal mechanism describes a path towards regional cooperation. The path starts with the regions' dependence on extra-regional investment inflows and export outflows. In order to improve their competitiveness in the global struggle for investment and export shares, the regional member states have an interest in cooperating in order to profit from the size and stability effects of regional markets. Although the member states may disagree about the concrete form of substantive and procedural institutions, regional cooperation is nevertheless likely to emerge in such battles of the sexes because all member states achieve absolute gains from regional integration. A likely consequence of successful regional cooperation and of the establishment of regional institutions is an improvement in the regions' competitiveness and an increase in extra-regional economic exchange, whereas the effects on intraregional economic exchange are likely to be limited in the short run.

The second causal mechanism differs from the first one in respect to the presence of extra-regional privileges for regional powers. Here, most member states share a general interest in improving their regions' competitiveness, but the regional powers enjoy important privileges in extra-regional economic relations. These privileges are at odds with regional

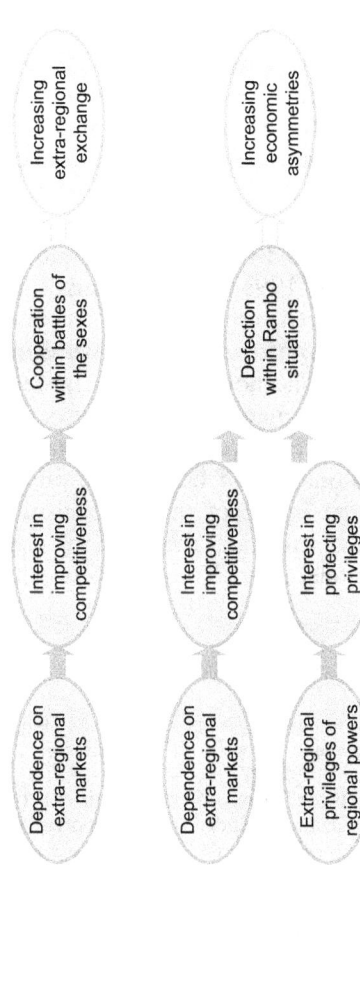

Fig. 3.1 The causal mechanisms behind regional cooperation and defection

cooperation when regional integration reduces the competitive differences between the regional member states. As a result, the regional powers become Rambos and defect in order to protect their privileges. This defection may occur before regional agreements, leading to deadlocks in decision-making, or after regional agreements, leading to non-compliance. The other member states still have interests in regional integration but are dependent on the regional powers' behaviours. Buying the regional powers' cooperation with side payments is expensive and can rarely be afforded by the smaller regional member states. A likely result of regional defection by the regional powers is that economic asymmetries within the regions increase because only the regional powers profit from extra-regional privileges in respect to investment and trade flows, whereas the other member states go away empty-handed.

The two mechanisms behind our hypotheses lead to different observable implications (King et al. 1994) along the causal chain links (see Table 3.3). Firstly, both causal mechanisms start with economic structures that are dominated by extra- instead of intraregional economic interdependence. The observable implications of this extra-regional dependence are that extra-regional investment and trade flows exceed intraregional exchange by far. In our trade network analyses, this dominance of extra-regional economic relations should lead to the observation that extra-regional actors are at the centre of the regional networks. The more central that extra-regional actors are, the more the respective regions are dominated by extra-regional trade. The (manifest or latent) existence of

Table 3.3 Observable implications of the causal mechanisms

	Causal mechanism for regional cooperation	*Causal mechanism for regional defection*
Incentive structure	Dominance of extra-regional economic interdependence	Existence of a regional power with important extra-regional privileges
Member states' interests	Emphasis on the extra-regional effects of regional integration	(*No official statements about the preferred unilateral strategies*)
Cooperation problem and outcome	Member states negotiate and cooperate in battles of the sexes	Deadlocks or implementation deficits in Rambo situations
Auxiliary outcome	Increasing extra-regional interdependence in the short run	Increasing economic asymmetries within the region

extra-regional privileges for the regional powers makes the difference for regional cooperation or defection. Dominant regional powers within the respective regions can be identified by the member states' share in extra- and intraregional trade, which is indicated by the size of their nodes within the regional trade networks. However, the existence of extra-regional privileges and their incompatibility with regional cooperation cannot be analysed at the macro-level within the regional trade networks. Here, case studies are needed to explore whether the regional powers enjoy extra-regional privileges that are at odds with further regional cooperation, or whether they can achieve such privileges by defecting from already-existing regional agreements.

Secondly, the member states' interests result from the economic structures of their respective regions, as well as from the presence or absence of extra-regional privileges. In developing regions where no member state enjoys important privileges in its extra-regional relations, all member states should have an interest in regional integration in order to improve their competitiveness in the global struggle for investment and export shares. The observable implications of this are that issues of regional competitiveness on the global market and the positive extra-regional effects of regional integration are discussed by the member states when negotiating regional agreements. This does not imply that intraregional effects of regional integration do not play a role during the negotiations. Our hypotheses do not rule out that regional integration has intraregional effects in developing regions, but these intraregional effects are unlikely to end the regions' dependence on extra-regional investment and trade flows, at least in the short run. In addition to following an extra-regional agenda, the member states of developing regions may also negotiate intraregional issues when cooperating with each other, but they will thereby be constrained by their extra-regional interests. What is probably more difficult to observe than member states' general interest in regional cooperation are the interests of regional powers that become regional Rambos in order to protect important extra-regional interests. Unilateral defection in the form of blocking or non-implementing regional agreements causes negative reputation effects for the regional Rambos. Thus, regional powers are unlikely to express particularistic interests openly. Although official statements about unilateral strategies would be 'smoking guns' (Mahoney 2012) for Rambo behaviour, the absence of such statements does not exclude the possibility that regional powers follow their extra-regional interests secretly.

Thirdly, the causal mechanisms differ from each other in respect to whether the member states of developing regions cooperate or defect. If no important extra-regional privileges are at stake, the member states play battles of the sexes with each other. Here, the observable implications are that the member states negotiate the distributive effects of regional integration, but cooperation and regional agreements are nevertheless the likely results. Agenda setting and majority decisions may help to reach agreements, but they are not essential because package deals and issue linkages may also solve distributive conflicts. Regional institutions that enforce implementation and solve disputes among the member states should be less prominent than in well-developed regions like the EU, because regional cooperation in battles of the sexes is self-enforcing as long as extra-regional actors punish non-compliance with declining investments or denied market access. In contrast, when regional powers act unilaterally in order to protect extra-regional privileges, the regional member states find themselves in Rambo situations. Then the cooperative behaviour of the regional Rambos is highly unlikely. In cases of pre-agreement Rambo behaviour, cooperation can only be achieved by large package deals or at the cost of granting side payments, but, due to the involved costs, it is more likely that Rambos will block regional agreements. In cases of implementation problems due to post-agreement Rambo behaviour, dispute settlement is unlikely to reinforce compliance because the Rambos do not free ride on the cooperation of others, but rather have no interests in regional cooperation at all, and their regional neighbours cannot effectively punish them.

Finally, although the consequences of regional cooperation and defection do not belong to the two causal paths, such auxiliary outcomes (Mahoney 2010) may nevertheless produce observable implications that improve our confidence in the two hypotheses. In cases of regional cooperation, the respective regions should be able to profit from size and stability effects and from improved competitiveness on the global market. Two consequences of this are that extra-regional investment inflows into the respective regions increase and that the regions engage in interregional or multilateral trade negotiations. Because of investment inflows and successful trade negotiations, extra-regional export outflows should also increase. Thus, the extra-regional economic exchange of such regions should increase in general, and this should become visible through diachronic analyses of regional trade networks. In contrast, in cases of regional defection, it is only one member state, namely the regional Rambo, that is able to profit from privileged extra-regional economic exchange. As a result, an increase of extra-regional investment inflows and export outflows should only become visible for this particular member state. In the long run, this means that the regional powers, which are the most likely member states to become regional Rambos, should receive relative gains in comparison to their smaller neighbours. Economic asymmetries are reinforced in this way, and this should become visible in the diachronic analysis of regional trade networks.

3 Conclusion

Our two hypotheses about regional economic cooperation and defection in developing regions are tested by qualitative and comparative case studies of collective or unilateral action in ASEAN, MERCOSUR, and SADC. These three regional organisations are selected because they constitute relatively unlikely and dissimilar cases. Firstly, ASEAN, MERCOSUR, and SADC are the economically most developed and integrated regional organisations on their continents, which implies that they can profit relatively well from the intraregional effects of regional integration. If the extra-regional logic of regional integration prevails nevertheless in these relatively well-developed regions of the developing world, it should be even more dominant in less-developed regions, where the intraregional gains from regional integration are low. Secondly, ASEAN, MERCOSUR, and SADC are all developing regions but are different in composition, as well as in respect to political and cultural homogeneity. If our hypotheses are confirmed by the analysis of such a heterogeneous sample, this improves our confidence that economic structures explain the success or difficulties of regional economic integration in the developing world, whereas alternative variables are likely to be less important. Besides the comparison of ASEAN, MERCOSUR, and SADC, we also compare different cases of regional cooperation and defection within the three regional organisations. Such in-case comparisons come as close as possible to controlled comparisons, as only one independent variable differs between observations and alternative variables are held constant. In our case, the independent variable of interest is the presence or absence of extra-regional privileges for the regional powers, and the case studies need to analyse whether this variable is able to explain the pattern of economic cooperation and defection in ASEAN, MERCOSUR, and SADC.

We employ different research techniques in order to test our hypotheses on cases of economic cooperation and defection in ASEAN, MERCOSUR, and SADC. Firstly, at the macro-level, we conduct diachronic network analyses of regional trade patterns. Such network analyses provide much more detailed pictures of the economic structures of the three regions than indicators like the share of intraregional trade could ever do. Thus, we avoid the shortcomings associated with stylised facts like the share of intraregional trade, and we are able to gain further information about potential regional powers and their economic interests within their respective regions. Secondly, at the micro-level of analysis, we conduct careful process tracing of six cases of regional cooperation or defection. The two hypotheses are based on two different causal mechanisms, and these causal mechanisms have various observable implications. The empirical analyses look for these observable implications, and they demonstrate that these observations are connected along a causal chain. Thus, process tracing does not only help us to simply increase the number of observations, but it also demonstrates that these observations follow logically on each other and can hardly be the result of alternative causal mechanisms.

Notes

1. The list of notified regional trade agreements can be found at the homepage of the WTO (rtais.wto.org/UI/PublicMaintainRTAHome.aspx).
2. The country groups are listed on the homepage of the World Bank (data.worldbank.org/about/country-classifications/country-and-lending-groups).
3. RIKS is an internet database published by the United Nations University Institute on Comparative Regional Integration Studies (www.cris.unu.edu/riks/web).
4. The intraregional trade intensity index divides the share of intraregional trade by the region's share in world trade. Thereby, it controls for the size of regions, which improves their comparability. The trade intensity index tells us how much more the regional member states trade with each other than could be expected from their respective shares in world trade, but it does not include information on how important intraregional trade is for them in absolute terms.
5. comtrade.un.org.
6. See, for example, the data of the UN Conference on Trade and Development (unctadstat.unctad.org).

REFERENCES

Axline, W. A. (1977). Underdevelopment, Dependence, and Integration: The Politics of Regionalism in the Third World. *International Organization, 31,* 83–105.
Bhagwati, J. N. (1988). Export-Promoting Trade Strategy. *World Bank Research Observer, 3,* 27–57.
Brandes, U., Kenis, P., & Raab, J. (2006). Explanation through Network Visualization. *Methodology, 2,* 16–23.
Brandes, U., Schneider, V., Wagner, D., Kenis, P., & Raab, J. (1999). Explorations into the Visualization of Policy Networks. *Journal of Theoretical Politics, 11,* 75–106.
Bulmer-Thomas, V. (Ed.). (2001). *Regional Integration in Latin America and the Caribbean: The Political Economy of Open Regionalism.* London: Institute of Latin American Studies.
De Lombaerde, P., Söderbaum, F., Van Langenhove, L., & Baert, F. (2010). The Problem of Comparison in Comparative Regionalism. *Review of International Studies, 36,* 731–753.
Doyle, M. W. (1997). *Ways of War and Peace.* New York: W.W. Norton.
Eckstein, H. (1975). Case Studies and Theory in Political Science. In F. Greenstein & N. Polsby (Eds.), *Handbook of Political Science* (Vol. 7, pp. 79–138). Reading: Addison-Wesley.
Frankel, J. A., & Wei, S.-J. (1998). *Open Regionalism in a World of Continental Trade Blocs* (IMF Working Paper).
Gehring, T. (1996). Integrating Integration Theory: Neo-functionalism and International Regimes. *Global Society, 10,* 225–253.
Gehring, T. (2002). *Die Europäische Union als komplexe internationale Organisation: Wie durch Kommunikation und Entscheidung soziale Ordnung entsteht.* Baden-Baden: Nomos Verlagsgesellschaft.
Genna, G. M., & De Lombaerde, P. (2010). The Small N Methodological Challenges of Analyzing Regional Integration. *European Integration, 32,* 583–595.
George, A. L., & Bennett, A. (2005). *Case Studies and Theory Development in the Social Sciences.* Cambridge: MIT Press.
Gilpin, R. (1981). *War and Change in World Politics.* Cambridge: Cambridge University Press.
Haas, E. B. (1976). Turbulent Fields and the Theory of Regional Integration. *International Organization, 30,* 173–212.
Hafner-Burton, E. M., Kahler, M., & Montgomery, A. H. (2009). Network Analysis for International Relations. *International Organization, 63,* 559–592.
Hafner-Burton, E. M., & Montgomery, A. H. (2009). Globalization and the Social Power Politics of International Economic Networks. In M. Kahler (Ed.),

Networked Politics: Agency, Power and Governance (pp. 23–42). Ithaca, NY: Cornell University Press.

Hix, S. (1998). The Study of the European Union II: The 'New Governance' Agenda and Its Rival. *Journal of European Public Policy, 5,* 38–65.

Hix, S., & Hoyland, B. (2011). *The Political System of the European Union* (3rd ed.). Basingstoke: Palgrave Macmillan.

Huntington, S. P. (1996). *The Clash of Civilizations and the Remaking of World Order.* New York: Simon & Schuster.

Iapadre, L. (2006). Regional Integration and the Geography of World Trade: Statistical Indicators and Empirical Evidence. In P. De Lombaerde (Ed.), *Assessment and Measurement of Regional Integration* (pp. 65–85). London: Routledge.

Kali, R., & Reyes, J. (2010). Financial Contagion on the International Trade Network. *Economic Inquiry, 48,* 1072–1101.

Kenis, P., & Schneider, V. (1991). Policy Networks and Policy Analysis: Scrutinizing a New Analytical Toolbox. In B. Marin & R. Mayntz (Eds.), *Policy Networks: Empirical Evidence and Theoretical Considerations* (pp. 25–59). Frankfurt: Campus.

Kindleberger, C. P. (1973). *The World in Depression: 1929-1939.* Berkeley, CA: University of California Press.

King, G., Keohane, R. O., & Verba, S. (1994). *Designing Social Inquiry: Scientific Inference in Qualitative Research.* Princeton, NJ: Princeton University Press.

Krasner, S. D. (1982). Structural Causes and Regime Consequences: Regimes as Intervening Variables. *International Organization, 36,* 185–205.

Langhammer, R. J. (1992). The Developing Countries and Regionalism. *Journal of Common Market Studies, 30,* 211–232.

Magnet, P., & Nicolaidis, K. (2004). The European Convention: Bargaining in the Shadow of Rhetoric. *West European Politics, 27,* 381–404.

Mahoney, J. (2007). Qualitative Methodology and Comparative Politics. *Comparative Political Studies, 40,* 122–144.

Mahoney, J. (2010). After KKV: The New Methodology of Qualitative Research. *World Politics, 62,* 120–147.

Mahoney, J. (2012). The Logic of Process Tracing Tests in the Social Sciences. *Sociological Methods and Research, 41,* 570–597.

Maoz, Z. (2011). *Networks of Nations.* Cambridge: Cambridge University Press.

Mattli, W. (1999). *The Logic of Regional Integration: Europe and Beyond.* Cambridge: Cambridge University Press.

McCormick, J. (2010). *Europeanism.* Oxford: Oxford University Press.

Merton, R. K. (1957). Social Theory and Social Structure, rev. ed. New York: Free Press.

Moravcsik, A. (1997). Taking Preferences Seriously: A Liberal Theory of International Politics. *International Organization, 51,* 514–553.

Nabers, D. (2003). The Social Construction on International Institutions: The Case of ASEAN+3. *International Relations of the Asia-Pacific, 3*, 113–136.
Olson, M. (1965). *The Logic of Collective Action: Public Goods and the Theory of Groups.* Cambridge: Harvard University Press.
Przeworski, A., & Teune, H. (1970). *The Logic of Comparative Social Inquiry.* New York: Krieger Publishing.
Ragin, C. C. (1987). *The Comparative Method: Moving Beyond Qualitative and Quantitative Strategies.* Berkeley, CA: University of California Press.
Robson, P. (1993). The New Regionalism and Developing Countries. *Journal of Common Market Studies, 31*, 329–348.
Schirm, S. A. (2002). *Globalization and the New Regionalism: Global Markets, Domestic Politics and Regional Cooperation.* Cambridge: Polity Press.
Schirm, S. (2009). Ideas and Interests in Global Financial Governance: Comparing German and US Preference Formation. *Cambridge Review of International Affairs, 22*, 501–521.
Scott, J. (2006). *Social Network Analysis: A Handbook.* London: Sage Publications.
Thurner, P. W., & Binder, M. (2009). European Union Transgovernmental Networks: The Emergence of a New Political Space Beyond the Nation-State? *European Journal of Political Research, 48*, 80–106.
Van Rijckeghem, C., & Weder, B. (2001). Sources of Contagion: Is It Finance or Trade? *Journal of International Economics, 54*, 293–308.
Venables, A. J. (2003). Winners and Losers from Regional Integration Agreements. *The Economic Journal, 113*, 747–761.
Von Bogdandy, A. (1993). *Die Europäische Option: Eine interdisziplinäre Analyse über Herkunft, Stand und Perspektiven der europäischen Integration.* Baden-Baden: Nomos Verlagsgesellschaft.

PART II

The Economic Structures of Different World Regions

CHAPTER 4

Trade Network Analyses

Economic Structures of the EC/EU, ASEAN, MERCOSUR, and SADC

Simon Fink and Daniel Rempe

Most European integration theories rely at least implicitly on intraregional economic interdependence, and especially trade interdependence, in order to establish causal claims about processes of regional integration. Despite the long-standing debate between neofunctionalism (Pierson 1996; Sandholtz 1998; Haas 1958) and intergovernmentalism (Moravcsik 1998), they agree that intraregional trade interdependence creates demands for regional integration (Mattli 1999). In neofunctionalism, trade interdependence creates spillovers to related fields of product regulation. For example, trade in foodstuffs generates the functional need to standardise regulations, harmonise safety measures, and introduce common standards of quality assessment and product labelling (e.g. Krapohl 2008). In intergovernmentalism, trade interdependence influences the preferences of domestic interest groups. Economic interest groups that

---

S. Fink (✉)
University of Bamberg, Bamberg, Germany
e-mail: simon.fink@uni-bamberg.de

D. Rempe
FocusEconomics, Barcelona, Spain

© The Author(s) 2017
S. Krapohl (ed.), *Regional Integration in the Global South*,
International Political Economy Series,
DOI 10.1007/978-3-319-38895-3_4

rely on exports for their revenue strongly support further integration and pressure their governments to act accordingly (Moravcsik 1998).

However, one should be cautious about the veracity of stylised facts about intraregional economic interdependence that stem from research on well-developed regions in general and the EU in particular. Most prominently, it is not clear whether these stylised facts also hold true for developing regions. The usual assumption is that regional interdependence is high in well-developed regions, but low in developing regions. In order to measure different degrees of intraregional economic interdependence, scholars of comparative regionalism often rely on more or less valid indicators like the share of intraregional trade in comparison to all international trade of the regions' member states. But such indicators of regional interdependence are overly simplified, and different indicators produce different assessments of regional interdependence (De Lombaerde et al. 2010). Consequently, one needs more finely tuned measures when analysing the intraregional interdependence patterns of regional organisations outside of Europe.

To remedy this methodological gap, this chapter uses network analysis to study regional trade patterns. The methodological claim is that the study of regional integration can benefit from the application of network analysis. Network analysis methods have recently been introduced into international relations, because their epistemological underpinnings provide an excellent match for many theories of international political economy (Hafner-Burton et al. 2009; Maoz 2009). Network analysis allows one to elucidate the magnitude and scope of interdependence, and to communicate the results in a convenient way without hiding the complexity of the underlying interdependence relations (Brandes et al. 1999).

Using network analysis, this chapter contributes to an analysis of the causal mechanisms laid out in Chap. 3. Most importantly, network analysis sheds light on the question whether intra- or extra-regional economic relations are more important for the members of a regional integration project as a whole. This question forms the starting point for both causal mechanisms, as dependence on extra-regional markets creates an interest constellation oriented towards external partners. Additionally, network analysis may contribute to an analysis of the probable distribution of interests among member states of regional integration projects. Network structures can hint at regional economic imbalances, which in turn may contribute to the emergence of Rambo situations in which one member sees its interests primarily served by closer ties to external partners and neglects regional integration.

The main result is that the starting point for both causal mechanisms can be empirically established. The interdependence patterns of the European Community (EC) show a high regional interdependence and comparatively little dependence on external partners. Thus, the EC had a viable internal market from the beginning and was not dependent on external partners. Moreover, the likelihood of a Rambo situation was low, as Germany and France—and later the UK—had nearly equal positions at the centre of the network so that there was no single dominating regional power. The picture for the Association of Southeast Asian Nations (ASEAN), the Common Market of South America (MERCOSUR), and the Southern African Development Community (SADC) is completely different. These regions exhibit a large dependence on trade with external partners. While there is no straightforward relation between economic interdependence patterns and likely integration outcomes, one can tentatively infer the interests of regional actors from the network analyses. Accordingly, regional integration in ASEAN, MERCOSUR, and SADC is most likely not due to intraregional market-making dynamics, but must be oriented towards external partners.

Moreover, the analyses show which actors dominate each region in economic terms and may consequently enjoy extra-regional economic privileges; this in turn increases the likelihood of Rambo behaviour. The extremely asymmetric trade pattern in SADC suggests that the dominant member state, South Africa, has little to gain from trade within SADC, but rather is very much focused on European export markets instead. To a lesser extent, a similar problem might be induced from the asymmetry between the dominant member state, Brazil, and its smaller neighbours in MERCOSUR. The least likely case for Rambo situations seems to be ASEAN, where Indonesia, Malaysia, Singapore, and Thailand balance each other, and where the gains from external trade are distributed relatively equally among these member states.

1 ANALYTICAL APPROACH

The basis for network analysis is relational data. Relational data characterise relations between two units, which in our case are member states of regional organisations. We use data about trade flows, which can be seen as an appropriate indicator of economic interdependence. They offer two advantages in comparison to other measurements like flows of foreign direct investments. Firstly, the available trade data are more comprehensive than data on foreign direct investments, as the former include information about the origins and addressees of goods, whereas investment data are either incomplete or only available in a highly aggregated manner. Secondly, trade data should also reflect with some time lag the developments of other important indicators. When foreign direct investment increases within a region, this should either lead to more intraregional trade, if investments are market driven, or to more extra-regional trade, if investments are driven by the search for cheap labour or natural resources (Markusen 2004; Kreinin and Plummer 2008). The source for trade data is the UN Comtrade database. Following the approach of Feenstra et al. (2005), we rely on the reports of importers to assess the quantity of trade flows (measured in US dollars, adjusted for inflation). As some countries are poor reporters, we use reports by exporters to fill in missing values.[1]

We use visone[2] to visualise the trade networks. In order to ensure a structured and focused comparison, all network graphs contain the same information (Fig. 4.1). For each regional integration project, we elucidate the three most important external trade partners and include them in the network. For each member state of a regional organisation, we plot the network connections to its three most important export partners and three most important import partners (which may be among the three external partners or among the internal trade partners). Trade between the external partners is omitted for visualisation reasons, and because trade between external partners does not pertain to our analytical goal, which centres on the regional organisation and its members. The width of the network ties reflects the intensity of trade relations. The arrows indicating

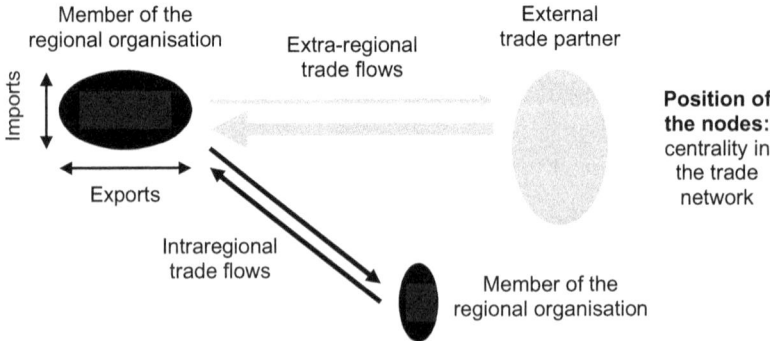

Fig. 4.1 Interpretation scheme for network graphs

intraregional trade are depicted using black lines, whereas extra-regional trade is depicted using grey lines. Member states of the regional integration project are depicted in dark grey, whereas external partners appear in light grey. The relative positions of countries as importers or exporters can be elucidated from the shape of their node symbols. The width of the node reflects the amount of exports (outdegree), whereas the height of the nodes reflects the amount of imports (indegree). The layout is an Multidimensional Scaling (MDS) solution that tries to depict patterns of similarities and dissimilarities in a two-dimensional space (Kruskal 1992). The idea behind the visualisation algorithm is to minimise the 'stress' in the system. Countries that have similar trade links (that are 'close together' regarding their trade patterns) are depicted closely together, while countries that are less connected to the network are depicted at the margins.

The algorithm and visualisation decisions create graphs that may be intuitively interpreted. The interpretation of the network graphs can focus on the configuration of countries and trade links. Visually central countries are central to the trade networks; countries at the margins are on the periphery. Countries that have close trade ties should emerge as clusters of closely placed countries. Changes in position of countries over time reflect changes in their relative positions in the regional trade network. The colour coding of project members and external actors allow us to determine who is more important in the network. Additionally, the differences in height and width of the network nodes allow us to elucidate whether countries are primarily exporters or importers, or both to a similar extent. Thus, considering Fig. 4.1 in light of the causal mechanisms set out in Chap. 3, we are interested in the relative strength of black and grey links (i.e. the relative importance of intra- and extra-regional economic links), in the size and position of black and grey nodes (i.e. the relative importance of intra- and extra-regional actors), and in the size of the black nodes in relation to each other (i.e. the degree of economic asymmetries in the region).

The network visualisations entail some simplifications. For example, the number of trade links displayed per country is confined to the three most important import and export partners. This choice may be justified by looking at trade concentration measures. For nearly all of the regional member states and years, the three most important partners account for more than 40 per cent of all international trade. Thus, the trade links depicted in the network graphs reflect a major share of the regions' international trade.

2 Empirical Analysis

The case selection for the network analyses centres on the regional integration projects analysed in this volume. Our chapter compares intraregional and extra-regional trade patterns of four regional organisations, namely the EC, MERCOSUR, ASEAN, and SADC. To provide a common ground for comparison, the chapter analyses the 'new' regional organisations in 1990, 1995, 2000, 2005, and 2010.[3] As Europe is the implicit reference point for most theories of regional integration, the 'early' EC from the 1960s to 1985 is analysed. In a way, the EC is the most dissimilar case to developing regions. Thus, we can use trade patterns of the early EC to highlight and contrast the specific economic patterns of developing regions. Our research design encompasses within-time and between-cases dimensions of comparison.

2.1 The European Community/European Union

The EC was founded with the Treaties of Rome in 1957. While it does not belong to the generation of the new regionalism, the EC is often used as a baseline example of regional integration. Figures 4.2 and 4.3 depict the early evolution of the EC's trade network from the implementation of the customs union during the 1960s until the Single European Act of the 1980s. Concerning the dependence on extra-regional actors—translated into the relative importance of intraregional and extra-regional trade links—the network graphs paint a clear picture. Black links, and hence intraregional trade ties, dominate the picture. A densely connected internal market already existed in the 1960s and the 1970s, despite the less-than-favourable political climate, with the empty chair crisis and Eurosclerosis marking critical moments in the political development of the EC (Armstrong et al. 1996; Dinan 2005). The network of intraregional trade links becomes even denser over time.

In effect, Figs. 4.2 and 4.3 depict the development of a viable internal market driven by the utilisation of economies of scale and comparative cost advantages through intraregional trade. Extra-regional trade—for example, with the USA—is important for many EC member states, but the network as a whole shows the paramount importance of intraregional trade. External trade partners occupy rather peripheral positions in the EC trade network. This can be discerned from the positions of internal and external actors. This pattern can already be seen in the 1960s and 1970s,

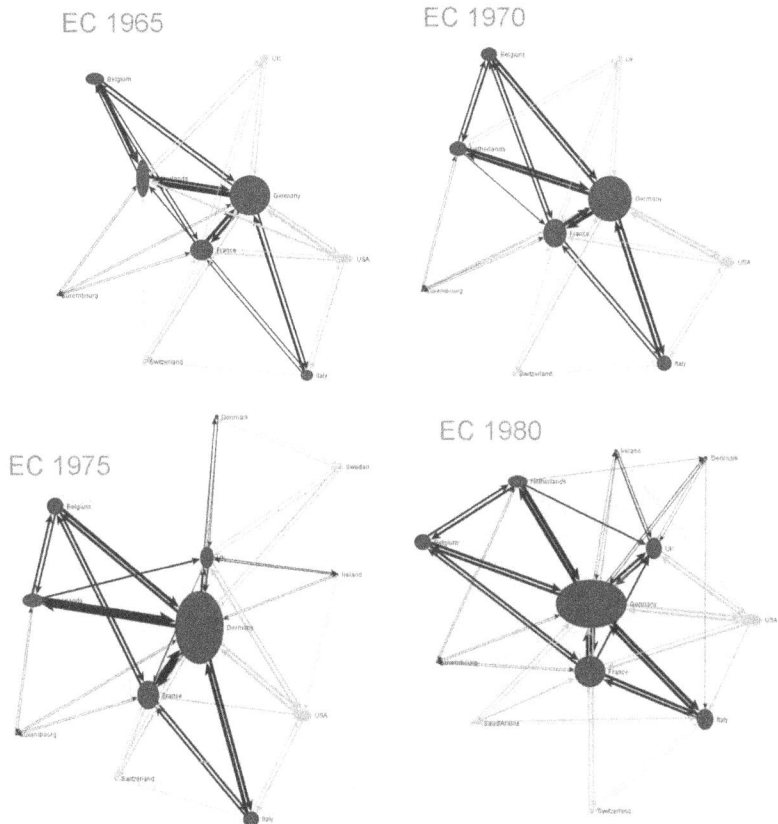

Fig. 4.2 Evolution of the EC trade network from 1965 to 1980

and persists in the 1980s (see the dominance of black network ties in Figs. 4.2 and 4.3). Thus, we would not expect external partners to play a large role in influencing the regional integration process. External feedback for regional integration is not as important as the internal dynamic of market creation.

A related conclusion from the network graphs—a conclusion that would not be obvious from aggregate statistics like the share of intraregional trade—is that most trade relations between the EC member states are symmetric. The European countries are mutually important trade partners. If we conceive of economic interdependence as mutual dependence,

Fig. 4.3 Trade interdependence in the EC in 1985

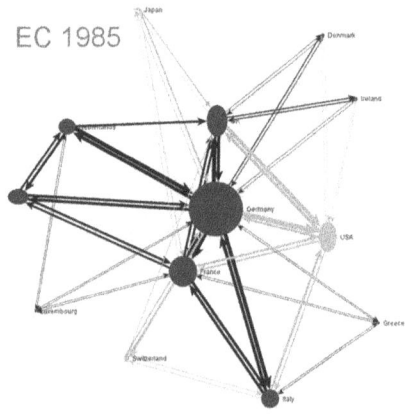

then the EC is a clear example of interdependence. Even back in 1965, most of the original member states are linked with reciprocal trade ties of nearly equal thickness (see Fig. 4.2). France is one of Italy's major trade partners, and vice versa. The same goes for Belgium and the Netherlands or Germany and France. Given the thesis that reciprocated trade ties indicate balanced relationships—A is important for B, and B also important for A—we may conclude that the whole system is integrated through relations of mutual importance. Thus, we can clearly support the thesis that relations of mutual dependence form the core of the European integration project (Stone Sweet and Sandholtz 1997).

Concerning distribution of interests within the region, it is equally clear that the region is not dominated by only one regional hegemon. In the 1960s, Germany is the major trade power, occupying a central role in the network (see Fig. 4.2). However, the development of the network demonstrates how France slowly gets drawn to the centre. Thus, the 'tandem' of Germany-France is not only a political alliance (Hyde-Price and Jeffery 2001), but builds upon a shared central role in European trade. After the accession of the UK, the tandem Germany-France develops into a strong trade triangle including the new member state in the 1980s (Fig. 4.3). The other original member states—the Benelux countries and Italy—are also closely integrated in the intraregional trade network, whereas the smaller new member states Denmark, Greece, Ireland, Portugal, and Spain establish a new rim of periphery around the old 'core'. Overall, increasing intraregional connections dominate the picture from the 1960s to the 1980s, and external trade partners never play a predominant role in the network. Thus, European countries have few incentives to defect from the course of European economic integration. Intraregional interdependence dominates their preference calculations, and there is no obvious Rambo with preferences for defection in order to protect important extra-regional economic relations.

To sum up, the early EC is an exemplary case of a well-developed region with intensive intraregional economic interdependence. Not only are the intraregional trade ties more important than extra-regional trade ties, but intraregional trade ties are also reciprocated. This pattern does not change over time. Instead, in a path-dependent development, this pattern of intraregional interdependence is reinforced (Krapohl and Fink 2013). A European market, based on the utilisation of comparative cost advantages and economies of scale through intraregional trade, develops. This corresponds to the classic analyses of neofunctionalism (Haas 1958; Stone Sweet and Sandholtz 1997; Rosamond 2005). However, the purpose of this section was not to test the claims of neofunctionalism, but to establish a baseline against which the economic structure of other regional integration projects can be evaluated.

2.2 *The Association of Southeast Asian Nations*

The original ASEAN was founded in 1967 by Indonesia, Malaysia, the Philippines, Singapore, and Thailand as a security community to fight the communist threat in Southeast Asia. However, the decisive economic integration step for our analysis of economic integration is the agreement to set up the Asian Free Trade Area (AFTA), a common preferential tariff scheme to promote the free flow of goods within ASEAN, which was signed in 1992. Since the beginning of AFTA, membership of ASEAN has expanded to include Brunei, Myanmar, Cambodia, Laos, and Vietnam (Tay 2000; Fukase 2003). The ASEAN now includes ten member states ranging from the poorer countries on the mainland to the well-developed city state Singapore.

Figure 4.4 shows the development of the ASEAN trade network from 1990 to 2005. At the start of the economic integration process, the region's trade patterns are dominated by trade with its most important external partners, which are the EU, the USA, and Japan. The only major trade relation within the region is that between Malaysia and Singapore. However, by 1995 the first signs of an internal market appear. Singapore

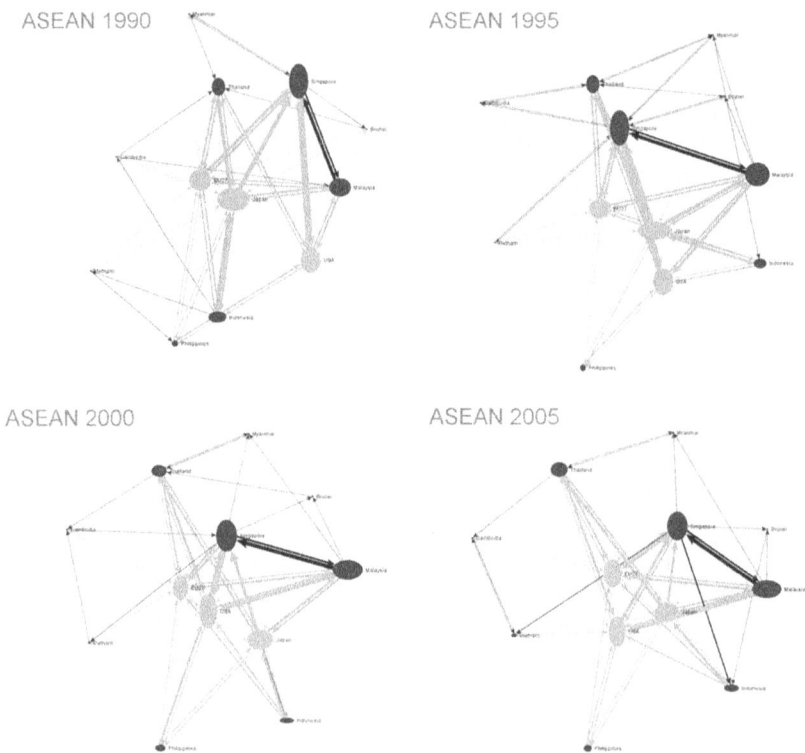

Fig. 4.4 Evolution of the ASEAN trade network from 1990 to 2005

moves towards the centre of the trade network, the relation between Singapore and Malaysia becomes of mutual importance, and many countries in the region start reorienting their trade towards Singapore (compare 1990 and 1995 in Fig. 4.4). Indonesia and the Philippines remain to some extent aloof from the integration process, but the nucleus for an internal market seems to be developing. However, the region's trade pattern changes dramatically with the beginning of the Asian crisis in 1997. The economic downturn damages intraregional trade and increases the role of the external partners (see the pattern in 2000 in Fig. 4.4). The trade patterns for 2005 and 2010 (Figs. 4.4 and 4.5) show a slight

Fig. 4.5 Trade interdependence in ASEAN in 2010

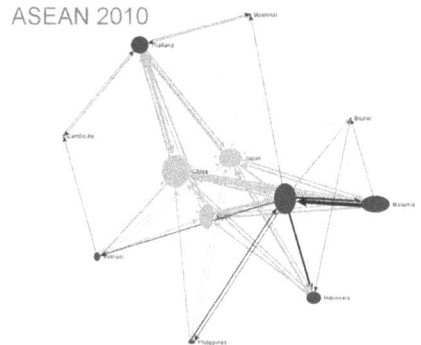

revival in intraregional trade. Black links between ASEAN members begin to reappear, and Singapore is again drawn to the centre of the network. However, the bulk of trade relations is still centred on external partners.

External actors are of paramount importance for trade in the region. Throughout the years under study, they occupy central roles in the trade network. Moreover, most regional member states seem to gain from extra-regional trade. This seems to indicate the success of the region's export-promoting development strategy. For example, in contrast to MERCOSUR, where mainly Brazil and to a lesser degree Argentina develop major extra-regional trade links (see Fig. 4.6), and Paraguay and Uruguay improve their extra-regional trade only little, most ASEAN members forged major trade links to external partners, either to the EU and the USA or to Japan and China. Especially, the rise of China is noteworthy in this regard. In 2010, it replaced the USA as one of the three most important trade partners of ASEAN (Fig. 4.5). As Japan is also among the three most important partners of the region, the ASEAN+3 process—the forging of closer ties between ASEAN on the one hand and China, South Korea, and Japan on the other hand—seems to be the logical consequence of the economic interdependence structure (Nabers 2003). In regard to potential Rambo behaviour, ASEAN is maybe the least likely case for defections of regional powers in order to protect privileges in their extra-regional economic relations. In contrast to SADC, there is no clear hegemon in the region who is likely to enjoy such privileges and who would thus profit from unilateral defection. Singapore and Malaysia are closely linked through major trade ties, so that a unilateral defection of one of them seems unlikely.

To sum up, the trade patterns of ASEAN from the 1990s to 2010 correspond to the macro pattern we would expect to arise from a successful export-based development strategy. Although its member states integrated their economies into a free trade area, their major economic partners are outside the regional organisation. As a result, intraregional trade grew only modestly from 1990 to 2010. As regards the scope conditions for the causal mechanisms, ASEAN shows a considerable dependence on external partners coupled with the lack of a clear regional power. Thus, ASEAN seems to be a case for the first causal mechanism, using regional integration to improve the standing of the region towards external partners.

2.3 The Common Market of South America

MERCOSUR was founded in 1991 by the Treaty of Asunción, which was amended in 1994 by the Protocol of Ouro Preto and in 2002 by the Protocol of Olivos (Estevadeordal et al. 2001; Veiga and Marchisio 2004). MERCOSUR's original member states are Brazil, Argentina, Paraguay, and Uruguay, and Venezuela joined the regional organisation in 2012. MERCOSUR has already established a customs union during the 1990s, which makes it one of the most advanced regional organisations of the developing world (Vaillant 2005). However, MERCOSUR is often criticised for lacking effective enforcement mechanisms and the customs union is consequently hardly implemented (Doctor 2013).

Figure 4.6 shows the evolution of the MERCOSUR trade network from 1990—shortly before the establishment of the regional organisation—until 2005. Concerning the interdependence pattern, the networks clearly demonstrate the importance of extra-regional trade for most MERCOSUR members and for MERCOSUR as a whole. In 1990, the most important trade ties are the extra-regional ones to the USA, the EU, and Japan. Hence, the MERCOSUR region does not show high intraregional economic interdependence at the beginning of the integration process, especially when compared to the early EC (see Fig. 4.2). Overall, the MERCOSUR trade network in 1990 resembles a star-shaped network with Brazil occupying the central position, and Brazil's extra-regional trade constituting the most important trade links. This pattern of regional trade changes slightly after the foundation of MERCOSUR. In 1995, the region exhibits a denser intraregional trade network. Especially, Brazil and Argentina intensify their trade (compare 1990 and 1995 in Fig. 4.6). However, over the course of time, it becomes clear that the development of MERCOSUR's intraregional trade stagnates. Although the importance of Brazil and Argentina as export markets for the smaller countries of the region has grown, the region still does not exhibit strong intraregional interdependencies. While intraregional trade clearly dominates the early EC trade network, the dominance of extra-regional trade relations—for example, between Brazil and the USA or the EU—is clearly visible in the MERCOSUR network. Thus, one can predict that the success or failure of regional integration in MERCOSUR should depend to a great extent on the feedback by external actors.

The Argentinean crisis hit MERCOSUR at the end of the 1990s. The country's economic downturn led to its shrinking importance as an export

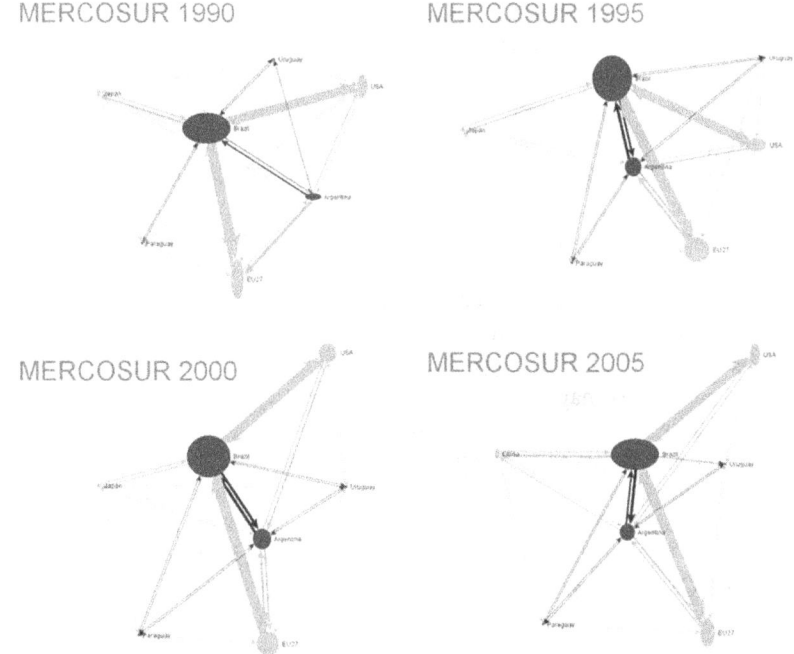

Fig. 4.6 Evolution of the MERCOSUR trade network from 1990 to 2005

Fig. 4.7 Trade interdependence in MERCOSUR in 2010

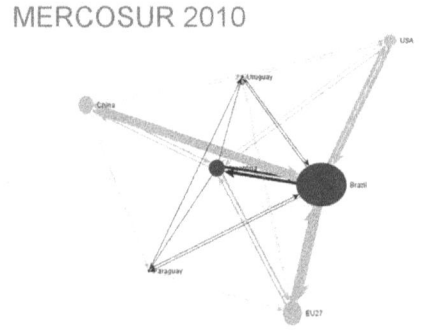

destination. This can be clearly seen when looking at the region's trade network and Argentina's network node. The Argentine economic crisis was not only dramatic for Argentina, but also for intraregional trade. Although the regional member states were able to overcome the economic crises in the following years, this has not initiated a new integrative dynamic for MERCOSUR. The regional trade network of 2010 (Fig. 4.7) shows the same thin trade connections within the region as the network of 1990 (Fig. 4.6). Brazil is an export market for all other regional member states, but the grey extra-regional ties dominate the picture, with China substituting Japan as one of the region's three most important extra-regional trade partners.

Economic asymmetries within developing regions increase the risk of Rambo situations, in which single member states of regional organisations lose incentives to integrate because they gain more from regional defection and bilateral cooperation with extra-regional partners. All network graphs of MERCOSUR (Figs. 4.6 and 4.7) suggest that the risk of such Rambo situations may be considerable in the region. The region consists of one major economic power, Brazil, one middle power, Argentina, and two economic dwarves, namely Paraguay and Uruguay. While Argentina suffered from a crisis in the late 1990s, Brazil became one of the world's most dynamic emerging markets and improved its trade relations with China, the EU, and the USA. Thus, we should expect conflicts between the MERCOSUR member states, because Brazil is likely to enjoy privileges in its extra-regional economic relations that it needs to protect as soon as they are at odds with regional integration.

To sum up, MERCOSUR has failed to create the dynamic process of intensifying intraregional trade connections as one can witness within the

EU (compare Fig. 4.6 with Fig. 4.2). Before the start of the regional integration process, the region's trade pattern resembled a star network with Brazil as the central player. Regional trade was highly asymmetrical, with the smaller countries depending on trade with Brazil, and Brazil in turn depending on extra-regional trade. During the formative years of MERCOSUR, this trade pattern gradually changed, and the Argentina–Brazil duo emerged as a motor for intraregional trade. However, the Argentine crisis at the turn of the millennium brought an end to this development. After the crisis, the intraregional economic interdependence that had developed in the 1990s was gone. The regional network has thinned out considerably, and extra-regional trade relations dominate again. Until today the region has not been able to regain the momentum for regional integration that it had created during the 1990s. Moreover, economic asymmetries between Brazil one the one hand and the smaller member states on the other hand suggest that Rambo situations may be a major problem for regional cooperation in MERCOSUR.

2.4 The Southern African Development Community

Today's SADC was founded in 1992, with the signing of the Windhoek declaration, as a successor of the previous Southern African Development Coordination Conference (SADCC), which had been set up in 1980. Whereas the main goal of the old SADCC was to build up a regional counterweight to apartheid-era South Africa, the new SADC concentrates on Balassa-like economic integration. Originally, SADC was established by Angola, Botswana, Lesotho, Malawi, Mozambique, Namibia, Swaziland, Tanzania, and Zambia, but South Africa joined the regional organisation after the end of apartheid, and Mauritius, the Seychelles, the Democratic Republic of Congo, and Madagascar followed during the 1990s (Oosthuizen 2006: 59–61). A first important step of SADC's economic integration was the implementation of the SADC FTA in 2008, but the region also aimed to establish a customs union in 2010 (which did not materialise), a common market in 2015, an economic union in 2016, and a monetary union in 2018.

The SADC trade network is marked by extremely few and asymmetrical trade ties within the region and high interdependence with extra-regional trade partners (Fig. 4.8). In stark contrast to the early EC (and similar to MERCOSUR), the grey extra-regional trade links dominate the picture. Moreover, the few intraregional trade links focus only on South Africa as the regional trade hub. Compared to the rather dense internal trade

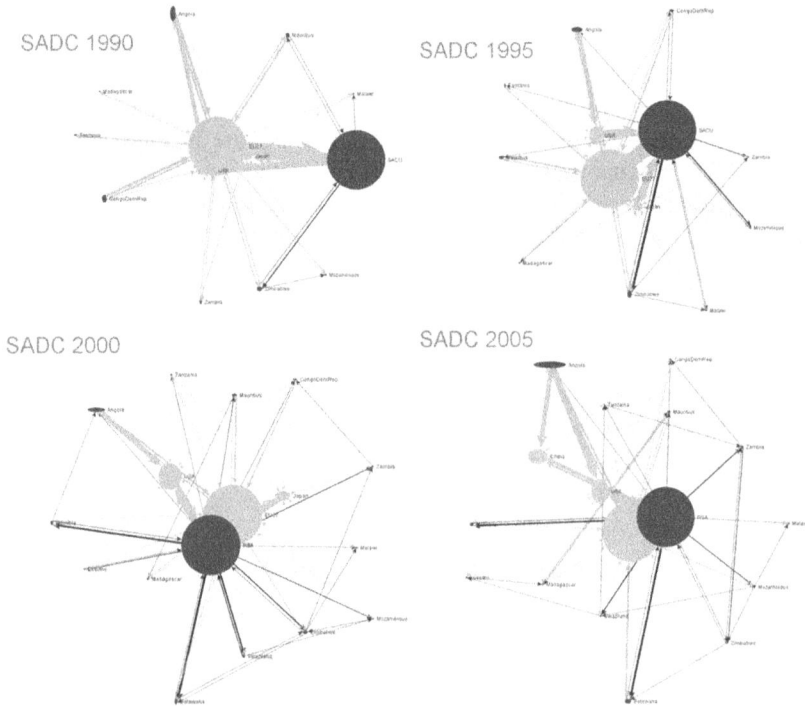

Fig. 4.8 Evolution of the SADC trade network from 1990 to 2005

network in the EC, there is no comparable development in SADC. Most of SADC's member states export primary products and do not constitute important markets for each other. Some members of the regional integration project—Angola for nearly all years, or Tanzania in the 1990s—have all of their most important trade partners outside of the region. The overall pattern of dominance of extra-regional trade does not change during the course of regional integration. In 1990, extra-regional trade links dominate the picture, the EU is the central trade power, and intraregional trade mainly means trade between South Africa and the other SADC member states. In 2010 (Fig. 4.9), this pattern has changed only very little. South Africa has been able to increase its intra- as well as extra-regional trade, and external actors still occupy central positions in the network. The network still resembles a hub-and-spoke network, centred on extra-regional trade partners and South Africa, with very tiny connections between the smaller SADC member states.

Fig. 4.9 Trade interdependence in SADC in 2010

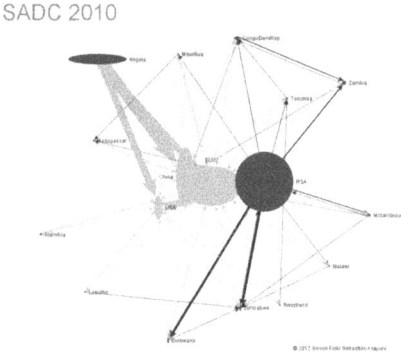

Even more than in MERCOSUR, SADC is dominated by only one regional power, which is South Africa. From 1995 on, South Africa is the only SADC member state that is at the centre of the regional trade network (Figs. 4.8 and 4.9). This means that South Africa is an important export market for most of the smaller SADC member states. However, the opposite does not hold, because the region cannot absorb all of the exports from the regional power. Consequently, South Africa's most important trade partner by far is an extra-regional one, namely the EU. Out of necessity, South Africa's most important interest is in securing its access to the European market and protecting its extra-regional economic relations with the EU. Such patterns of economic asymmetries together with the dominance of extra-regional trade mean a relatively high risk for Rambo situations within the region. Whenever its extra-regional interests are at odds with its intraregional ones, the regional power needs to opt for the former and to protect privileges in its extra-regional economic relations. It becomes a regional Rambo with a dominant strategy of defecting within the region, and this may considerably harm the regional integration process in SADC.

To sum up, the SADC integration process started from an extremely low level of intraregional trade, and this pattern did not change very much. While some intraregional trade ties developed, the majority of increased trade is due to the extra-regional trade links of South Africa. The region shows a high reliance on extra-regional trade, which indicates that the extra-regional effects of regional cooperation are important in pushing or impeding the regional integration process. Moreover, SADC seems a most likely case where Rambo situations may occur. South Africa's role as a regional hegemon is clearly visible in the trade network. It is not only economically more powerful than the other SADC members, but it is also at the centre of most intraregional trade. Thus, on the one hand, its continuing support is crucial for regional integration, but on the other hand, this support is highly precarious, as South Africa's main trade interests seem to lie outside the region.

3　Conclusion

The empirical conclusion from the network analyses is that the economic interdependence structures that form the basis for regional integration vary considerably across the various regions. The causal mechanisms to explain regional integration in developing regions start with the argument that extra-regional economic relationships are more important than intraregional ones. Thus, the extra-regional effects of regional integration are a major motivation and constraint for regional integration (see Chaps. 2 and 3). While the network analyses cannot test the second part of the argument, the analyses have clearly shown the paramount importance of external partners for ASEAN, MERCOSUR, and SADC. This paramount importance is visible in the relative importance of extra-regional versus intraregional trade ties, and also in the fact that in two of the three regional organisations—SADC and ASEAN—external actors occupy central roles in the regional trade network. In contrast, the EC has from its beginning exhibited a densely interconnected internal market between its member states.

Thus, the theoretical argument can be corroborated that regional integration in developing regions follows a different rationale than regional integration in Europe due to differing underlying economic structures. Intraregional market creation has been the major impetus behind European integration, and the network analyses show how successful these attempts have been. However, none of the other analysed projects has been able to develop a similarly viable and stable internal market. ASEAN and MERCOSUR show some signs of increasing intraregional trade, as does SADC to a lesser degree, but the major driver of trade in these regions is extra-regional trade.

The network analyses also allow some tentative conclusions concerning the likelihood of Rambo situations in the respective regional organisations. The causal mechanisms argue that in developing regions, member states that are able to preserve or gain privileges in their extra-regional relations by acting unilaterally become regional Rambos. The likeliness of Rambo situations increases with economic asymmetries between the regional member states (Chaps. 2 and 3). The network analyses allow a refinement of this argument, the formulation of more precise observable implications and identification of potential Rambo situations. If we take the asymmetry of trade relations as a major indicator of economic asymmetries, we would expect SADC to be most vulnerable to Rambo situations. South Africa is the regional hegemon, but with small trade ties within the region. MERCOSUR holds a middle ground. On the one hand, the economic asymmetries are not as pronounced as in SADC; on the other hand, Brazil resembles South Africa in that its major trade interests lie outside the region. Judging from its trade structure, ASEAN is probably the least likely candidate for Rambo situations.

Complementing the substantive conclusions of the chapter are the methodological lessons. So far, the field of comparative regionalism has mainly used highly aggregated indicators, characterising regions 'as a whole'. This line of inquiry has been criticised for paying too little attention to nuances in development patterns and differences between regional member states (Frankel and Wei 1998; De Lombaerde et al. 2010). While a comparison of the classical indicators may come to similar conclusions as the network analysis, the network graphs allow for a more fine-grained analysis. The network graphs do not only show clear differences between different world regions, but also alert one to the complexity within the regions. For example, they demonstrate the high degree of symmetry of trade relations in the EC and the striking asymmetry of SADC trade. Thus, the networks allow us not only to find empirical regularities, but also help to elucidate more complex relations within the regional organisations, and to discern single countries and interesting patterns for further research.

Notes

1. Especially the SADC countries proved difficult in this respect. We used four data sources to construct our dataset. Firstly, we used the UN Comtrade data as reported by the importers. We filled in the missing values with UN Comtrade exporters' reports, with SADC Trade Database importers' reports, and with SADC Trade Database exporters' reports. Nevertheless, even with these four sources, valid and comparable data for Lesotho, Botswana, Namibia, and Swaziland were not available until 1999, because most of their trade was carried out through and reported by South Africa. Thus, we aggregate these countries to the Southern African customs union (SACU), a customs union today included in the SADC free trade area

(Walters 1989). After 1999, valid data are available, and we disaggregate SACU into its components.
2. www.visone.info
3. Most of the 'new' regional organisations were founded or refounded at the beginning of the 1990s. Thus, we use 1990 as the baseline year to elucidate the situation shortly before the foundation of the organisations. Even though the regional integration projects were not established in 1990, we show the 'prospective' member states and their external trade partners.

REFERENCES

Armstrong, D., Lloyd, L., & Redmond, J. (1996). *From Versailles to Maastricht: International Organisation in the Twentieth Century*. London: Palgrave Macmillan.
Brandes, U., Schneider, V., Wagner, D., Kenis, P., & Raab, J. (1999). Explorations into the Visualization of Policy Networks. *Journal of Theoretical Politics, 11*, 75–106.
De Lombaerde, P., Söderbaum, F., Van Langenhove, L., & Baert, F. (2010). The Problem of Comparison in Comparative Regionalism. *Review of International Studies, 36*, 731–753.
Dinan, D. (2005). *An Ever Closer Union: An Introduction to European Integration*. Basingstoke: Palgrave Macmillan.
Doctor, M. (2013). Prospects for Deepening MERCOSUR Integration: Economic Asymmetry and Institutional Deficits. *Review of International Political Economy, 20*, 515–540.
Estevadeordal, A., Goto, J., & Saez, R. (2001). The New Regionalism in the Americas: The Case of MERCOSUR. *Journal of Economic Integration, 16*, 180–202.
Feenstra, R. C., Lipsey, R. E., Deng, H., Ma, A. C., & Mo, H. (2005). *World Trade Flows: 1962-2000* (NBER Working Paper).
Frankel, J. A., & Wei, S.-J. (1998). *Open Regionalism in a World of Continental Trade Blocs* (IMF Working Paper).
Fukase, E. (2003). Possible Dynamic Effects of AFTA for the New Member Countries. *World Economy, 26*, 853–872.
Haas, E. B. (1958). *The Uniting of Europe: Political, Social and Economic Forces, 1950-1957*. Stanford, CA: Stanford University Press.
Hafner-Burton, E. M., Kahler, M., & Montgomery, A. H. (2009). Network Analysis for International Relations. *International Organization, 63*, 559–592.
Hyde-Price, A., & Jeffery, C. (2001). Germany in the European Union: Constructing Normality. *Journal of Common Market Studies, 39*, 689–717.
Krapohl, S. (2008). *Risk Regulation in the Single Market: The Governance of Pharmaceuticals and Foodstuffs in the European Union*. Basingstoke: Palgrave Macmillan.

Krapohl, S., & Fink, S. (2013). Different Paths of Regional Integration: Trade Networks and Regional Institution-Building in Europe, Southeast Asia and Southern Africa. *Journal of Common Market Studies, 51*, 472–488.

Kreinin, M. E., & Plummer, M. G. (2008). Effects of Regional Integration on FDI: An Empirical Approach. *Journal of Asian Economics, 19*, 447–454.

Kruskal, J. B. (1992). *Multidimensional Scaling.* Beverly Hills, CA: Sage Publications.

Maoz, Z. (2009). The Effects of Strategic and Economic Interdependence on International Conflict Across Levels of Analysis. *American Journal of Political Science, 53*, 223–240.

Markusen, J. R. (2004). Regional Integration and Third-Country Inward Investment. *Business and Politics, 6*, 1082–1108.

Mattli, W. (1999). *The Logic of Regional Integration: Europe and Beyond.* Cambridge: Cambridge University Press.

Moravcsik, A. (1998). *The Choice for Europe: Social Purpose and State Power from Messina to Maastricht.* Ithaca, NY: Cornell University Press.

Nabers, D. (2003). The Social Construction on International Institutions: The Case of ASEAN+3. *International Relations of the Asia-Pacific, 3*, 113–136.

Oosthuizen, G. H. (2006). *The Southern African Development Community: The Organisation, Its Policies and Prospects.* Midrand: The Institute for Global Dialogue.

Pierson, P. (1996). The Path to European Political Integration: A Historical Institutionalist Analysis. *Comparative Political Studies, 29*, 123–163.

Rosamond, B. (2005). The Uniting of Europe and the Foundation of EU Studies: Revisiting the Neofunctionalism of Ernst B. Haas. *Journal of European Public Policy, 12*, 237–254.

Sandholtz, W. (1998). The Emergence of a Supranational Telecommunications Regime. In W. Sandholtz & A. Stone Sweet (Eds.), *European Integration and Supranational Governance* (pp. 134–163). Oxford: Oxford University Press.

Stone Sweet, A., & Sandholtz, W. (1997). European Integration and Supranational Governance. *Journal of European Public Policy, 4*, 297–317.

Tay, S. (2000). *A New ASEAN in a New Millennium.* Jakarta: Center for Strategic and International Studies and Singapore Institute of International Affairs.

Vaillant, M. (2005). MERCOSUR: Southern Integration Under Construction. *Internationale Politik und Gesellschaft, 2*, 52–71.

Veiga, P. L. d. M., & Marchisio, M. (2004). *MERCOSUR's Institutionalization Agenda.* Buenos Aires: Institute for the Integration of Latin America and the Caribbean.

Walters, J. (1989). Renegotiating Dependency: The Case of the Southern African Customs Union. *Journal of Common Market Studies, 28*, 29–52.

PART III

Cases of Regional Cooperation and Defection in Developing Regions

CHAPTER 5

ASEAN

Extra-Regional Cooperation Triggers Regional Integration

Sebastian Krapohl

The evaluations of regional integration efforts in Southeast Asia differ widely between academic observers. On the one hand, critics argue that there is a huge gap between the stated goals of the Association of Southeast Asian Nations (ASEAN) and the actual achievements of the regional organisation (Cuyvers and Pupphavesa 1996; Ravenhill 1995; Wong 1989). Accordingly, the informal, consensual style of decision-making—the so-called ASEAN way (Capie and Evans 2002)—does not commit the member states sufficiently enough for integration to proceed and agreements to be implemented (Jetschke and Rüland 2009). Especially when ASEAN was not able to find a regional answer to the Asian crisis of the late 1990s, many observers regarded ASEAN as being obsolete and predicted its decline in the years following (Rüland 2000). On the other hand, proponents of ASEAN stress the organisation's achievements in maintaining peace and

S. Krapohl (✉)
University of Amsterdam, Amsterdam, The Netherlands
e-mail: s.krapohl@uva.nl

© The Author(s) 2017
S. Krapohl (ed.), *Regional Integration in the Global South*,
International Political Economy Series,
DOI 10.1007/978-3-319-38895-3_5

realising economic development within the region (Acharya 2011; Narine 2008). For them, the ASEAN way is a pragmatic approach to achieve realistic decisions that do not overburden member states in terms of having to give up sovereignty (Nesadurai 2001). The fact that ASEAN managed to survive the Asian crisis[1] and to integrate even further during the 2000s seems to support this optimistic view (Stubbs 2014).

The question as to whether the glass of Southeast Asian regionalism is in fact half-full or half-empty cannot be answered per se, but ASEAN's development can be compared with that of other regional organisations. Compared with MERCOSUR (see Chap. 6) and SADC (see Chap. 7), ASEAN has seemed to do well since the 1990s. The ASEAN member states do not form a customs union like MERCOSUR, but rather only a free trade area like SADC. However, at least during the 2000s, regional integration proceeded more dynamically in Southeast Asia than in South America and Southern Africa. Unlike the Argentinean crisis in South America, the Asian crisis did not stop regional integration in Southeast Asia. There was no regional power within ASEAN to defect from regional cooperation in order to follow extra-regional interests, as was the case with Brazil in MERCOSUR and South Africa in SADC. Thus, despite its problems of weak regional institutions and a lack of implementation, ASEAN seems to be the most successful regional organisation in the Global South at the present time.

Much of ASEAN's current success is due to the fact that the regional organisation became the focal point of regionalism in the whole of East Asia and the Pacific. Although ASEAN could not effectively support its member states during the Asian crisis, the extra-regional countries China, Japan, and South Korea became aware that they needed to support ASEAN in order to stabilise their neighbourhood in economic terms (Krapohl 2015). The result is the so-called ASEAN+3 process, which has so far led to a regional liquidity arrangement to prevent further financial crises and to separate trade agreements between ASEAN and each of the +3 countries. Australia, India, and New Zealand are showing some interest in regional cooperation as well, which would lead to an ASEAN+6 formation or even an East Asian Community (EAC) (Chirathivat 2006; Dieter 2008; Gilson 2006; Stubbs 2002). ASEAN+3 and ASEAN+6 are not independent regional organisations on their own, but they rely on the existence of ASEAN. The ASEAN member states act as one block within these extra-regional cooperation schemes. Thereby, they gain economic benefits that they could hardly achieve by acting independently on their own. This successful extra-regional cooperation makes regional integration within ASEAN more attractive, which explains the new dynamic of ASEAN itself after the Asian crisis and in parallel to the ASEAN+3 process (Stubbs 2014).

This chapter proceeds in three steps in order to demonstrate that cooperation of the ASEAN member states has mainly been driven by extra-regional considerations. The first section provides an analysis of the ASEAN Free Trade Area (AFTA), which was adopted in 1992 and implemented during the 1990s. AFTA is a textbook example of the new regionalism, as it predominately aimed to improve the region's competitiveness in order to attract extra-regional investments. Secondly, in order to understand ASEAN's development after the Asian crisis, it is necessary to have a brief aside on the Asian crisis itself and the subsequent ASEAN+3 process. The third section analyses the agreements on the ASEAN Charter and on the ASEAN Economic Community (AEC) in 2007. The ASEAN Charter in particular strengthens the regional organisation and its standing in extra-regional negotiations. Finally, the conclusion summarises the findings and reflects on the hypotheses developed in Chap. 2.

1 THE ESTABLISHMENT OF THE ASEAN FREE TRADE AREA DURING THE EARLY 1990s

ASEAN was founded in 1967 by Indonesia, Malaysia, the Philippines, Singapore, and Thailand. During its first 25 years, ASEAN was mainly a security community standing against the Communist threat in East Asia during the Cold War (Acharya 2001). ASEAN's founding document—the Bangkok Declaration[2]—mentioned economic integration and development as one fundamental goal, but the organisation's success was very marginal in this respect, because the economic strategies of its member states varied widely between free trade (e.g. Singapore) and protectionism (e.g. Indonesia) (Dosch 1997). The ASEAN member states achieved a preferential trade agreement in 1977, but its effects on intraregional trade were marginal, because the member states excluded the most-traded products (Chirathivat 1996; Ravenhill 1995). A swap agreement between the member states was signed in the same year, but its volume was very small (first US$100 mn, later US$200 mn).[3] More significant were ASEAN's achievements with respect to regional security. The member states created a Zone of Peace, Freedom and Neutrality (ZOPFAN) in 1971 and signed the Treaty of Amity and Cooperation in Southeast Asia (TAC) in 1976. Besides, ASEAN was relatively successful in dealing with Vietnam's invasion of Cambodia in 1978 (Koga 2014; Narine 2008).

At the beginning of the 1990s, the Communist threat disappeared with the end of the Cold War and its bipolar world order, and ASEAN needed a new raison d'être (Katzenstein 2000; Yuan 1994). At the same time, new regionalism spread around the world (Mansfield and Milner 1999), and ASEAN followed the global trend by restarting its regional integration process with a new focus on economic cooperation. In accordance with the dominant paradigm of liberalism at that time, the ASEAN member states forwent import substitution and protectionism in order to concentrate on deregulation, privatisation and export promotion to develop their economies (Yuen and Wagner 1989). Economic integration in ASEAN was seen as an instrument for improving the region's standing on the global market, and the most important project was therefore AFTA, which was signed in 1992 (Bowles 1997; Stubbs 2000). Here, the ASEAN member states committed themselves to reducing their tariffs against each other by 2008 under the Common Effective Preferential Tariff scheme (CEPT scheme).

1.1 ASEAN's Dependence on Extra-Regional Investments and Exports

Although ASEAN has the highest share of intraregional trade from all regions analysed in this book, it is nevertheless far away from the economic interdependence of well-developed regions like the EU or the North American Free Trade Agreement (NAFTA). During the early 1990s, when the ASEAN member states agreed on AFTA, the share of intraregional trade was at around 18 per cent—much below the 65 per cent for intraregional trade in the EU at that time.[4] Besides, the small city state of Singapore adds a lot to the intraregional trade figure. However, many goods traded via Singapore are either intraregional imports that are directly re-exported to extra-regional markets, or extra-regional imports that are redistributed within the region (Ariff 1994). If such re-exports were not counted, ASEAN's share of intraregional trade would be considerably smaller (Stubbs 2000). Also, the official trade numbers do not of course reflect informal trade between ASEAN member states with common borders (Ariff 1994).

In the early 1990s, the most important export markets for the ASEAN member states were extra-regional markets in Europe, North America,

Table 5.1 The three most important export destinations of the ASEAN member states in 1991

	First	Second	Third
Brunei	Japan 56 %	South Korea 11 %	Thailand 7 %
Cambodia[a]	EU 35 %	Thailand 21 %	Malaysia 18 %
Indonesia	Japan 45 %	EU 13 %	USA 13 %
Laos[a]	Thailand 56 %	EU 22 %	Japan 5 %
Malaysia	Singapore 26 %	Japan 17 %	USA 17 %
Myanmar[a]	Thailand 29 %	China 16 %	Singapore 14 %
Philippines	USA 37 %	Japan 23 %	EU 16 %
Singapore	USA 24 %	EU 19 %	Malaysia 13 %
Thailand	USA 24 %	EU 21 %	Japan 20 %
Vietnam[a]	Japan 40 %	Hong Kong 10 %	Thailand 7 %

Calculation based on the UN Comtrade database (comtrade.un.org)
[a]Cambodia, Laos, Myanmar, and Vietnam (the so-called CLMV countries) were not yet ASEAN member states in 1991

and Northeast Asia (see Table 5.1). The EU and the USA are among the three most important export destinations for all five original ASEAN member states. Intraregional trade is only significant between the new ASEAN member states (Cambodia, Laos, Myanmar, and Vietnam; the so-called CLMV countries) and Thailand, as well as between Malaysia and Singapore. It is a huge difference with MERCOSUR and SADC that neighbouring East Asian countries—namely China, Japan, and South Korea—are as important for Southeast Asian exports as the EU and the USA are. In 1991, before the dramatic rise of the Chinese economy, Japan in particular dominated the East and Southeast Asian trade networks. Thus, some of ASEAN's most important extra-regional partners are geographically very close to the regional organisation. This may be an advantage for regional integration in Southeast Asia if the East Asian neighbours develop an own interest in cooperating with ASEAN thanks to being economically affected by developments within the regional organisation.

A second advantage for regional cooperation within ASEAN is that none of the member states dominates the whole region on its own (see Chap. 4). Indonesia, Malaysia, Singapore, and Thailand are obviously more important for the intraregional trade network than the other member states, but they balance each other out and none of them is big enough to become an undisputed regional power. Indonesia is economically not developed enough to dominate the region (Emmers 2014), whereas the very well-developed Singapore is only a small city state (Thompson 2006). Because there is no clear regional power, there is also no country that is a priori more important and more attractive for extra-regional actors. Thus, the likelihood that one of the member states enjoys extra-regional privileges declines. And, if no member state needs to protect such privileges in its extra-regional economic relations, Rambo situations and a defection from regional cooperation become less likely. Consequently, one may expect that the chances for successful regional cooperation within ASEAN were relatively high.

The patterns seen in trade are also reflected in the patterns of investment inflows into the ASEAN member states. Generally, Southeast Asia had already improved its economic attractiveness and received growing investments during the 1980s. At the beginning of the 1990s, the region received the most investments of the developing world (Yue 1999). The size and stability effects of ASEAN and AFTA were expected to contribute positively to this trend (Athukorala and Menon 1996; Bowles 1997). Most of the investment inflows to ASEAN member states traditionally originate from Europe and the USA, but Japanese firms also invest heavily in the region (Igusa and Shimada 1996). In comparison, intraregional foreign investment is very low in ASEAN (Yue 1999). Although the small but well-developed Singapore attracts a high share of the extra-regional investment inflows, it is not the only country that benefits. Indonesia, Malaysia, and Thailand are also among ASEAN's most attractive investment destinations (Yue 1999). Thus, there is again no single country that dominates the picture, enjoys extra-regional privileges, and is tempted to protect these privileges at the cost of regional cooperation.

1.2 Consensus on the New Regionalism during the 1990s

During the 1990s, a new consensus on economic development in the global south emerged in parallel with the end of the Cold War and the rise of the new regionalism. Until the 1980s, dependency theory had dominated the academic debate on economic (under)development, and import substitution was seen as the main instrument for protecting developing economies against harmful competition on the global market. This changed when it became evident during the 'lost decade' of the 1980s that sustainable economic development did not really happen behind high tariff walls, and countries with liberal trade policies, like Hong Kong, South Korea and Taiwan, generally showed more economic success (Krueger 1997). The new development paradigm of export promotion required attracting foreign investments and getting free access to important export markets in Europe and North America (Bhagwati 1988). The ASEAN member states were afraid that regional integration in other world regions (especially NAFTA, with the participation of Mexico) and the rise of the Chinese economy would distort competition and distract investments away from Southeast Asia (Bowles 1997; Ravenhill 1995). In this situation, regional economic integration in the form of AFTA was an instrument for making the region more attractive for extra-regional investments. Thus, AFTA was clearly an example of an outwardly oriented, open regionalism (Bowles 1997).

Due to the neoliberal turn at the beginning of the 1990s, a new consensus emerged between the ASEAN member states. Before that, nearly all of the original ASEAN member states (Indonesia, Malaysia, the Philippines, and Thailand) had protected their markets heavily, and only Singapore had adopted a very liberal external trade policy (Dosch 1997; Stubbs 2000). As a result, early attempts at market integration in ASEAN had little effect because the member states excluded nearly all relevant sectors from intra-regional trade liberalisation (Chirathivat 1996; Ravenhill 1995). However, all ASEAN member states gave up their protectionist trade strategies at roughly the same time at the beginning of the 1990s (Obermeier 2013). In Indonesia and Malaysia, recessions of the 1980s and the following balance of payment problems strengthened the position of liberal reformers, who gained decisive influence in the early 1990s. The Philippines even became dependent on support from the International Monetary Fund (IMF) and the World Bank, which pushed for economic reforms. And in Thailand, a military coup brought liberal economists to power in 1991. These political changes in the original ASEAN member states opened up a policy window that allowed Thailand's government to bring forward the proposal for an ASEAN-wide free trade area (Stubbs 2000).

Despite the general consensus on intraregional trade liberalisation, the ASEAN member states nevertheless disagreed about the concrete form of AFTA. Here, conflicts emerged about the pace of trade liberalisation and transitional periods, as well as about exceptions and the protection of sensitive industries in some member states. Domestic firms in Indonesia pushed for protection, Malaysia did not want to risk its young automobile industry, the Philippines saw its textile and steel industries endangered, and Thailand's petrochemical industry was afraid of losing out to competitors from Singapore. The struggle over these issues was reinforced by political instability in the Philippines and Thailand that put the countries' commitment to AFTA in question (Stubbs 2000). The situation resembled a classic battle of the sexes wherein the member states agreed on the general goal of cooperation but negotiated over the distributive consequences in the form of exceptions and transition periods. A formula was needed that would accommodate the different distributive interests of the member states without endangering the common project of market integration in Southeast Asia.

1.3 Cooperation towards the Free Trade Area

The ASEAN member states finally decided to establish AFTA at a summit meeting in Singapore in January 1992 (Bowles 1997; Ravenhill 1995).[5] Accordingly, the member states committed themselves to reducing the tariffs on their intraregional trade to 5 per cent or less within a period of 15 years, starting in January 1993. The CEPT scheme laid down a timetable for the stepwise reduction of tariffs on intraregional trade (Cuyvers and Pupphavesa 1996; Nesadurai 2001; Pangestu et al. 1992).[6] The scheme applied to all manufactured goods, including capital goods and processed agricultural products, with values created of up to 40 per cent in one of the ASEAN member states. Unprocessed agricultural products and goods produced to more than 60 per cent outside the region were excluded from intraregional trade liberalisation. The CEPT prescribed that tariffs above 20 per cent should be reduced to 20 per cent within five to eight years and further to 5 per cent or less within another seven years. Within a so-called fast track, two or more member states could agree to reduce tariffs mutually at an accelerated pace. Tariff concessions took place on a mutual basis, so that only complying member states enjoyed the concessions of the other member states. Each member state could place certain products on a temporary exclusion list if tariff reductions on imports of these goods endangered the existence of domestic industries or the balance of payment situation of the respective country. The exclusion list was to be cut down over the years. Also, every member state could still adopt trade restrictions in order to protect national security, public health, and the country's cultural heritage.

The final form of AFTA resembles a classic compromise at the lowest common denominator between trade liberalisation on the one hand and the need of some member states to protect their infant industries on the other hand. Although the member states agreed on the general goal of establishing AFTA, the CEPT scheme was rather unspecific, its implementation period was rather long, the annual cuts in tariffs were modest, and the member states reserved the right to exempt some sectors from trade liberalisation at will. These compromises undermined the general goal of intraregional trade liberalisation to a significant degree. As a result, AFTA and the CEPT scheme were criticised from the very beginning for having a limited effect on intraregional trade (Cuyvers and Pupphavesa 1996; Stubbs 2000). Observers were in doubt as to whether AFTA added anything more to the level of trade liberalisation that had been accepted by the 'old' ASEAN member states during the Uruguay round of trade negotiations under the General Agreement on Tariffs and Trade (GATT) (Ariff 1994).

Trade liberalisation was especially problematic for the CLMV countries that joined ASEAN during the 1990s (Ariff 1996; Menon 1998). Originally, AFTA was negotiated between the original member states and Brunei, which joined the regional organisation in 1984. Thus, AFTA did not take into account the interests of the very poor economies in mainland Southeast Asia, which were significantly less developed than the 'old' ASEAN member states. The CLMV countries had just started to introduce free-market economies (Laos and Vietnam), recovered from war and occupation (Cambodia) or suffered from military and authoritarian rule (Myanmar). Nevertheless, it was assumed that new member states would have to accept the same commitments to tariff reductions and trade liberalisation under the CEPT scheme as the old member states. However, the implementation periods of the CEPT scheme would not start in 1993, but rather only when the respective countries joined ASEAN (Ariff 1996; Menon 1998). This granted the respective economies some more time to prepare for competition on the regional market.

1.4 Effects of the Free Trade Area

Despite the modest scope of trade liberalisation and the criticism of contemporary observers (Ariff 1994; Cuyvers and Pupphavesa 1996; Cuyvers et al. 2005; Ravenhill 2008), AFTA achieved its goals until the Asian crisis in the late 1990s. AFTA's relative success can be illustrated by three different developments. Firstly, the CEPT scheme was extended in scope and implemented quicker than had been envisaged (Chirathivat 1996; Menon 1998; Stubbs 2000). In December 1995,[7] the ASEAN member states decided to include unprocessed agricultural products—which had been deliberately excluded three years prior—in tariff reductions under the CEPT scheme.

At the same time, the implementation period of the scheme was reduced from 15 to 10 years so that AFTA could enter into force in 2003 instead of 2008. Only the new ASEAN member states would participate somewhat later in AFTA, because the implementation period of ten years only started at the date when the respective countries joined ASEAN (Vietnam joined ASEAN in 1995, Myanmar and Laos in 1997, and Cambodia in 1999).

Secondly, intraregional trade in Southeast Asia increased during the implementation of the CEPT scheme. Due to the shift towards an export-promoting development strategy, exports of the regional member states increased drastically in absolute terms and in relation to gross domestic product (GDP) (Yue 1999). Most of these exports still addressed extra-regional markets like that of the EU, Japan, and the USA, but intraregional trade grew even faster than extra-regional trade. In 1990, before the member states had agreed on AFTA, the share of intraregional trade in ASEAN had been at 17 per cent, and it then grew during the implementation of the CEPT scheme to 21 per cent in 1996 before the outbreak of the Asian crisis.[8]

And thirdly, ASEAN enjoyed growing investments from extra-regional actors during the 1990s. Before the Asian crisis hit the region, one could even speak of an investment boom in Southeast Asia (Bowles 1997; Yue 1999). Between 1990 and 1996 (just before the beginning of the Asian crisis), the stock of foreign direct investment in the ASEAN economies more than tripled from US\$61 bn to US\$192 bn.[9] This investment boom was probably not only due to AFTA and the implementation of the CEPT scheme because the general policies of deregulation and privatisation within the region had a positive effect as well (Yuen and Wagner 1989). However, the creation of a larger and more stable regional market is likely to have contributed to the increasing investment amounts to a significant degree (Bowles 1997; Athukorala and Menon 1996).

2 The Asian Crisis and Its Consequences

The Asian crisis marked a turning point in Southeast Asian regionalism (Acharya 1999; Bowles 2002). Between the end of the Cold War and the beginning of the Asian crisis, AFTA was a textbook example of the new regionalism in ASEAN. Extra-regional investments, as well as extra- and intraregional exports, increased enormously. The new export-promoting development strategy seemed to be a success for the ASEAN member states. Indonesia, Malaysia, the Philippines, and Thailand even became known as Tiger Cub Economies, and were expected to follow in the footsteps of the advanced Tiger Economies: Hong Kong, Singapore, South Korea, and Taiwan. However, the Asian crisis, which came as a surprise for many observers, put an end to such high hopes. The Southeast Asian economies stumbled, and ASEAN proved to be badly prepared to support its member states during the crisis (Rüland 2000). The regional organisation stayed passive, and the crisis-suffering countries needed to approach the IMF for financial support. In the aftermath of the crisis, many contemporary observers expected the marginalisation of ASEAN (Webber 2001). However, China, Japan, and South Korea started to engage in the region, and the so-called ASEAN+3 process was born (Chirathivat 2006; Dieter 2008; Gilson 2006; Stubbs 2002). This successful extra-regional cooperation with the economic powers of Northeast Asia provided new impetus to regional integration within ASEAN itself (see Sect. 3).

2.1 The Failure of ASEAN

Due to Southeast Asia's economic success during the 1990s, a lot of capital was invested within the region (Radelet and Sachs 1998). Like in many developing countries, the weak financial systems of the ASEAN member states suffered from balance sheet mismatches. Domestic banks borrowed money short term on the international market in US dollar, but they loaned in the long-term and in domestic currencies. This was not a problem as long as the domestic central banks kept exchange rates to the US dollar stable and creditors were willing to roll over outstanding debts. However, during the mid-1990s the Southeast Asian countries faced increasing competition from the rising Chinese economy and from Mexico, which profited from the NAFTA agreement with the USA. As a result, the growth of exports from Southeast Asia to extra-regional markets stagnated, and foreign exchange reserves tightened. In this situation, international investors lost confidence in the sustainability of the Asian economic miracle. The withdrawal of capital from Southeast Asia had a self-reinforcing effect, and investors flew from the region in a herd-like panic (Radelet and Sachs 1998). The outflow of capital led to pressure on the local currencies to devaluate, but such devaluations meant sharp increases in international debts in the values of domestic currencies. The first country hit by the crisis was Thailand, which was running out of currency reserves and had to float the Bhat in July 1997.

Because international investors did not evaluate the regional economies independently from each other, the crisis spread further from Thailand to Indonesia, Malaysia, the Philippines, and South Korea (MacIntyre 2001). All these countries had to float their currencies, suffered from collapsing financial institutions, and could not serve private and public debts anymore at the end of 1997.

ASEAN was of little help for the member states that were affected by the Asian crisis (Rüland 2000; Webber 2001; Wesley 1999). This can be demonstrated in two different areas of economic integration. Firstly, intraregional capital and trade flows within AFTA did not bolster the ASEAN member states against the volatility of international markets. The share of intraregional trade was at just about 21 per cent, and it even decreased slightly in 1998, because of the general contraction of demand within the region.[10] Thus, the ASEAN member states were still dependent on extra-regional exports, whose decline marked the beginning of the crisis (Radelet and Sachs 1998). Intraregional financial flows within ASEAN were even lower and could certainly not replace the capital that was withdrawn from the region on a large scale (MacIntyre 2001). And secondly, although the ASEAN member states had a swap agreement from 1977,[11] the volume of this agreement was far too small to support even one of the ASEAN member states during the crisis. A sum of US$200 m. within the swap agreement stood against the financial needs of approximately US$40 bn for Indonesia alone (Radelet and Sachs 1998). Thus, only bailing out Indonesia would have required 200 times as much capital as was available under the old agreement from 1977, and on top of that three other ASEAN member states were also affected by the Asian crisis. Not surprisingly, none of the ASEAN member states activated these highly insufficient swap agreements during the Asian crisis (Henning 2002). Besides, not only ASEAN but also the Asia Pacific Economic Cooperation (APEC) remained passive during the crisis—although for different reasons. Whereas ASEAN was too small and powerless to handle the economic problems, APEC was too big and heterogeneous to provide an Asian answer to the Asian crisis (Webber 2001, 2010). Thus, both existing regional organisations were of no help for the crisis-suffering countries in South- and Northeast Asia.

Indonesia, the Philippines, South Korea, and Thailand had to go to the IMF in order to get help during the Asian crisis, whereas Malaysia went through the crisis without IMF intervention (MacIntyre 2001). The IMF provided the necessary liquidity for the crisis-suffering countries, but its loans were connected to very strict conditions. In order to restore investors' confidence, the IMF demanded that the four countries implement structural reforms like privatisation and deregulation, as well as adopt tight fiscal and monetary policies (Radelet and Sachs 1998). However, it turned out that these measures proved insufficient to stop the outflow of capital from Asia. In parallel to the ongoing capital flight, the strict fiscal policies and high interest rates led to a further contraction of the Asian economies (Stiglitz 2003). Together, the panic-like behaviour of creditors and the conservative policies of the IMF reinforced the Asian recession, which became much worse than pre-crisis economic data had suggested it would be (Radelet and Sachs 1998). Of course, the IMF's behaviour during the Asian crisis was heavily criticised, and a general dissatisfaction with the influence of global economic institutions, which were deemed to be dominated by EU and US interests, emerged within the region (Katzenstein 2000).

The Asian crisis led to widespread discontent with global and regional economic institutions in East Asia. On the one hand, it became evident that ASEAN alone could not handle an economic crisis of such a scale. The ASEAN member states were too dependent on the inflow of capital from and the outflow of goods to other world regions. Important regional powers of East Asia—namely, China and Japan—were not members of ASEAN and would consequently not stabilise the region effectively in cases of economic turmoil. On the other hand, global institutions like the IMF were dominated by the EU and the USA, and by their views about sound economic policies (for the so-called Washington consensus, see Williamson 1993). The IMF would not take the particular interests of Asian countries into account, despite their growing economic presence on the global stage. This general dissatisfaction opened a policy window (for the concept of policy windows, see Kingdon 1995), and new economic institutions could therefore emerge in East Asia.

2.2 The Emergence of ASEAN+3

In the aftermath of the Asian crisis, the two regional powers China and Japan started to get more involved in regionalism in East Asia. Although both countries were not directly affected by the Asian crisis themselves, they suffered from the negative externalities of the crisis in neighbouring countries (Krapohl 2015). Japanese companies in particular had started to invest heavily in production networks in Southeast Asia during the 1980s and 1990s (Gilson 2004; Stubbs 2002). Financial crises in this region brought the risks that some of the Japanese investments in cheap suppliers of labour-intensive inputs would be lost. Thus, Japan had an interest in stabilising its regional neighbourhood in financial terms. At the turn of the millennium, China was economically less involved in the region, but its ongoing economic rise and its rivalry with Japan motivated the country to take a more proactive role in regional politics (Jiang 2010). China was not willing to leave the regional playing field to Japan, and, consequently, both regional powers competed (and still compete) for regional leadership in East Asia.

The main policy innovation of ASEAN+3 (which includes ASEAN, China, Japan, and South Korea) is the Chiang Mai Initiative (CMI), which aims to create a regional instrument in order to support East Asian countries in financial distress (Dieter and Higgott 2003). Originally, Japan had proposed the establishment of an Asian Monetary Fund (AMF) at the peak of the Asian crisis in 1997 (Nair 2008). The AMF proposal met with resistance from the USA and failed to get support within East Asia, but the finance ministers of the ASEAN+3 countries decided to establish a network of bilateral swap agreements at a meeting in Chiang Mai (Thailand) in 2000.[12] Originally, the CMI was not really a multilateral liquidity fund, but only a web of bilateral agreements, and it was undercapitalised with a volume of only US$40 bn. Besides, the CMI was not independent from the IMF, but more of a regional complement to the global rescue mechanism (Grimes 2011a). The member states could only draw up to 10 per cent of their quotas independently from the IMF, and more capital would only be granted if the crisis-suffering member states negotiated an agreement with the IMF. However, the volume and independence of the CMI were increased repeatedly in the following years (Grimes 2015). Today, the available capital adds up to US$240 bn, and the member states may withdraw up to 30 per cent of their quota without the involvement of the IMF. The most important reform was decided by the ASEAN+3 states in 2009 with the Chiang Mai Initiative Multilateralization (CMIM), which created a real regional liquidity fund (Grimes 2011a).[13] The CMIM is in fact an instrument of China and Japan for stabilising the ASEAN member states and South Korea in financial terms. The two regional powers provide the bulk of the available capital, and they themselves can only withdraw half of their own contributions in cases of crises. In contrast, the original ASEAN member states may borrow up to 2.5 times as much as they themselves contribute, and for CLMV countries and Brunei that figure is 5 times (Grimes 2011a). Whereas it is very doubtful that the CMIM is sufficiently equipped to support the bigger Northeast Asian economies in cases of financial crises (Grimes 2011b), its utility for the Southeast Asian countries is much more apparent.

In addition to financial cooperation on the CMIM, ASEAN also managed to cooperate with each of the +3 countries in trade matters. In contrast to ASEAN itself, the share of intraregional trade in ASEAN+3 is almost 50 per cent greater, and China and Japan are important export markets for the ASEAN member states (Krapohl and Fink 2013). The beginning of the ASEAN+1 trade agreements was the ASEAN-China Free Trade Area (ACFTA), which was signed in 2002 and implemented in 2010 (Ba 2003; Cai 2003). Japan followed soon and successfully negotiated with the ASEAN member states for a Comprehensive Economic Partnership Agreement between 2003 and 2008 (Corning 2009). And, South Korea signed an agreement to establish a free trade area with ASEAN in 2005. In addition to AFTA and the three ASEAN+1 trade agreements, there exist several bilateral trade agreements between single ASEAN member states and Northeast Asian countries. This 'spaghetti-bowl' (Baldwin 2006; Baldwin and Seghezza 2010) of trade agreements in East Asia could best be harmonised within a single ASEAN+3 trade agreement (Park 2009), but this fails due to the rivalry between China and Japan (Webber 2010). So far, the ASEAN+1 trade agreements are the most promising buildingblocs of an ASEAN+3 free trade area, and they grant all ASEAN member states privileged access to the important export markets in Northeast Asia.

Another issue for East Asian regionalism is the formation of ASEAN+6 and the East Asian Summit (EAS). The ASEAN+6 includes the ASEAN+3 member states plus Australia, India, and New Zealand, which all signed ASEAN+1 trade agreements with ASEAN itself (Terada 2010). These 16 states of East Asia and the Pacific meet regularly at the East Asian Summit (EAS), and proposals to establish an East Asian Community (EAC) are discussed from time to time. So far, several bilateral and plurilateral trade agreements have been signed between members of this group, but a comprehensive EAC seems to be a long way off. In any case, Australia, India, and New Zealand do not have the same economic importance for ASEAN as do China, Japan, and South Korea, and they are much less integrated into the regional trade network (see Chap. 4).

All the different regional agreements in East Asia are based on ASEAN as a focal point for East Asian regionalism. There would not be any ASEAN+3 or ASEAN+6 without ASEAN. The regional organisation provides the necessary forum for all these regional initiatives. Despite the fact that ASEAN is relatively weak in economic and military terms, it nevertheless fulfils a leadership role for regional cooperation in East Asia (Stubbs 2014). The regional powers China and Japan distrust each other, and neither one nor the other nor both can act as undisputed regional leaders (Dieter 2008; Webber 2001). But while they mistrust each other, they do not mistrust ASEAN, which is not an economic or political threat to them. And, of course, ASEAN can play its role in East Asian regionalism more successfully if it is able to speak with one voice. The more ASEAN is integrated, the better is its position between the rivalling regional powers. The ASEAN member states profit from extra-regional cooperation within the CMIM and the different trade agreements, and this provides additional incentives for regional integration within ASEAN itself in order to improve ASEAN's standing within the region.

Whereas the ASEAN member states managed to speak with one voice in the ASEAN+3 and ASEAN+6 framework, extra-regional relations with the EU and the USA were more complicated. The EU started interregional negotiations for a free trade agreement with the whole ASEAN in 2007. However, these negotiations became difficult, and the EU switched towards bilateral negotiations with single ASEAN member states (Malaysia, Singapore, Thailand, and Vietnam; Garcia 2013). Similarly, the Trans-Pacific Partnership Agreement (TPP) under the lead of the USA also includes only a minority of ASEAN's member states (Brunei, Malaysia, Singapore, and Vietnam; Capling and Ravenhill 2011). Although the relative importance of the EU and the USA as destinations for ASEAN's exports is less than that of China and Japan, a fragmentation of ASEAN's external trade regime towards the EU and the USA may nevertheless be an obstacle for further integration within ASEAN itself. However, one has to keep in mind that AFTA is only a free trade area without a harmonised external trade regime. Thus, it does not stand in direct conflict with bilateral trade agreements between ASEAN member states and extra-regional partners.

3 THE ASEAN CHARTER AND THE ASEAN ECONOMIC COMMUNITY

ASEAN was in a state of crisis at the turn of the millennium (Jetschke and Murray 2012; Ravenhill 2008). The regional organisation proved unable to support its member states during the Asian crisis, and a rise of other bilateral, plurilateral, and multilateral agreements in East Asia threatened the unity of ASEAN. Many observers at this time expected the marginalisation of ASEAN and put their hope in regional cooperation on ASEAN+3 instead (Bowles 2002; Dieter and Higgott 2003; Webber 2001). Their criticism was that ASEAN would be unable to solve the economic and political problems of East Asia on its own because it lacked the participation of the two regional powers, China and Japan. The cooperation of the two regional powers was deemed necessary in order to solve security problems like the conflict about the Spratly Islands in the South China Sea or economic problems like the Asian crisis (Simon 2008).

Observers were not wrong to expect an important role for the ASEAN+3 framework after the Asian crisis, but they did not foresee the positive effects of this development on ASEAN itself. In the shadow of regional cooperation in East Asia, a new regional integration dynamic emerged in ASEAN during the first decade of the new millennium. In 2007, the ASEAN member states adopted the ASEAN Charter, which represents the first step away from the old ASEAN way towards a more rule-based regional organisation (Freistein 2013; Jetschke and Murray 2012; Yoshimatsu 2006). Parallel to that, the member states decided to establish the AEC, which is built up on the basis of AFTA and pushes regional integration significantly forward (Petri et al. 2012; Simon 2008). These steps cannot be explained by intraregional developments within ASEAN alone; they are driven forward by ASEAN's successful extra-regional cooperation with China, Japan, and South Korea in the ASEAN+3 framework.

3.1 Extra-Regional Economic Relations with China and Japan

Although the implementation of AFTA and the CEPT was criticised for being cumbersome and incomplete (Cuyvers et al. 2005; Ravenhill 2008), the share of intraregional trade within ASEAN grew from approximately 18 per cent in 1991 to around 21 per cent shortly before the Asian crisis, and to 25 per cent in the mid-2000s.[14] Although these numbers are high for a developing region and mark a significant improvement in intraregional trade, they also show that the ASEAN member states are

Table 5.2 The three most important export destinations of the ASEAN member states in 2006

	First	Second	Third
Brunei	Japan 30 %	Indonesia 20 %	South Korea 15 %
Cambodia	USA 58 %	EU 24 %	Vietnam 4 %
Indonesia	Japan 20 %	EU 14 %	USA 12 %
Laos	Thailand 48 %	EU 20 %	Vietnam 16 %
Malaysia	USA 20 %	Singapore 16 %	EU 13 %
Myanmar	Thailand 51 %	India 15 %	EU 9 %
Philippines	China 26 %	USA 15 %	EU 13 %
Singapore	EU 16 %	Hong Kong 13 %	USA 11 %
Thailand	USA 17 %	EU 15 %	China 13 %
Vietnam	EU 23 %	USA 22 %	Japan 13 %

Calculation based on the UN Comtrade database (comtrade.un.org)

still largely dependent on trade with extra-regional economic partners. In 2006, shortly before the ASEAN Charter and the AEC were adopted, the main trade partners for Southeast Asian countries were still the EU, Japan, and the USA (see Table 5.2). The importance of the EU and the USA for ASEAN's exports had increased in comparison to 1991, whereas the dominance of Japan declined due to the ongoing economic stagnation of that country. Japan's central position was replaced by the EU's, which was among the three most important export destinations for nearly all ASEAN member states in 2006.

The cursory data of 2006 misses one important change in ASEAN's trade network: the rise of China as an important trade partner for Southeast Asia.[15] The dynamic economic growth of China was one of the most important developments on the global market during the first decade of the new millennium (Ikenberry 2008). Of course, China became a much more important export destination for the ASEAN member states due to this development. ASEAN's trade network of 2010 demonstrates this very clearly (see Fig. 4.5 in Chap. 4). Whereas China was not yet represented among ASEAN's three most important extra-regional trade partners in 2005, it became one of the most central actors in ASEAN's trade network of 2010. The EU lost relevance for Southeast Asian trade and the USA was not among ASEAN's three most important trade partners anymore in 2010, because the global financial crisis of 2008–2010 led to weakening demand in the Western World. In 2010, the most important trade partners for ASEAN became the two regional powers China and Japan, which cooperated with ASEAN in the ASEAN+3 framework.

The economic weights within ASEAN did not change a lot between the 1990s and the 2000s. There were still four member states—Indonesia, Malaysia, Singapore, and Thailand—that were more economically important than the six remaining member states (see Chap. 4). However, none of these bigger member states were large and wealthy enough to dominate the region in economic terms and to be of outstanding economic importance for extra-regional actors. This reduced the risk that any member state would enjoy privileges in its extra-regional economic relations with the EU and the USA at the beginning of the decade or with China and Japan at its end. This situation would have allowed for cooperation between the member states in order to improve their common position in relation to extra-regional partners. It was unlikely that one of the member states would have had to protect important privileges in its extra-regional relations at the cost of regional integration.

3.2 ASEAN's Growing Win-Set

Successful extra-regional cooperation within the ASEAN+3 framework enlarged the win-sets for further regional cooperation within ASEAN itself. Due to limited intraregional economic interdependence, the intraregional gains of regional integration were relatively modest for the ASEAN member states. However, due to China's economic growth, the two regional powers China and Japan together became ASEAN's most important economic partners during the late 2000s. ASEAN was able to achieve important gains from extra-regional cooperation with China and Japan within ASEAN+3. The ASEAN member states profit from financial stabilisation through the CMIM (Dieter and Higgott 2003; Dieter 2008), and they enjoy privileged market access to China, Japan, and South Korea through the ASEAN+1 trade agreements (Krapohl and Fink 2013; Park 2009). These gains through extra-regional cooperation make participation in ASEAN more worthwhile for its member states. If they were not part of ASEAN, the Southeast Asian countries would lose these privileges in their economic relations to China and Japan. As a result, the win-set for regional cooperation within ASEAN is larger, because the exit option is much less attractive for the ASEAN member states. Thus, the success of ASEAN+3 widens the possibilities for regional cooperation within ASEAN itself.

The ASEAN member states aimed to use the enlarged win-sets for regional cooperation in order to strengthen ASEAN's position within the ASEAN+3. ASEAN was in a crisis at the beginning of the new millennium, and the Southeast Asian influence in ASEAN+3 could only be improved by strengthening ASEAN itself (Jetschke and Murray 2012). Firstly, regional economic integration within Southeast Asia had to be pushed beyond the achievements of AFTA (Ravenhill 2008; Webber 2010). Although AFTA had made some progress during the 1990s and intraregional trade increased within ASEAN, intraregional market liberalisation was still not far-reaching. The differences between the remaining intraregional tariffs of up to 5 per cent within AFTA and the tariffs applied to extra-regional trade partners within the WTO were small. Besides, customs procedures were cumbersome even within AFTA, and non-tariff trade barriers were not addressed by trade liberalisation. As a result, the privileges of AFTA were rarely used for intraregional trade, and businesses often preferred to pay tariff premiums in order to avoid overly bureaucratic procedures at intraregional borders (Cuyvers et al. 2005; Hayakawa et al. 2013). Further steps in economic integration needed to be taken in order to improve ASEAN's attractiveness for the production chains of Chinese and Japanese investors.

Secondly, and even more importantly, ASEAN lacked an adequate institutional setup in order to commit its own member states to common policies and to cooperate with the +3 countries. ASEAN's founding document—the Bangkok Declaration from 1967[16]—was not an international treaty and ASEAN had no legal personality in international law (Ravenhill 2008; Simon 2008). The ASEAN way, with its emphasis on consensual decision-making and state sovereignty, prevented quick progress in regional integration and effective oversight of implementation by the member states (Jetschke and Rüland 2009). The informality of ASEAN and the lack of formalised dispute settlement led to a deficit of legal certainty and of the predictability of member states' actions. All these institutional deficits endangered the unity of ASEAN in the international system and in negotiations with China and Japan. New regional institutions were needed to ensure both the development of a common ASEAN position and the effective representation of this position in extra-regional negotiations.

Not all ASEAN member states were willing to proceed with economic integration and institutional commitment to the same degree. The readiness to go on with market integration correlated positively with the economic development of the member states. The more-developed countries wanted to proceed further, whereas the less-developed ones were afraid of increasing competition on the regional market (Ravenhill 2008). The willingness to accept stronger regional institutions depended on the level of democracy within the member states. The more democratic countries agreed to more institutional commitment, whereas the more authoritarian states were afraid to give up sovereignty and to accept interference into their own matters (Simon 2008). Both issues led to a cleavage between the old and the new ASEAN member states (Yoshimatsu 2006). The original member states were economically much more developed than the CLMV countries in mainland Southeast Asia. And ASEAN's more democratic member states—Indonesia, the Philippines, and Thailand—also belonged to the old member states, whereas the CLMV countries were all more or less subject to authoritarian rule. Thus, a compromise between the old and the new ASEAN was needed.

3.3 Towards an ASEAN Community

ASEAN celebrated the 40th birthday of the Bangkok declaration in November 2007. At this time, the member states adopted a blueprint to establish the AEC[17] and launched the ASEAN Charter.[18] Firstly, the idea for the AEC went back to the ASEAN Vision 2020 of 1997 and the Bali Concord II of 2003, which together envisioned the establishment of an ASEAN Community, including an ASEAN Economic Community, an ASEAN Political-Security Community and an ASEAN Socio-Cultural Community (Cuyvers et al. 2005). The AEC was aimed at creating a Southeast Asian single market for the free movement of goods, services, investments, and skilled labour, and a freer flow of capital, by 2015. This included the reduction of all tariffs to zero, but it did not include the establishment of common external tariffs—such a customs union could not be set up because of the extremely diverse external trade regimes of the ASEAN member states (Ravenhill 2008). The AEC Blueprint also listed some measures for reducing non-tariff barriers to trade and simplifying customs procedures. In order to meet the concerns of the CLMV countries, the blueprint promised to enhance the Initiative for ASEAN Integration (IAI), which had already been launched in 2000 in order to close the development gap between old and new member states. The AEC Blueprint repeatedly stressed the outward orientation of the AEC, which was to establish a competitive regional production base integrated into the global economy.

Secondly, the ASEAN Charter—sometimes called the constitution of ASEAN (Freistein 2013)—was the first international treaty to give ASEAN a legal personality in international law. First recommendations for the

Charter were submitted by an Eminent Person Group of elder statesmen in 2006.[19] This was the basis for negotiations within the High Level Task Force of member states' representatives, which worked in close contact with the member states' foreign ministers (Koh 2009). The final Charter adopted at an ASEAN summit was diluted in comparison to the recommendations of the Eminent Persons Group (Chalermpalanupap 2009). Although it is sometimes claimed that the ASEAN Charter represents a step towards a more rule-based, EU-style regional organisation (Jetschke and Murray 2012), the improvements towards more institutional commitment by the member states are very modest. The Charter does not establish any supranational institutions. ASEAN remains a purely intergovernmental organisation, wherein unanimity prevails as the only method of decision-making. The Charter does not allow for majority vote in order to facilitate regional cooperation. The secretariat has the responsibility to monitor the implementation of regional agreements by the member states, but there is no regional court that could rule on cases of insufficient compliance. Dispute settlement between the member states are to be governed by the 'ASEAN Protocol of Enhanced Dispute Settlement Mechanism',[20] which established a WTO-like procedure in 2004 and which was reformed in 2010.[21] However, to the knowledge of the author, the formal procedure has never been applied by ASEAN member states, which prefer to settle disputes informally and through negotiations (see also Woon 2009).

The AEC Blueprint and the ASEAN Charter were compromises at the lowest common denominator between the member states. Firstly, the AEC excluded disputed issues like a common external tariff, for which the positions of member states like the free port Singapore and the less-developed countries on mainland Southeast Asia were irreconcilable. The acceptance of the CLMV countries to the AEC was achieved by stressing the common efforts to close the development gap within ASEAN. And secondly, the ASEAN Charter more or less formalised the already existing structures of ASEAN, but it did not revolutionise its institutional setup. Consensual decision-making and member states' sovereignty were not touched, and the regional institutions were not significantly strengthened by the Charter. What the Charter did, however, was to give ASEAN a legal personality and stress ASEAN's centrality for member states' foreign economic policies (Ravenhill 2008). This undoubtedly improved ASEAN's position in the international system (Jetschke and Murray 2012) and in relation to the regional powers China and Japan within the ASEAN+3.

3.4 A Strengthened ASEAN in East Asian Regionalism

The AEC and the ASEAN Charter were heavily criticised in the academic literature (Dosch 2008; Jones 2008; Leviter 2010; Ravenhill 2008; Simon 2008; Tay 2010). According to this criticism, the two projects did not take the necessary steps in order to proceed in a meaningful way with economic integration and to commit the member states sufficiently to common decision-making and the implementation of regional agreements. Indeed, like many other ASEAN agreements, the AEC Blueprint lists very ambitious goals, but is rather unspecific on how to implement them. Besides, the refusal to harmonise the member states external tariffs towards a customs union seems to be inconsistent with the objective of establishing a more far-reaching single market. The ASEAN Charter does not establish a completely new institutional structure, but it formalises to some degree the traditional ASEAN institutions. In particular, the lack of majority rule and effective dispute settlement demonstrate that the ASEAN member states are not really willing to give up some sovereignty in favour of regional integration.

Despite its deficiencies, the AEC Blueprint and especially the ASEAN Charter are cases of successful regional cooperation and mark a turning point in ASEAN's integration history (Freistein 2013; Jetschke and Murray 2012). The question is whether these agreements should be assessed in comparison with an ideal conception of regional integration or with the EU. Such ambitious comparisons draw almost necessarily negative pictures of the agreements, which are shaped by member states' particular interests and the need to find compromises. But in fact, the AEC Blueprint and the ASEAN Charter represent progress in regional integration in at least two respects. Firstly, economic integration within the AEC goes much beyond what was already achieved through AFTA, even if it does not really lead to a single market as it is known in Europe. And secondly, the ASEAN Charter establishes a regional organisation with a legal personality, even if the member states do not accept supranational institutions as in Europe.

The main success of the AEC and the ASEAN Charter is that the ASEAN member states managed to cooperate and to keep their unity in relation to extra-regional actors. In this respect, ASEAN was more successful than MERCOSUR (see Chap. 6) and SADC (see Chap. 7). In the latter two regional organisations, the regional powers Brazil and South Africa defected from regional cooperation on important occasions in order to protect privileges in their extra-regional economic relations. This did not happen in ASEAN, where the member states acted as one block when cooperating with extra-regional actors in the ASEAN+3 or ASEAN+6 frameworks (the so-called ASEAN first principle). The common position of the ASEAN member states may have resembled an unambitious lowest common denominator among them, but the region was not divided into different groups due to diverging extra-regional interests.

The AEC and the ASEAN Charter are a necessary (but probably not sufficient) building block for East Asian regionalism. Neither ASEAN+3 nor the East Asian Summit (i.e. ASEAN+6) would exist without the leadership of the regional organisation ASEAN (Stubbs 2014). The unity of ASEAN is essential for any kind of regional cooperation in East Asia, and ASEAN+3 would fail if ASEAN itself failed. Even if the AEC and the ASEAN Charter are not a great leap forward in regional integration, they nevertheless represent a necessary unity of the ASEAN member states. In this way, successful cooperation within ASEAN stabilises extra-regional cooperation within ASEAN+3. In return, extra-regional cooperation within ASEAN+3 makes regional cooperation within ASEAN worthwhile for the member states. Thus, the two levels of regionalism in Southeast and East Asia mutually reinforce and stabilise each other.

4 Conclusion

The 1991 decision to liberalise intraregional trade in Southeast Asia and to establish AFTA by 2008 (later brought forward to 2003) was a textbook example for the new regionalism of the 1990s. After the end of the Cold War and the bipolar order in the international system, economic integration became the new raison d'être of ASEAN. The member states were aware that the potential for intraregional trade in ASEAN was low and that the intraregional gains of economic integration were marginal. Thus, the main goal of AFTA was not to utilise comparative cost advantages and economies of scale within the region, but to attract investments from extra-regional actors. The region saw itself in a competition with other world regions and with an awakening China, which threatened to distract investments away from Southeast Asia. AFTA was criticised for its low ambitions and a range of exceptions, but it was implemented successfully five years before the original deadline (in 2003 instead of 2008). In parallel to AFTA's implementation, Southeast Asia became one of the world's most dynamic regions in economic terms. The Southeast Asian countries enjoyed an investment boom and increasing intraregional trade during the 1990s. Only the unexpected Asian crisis of 1997 put an end to this positive development. During the crisis, declining exports and capital flight by international investors pushed the region into disastrous economic turmoil. It turned out that ASEAN itself had not yet developed the necessary means to support its member states in such a situation.

The strengthening of ASEAN through the AEC and the ASEAN Charter was an answer to the organisation's failure during the Asian crisis. However, once again, this development cannot be understood without taking the extra-regional environment of ASEAN into account. The ASEAN member states did not develop the necessary means to fight financial crises within ASEAN itself. Instead, a regional liquidity fund to stabilise Southeast Asia in financial terms was established in form of the CMIM within the ASEAN+3 framework. And the ASEAN+1 trade agreements with China, Japan, and South Korea had more potential to bolster Southeast Asian exports against fluctuations on the global market than intraregional trade within AFTA could ever have done. ASEAN could not protect itself effectively against future crises without the support of its economically more powerful neighbours in Northeast Asia. The AEC and the ASEAN Charter were established in order to improve the Southeast Asian position within the ASEAN+3 framework. The more the ASEAN member states build up a unified block, the better are they able to represent their own interests in negotiations with the regional powers China and Japan. In fact, ASEAN+3 would not exist without a well-functioning ASEAN, and the member states would lose their gains from successful extra-regional cooperation if they failed to cooperate with each other within ASEAN itself.

The two cases analysed in this chapter clearly support Hypothesis 1 (see Chap. 2). The member states of a developing region (here ASEAN) are able to cooperate sufficiently if such cooperation is rewarded by extra-regional actors. Here, the extra-regional gains of regional integration are growing investment inflows during the 1990s (first case), as well as financial stabilisation through the CMIM and improving market access to China, Japan, and South Korea through the ASEAN+1 trade agreements during the 2000s (second case). Thus, even if the intraregional gains due to regional integration are small, the extra-regional gains may be sufficient to push economic integration in developing regions. Two special characteristics of ASEAN are supportive of such successful, externally driven regional integration. Firstly, ASEAN is not dominated by a single regional power that would be likely to enjoy privileges in its economic relations to important extra-regional actors. Indonesia, Malaysia, Singapore, and Thailand balance each other out, and none of them is strong enough to dominate the region. They all do better if they develop a common position towards China and Japan than if each of them looks for privileged relations with the regional powers. As a result, Hypothesis 2 could not be tested in the case of ASEAN. Secondly, and going beyond the expectations of the theoretical framework (see Chap. 2), ASEAN profits from the fact that important extra-regional actors are located in the wider regional neighbourhood and provide positive feedback for regional cooperation. China and Japan have economic interests in Southeast Asia, and they profit from a stable regional neighbourhood. Consequently, they provide capital to stabilise the region in financial terms, and they negotiate trade agreements with ASEAN. Such stable extra-regional support is less likely for developing regions whose most important trade partners are located far away and therefore have less interest in supporting the regions in question.

Notes

1. After almost a decade of very dynamic economic development, the Asian financial crisis hit East Asia in 1997. That was when international investors abruptly lost confidence in the region's economies and withdrew capital on a large scale. The crisis originated in Thailand, which had to float the baht in July 1997, and then spread further to Indonesia, Malaysia, the Philippines, and South Korea. The crisis was a major challenge for the whole region, but ASEAN was of little help to its member states on that occasion.
2. ASEAN (1967): 'The ASEAN Declaration (Bangkok Declaration) Bangkok, 8 August 1967' (http://www.asean.org/the-asean-declaration-bangkok-declaration-bangkok-8-august-1967/).
3. ASEAN (1977): 'Memorandum of Understanding on the ASEAN Swap Agreements, Kuala Lumpur, 5 August 1977' (cil.nus.edu.sg/rp/pdf/1977%20Memorandum%20of%20Understanding%20on%20the%20ASEAN%20Swap%20Arrangements-pdf.pdf).
4. These numbers are taken from the database of the Regional Integration Knowledge System (RIKS) of the United Nations University Institute on Comparative Regional Integration Studies (UNU-CRIS) (www.cris.unu.edu/riks/web/data).

5. ASEAN (1992): 'Framework Agreements on Enhancing ASEAN Economic Cooperation' (agreement.asean.org/media/download/20140119154919.pdf).
6. ASEAN (1992): 'Agreement on the Common Effective Preferential Tariff (CEPT) Scheme for the ASEAN Free Trade Area' (agreement.asean.org/media/download/20140119155006.pdf).
7. ASEAN (1995): 'Protocol to Amend the Agreement on the Common Effective Preferential Tariff Scheme for the ASEAN Free Trade Area' (http://www.asean.org/storage/images/2012/Economic/AFTA/Common_Effective_Preferential_Tariff/Protocol%20to%20Amend%20the%20Agreement%20on%20the%20Common%20Effective%20Preferential%20Tariff%20(CEPT)%20Scheme%20for%20the%20ASEAN%20Free%20Trade%20Area%20(AFTA)%20for%20the%20Ilimination%20of%20Import%20Duties.pdf).
8. These numbers are taken from the database of RIKS of the UNU-CRIS (www.cris.unu.edu/riks/web/data).
9. Calculation based on data of the UN Conference on Trade and Development (unctadstat.unctad.org).
10. The share of intraregional trade in ASEAN was 21.4 per cent in 1997 and 20.8 per cent in 1998. These numbers are taken from RIKS, an internet database published by the UNU-CRIS (www.cris.unu.edu/riks/web/data).
11. ASEAN (1977): 'Memorandum of Understanding on the ASEAN Swap Agreements, Kuala Lumpur, 5 August 1977' (cil.nus.edu.sg/rp/pdf/1977%20Memorandum%20of%20Understanding%20on%20the%20ASEAN%20Swap%20Arrangements-pdf.pdf).
12. ASEAN+3 (2000): 'The Joint Ministerial Statement of the ASEAN+3 Finance Ministers Meeting, Chiang Mai, Thailand, 6 May 2000' (www.mof.go.jp/english/international_policy/convention/asean_plus_3/20000506.htm).
13. ASEAN+3 (2009): 'Joint Media Statement of the ASEAN+3 Finance Ministers' Meeting: Action Plan to Restore Economic and Financial Stability of the Asian Region' (www.mof.go.jp/english/international_policy/convention/asean_plus_3/20090222.pdf).
14. These numbers are taken from the database of RIKS of the UNU-CRIS (www.cris.unu.edu/riks/web/data).
15. Table 5.2 shows only the three most important export destinations of the ASEAN member states in 2006. The rise of China cannot be reflected within that table as long as China is not among ASEAN's three most important trade partners.

16. ASEAN (1967): 'The Asean Declaration (Bangkok Declaration) Bangkok, 8 August 1967' (http://www.asean.org/the-asean-declaration-bangkok-declaration-bangkok-8-august-1967/).
17. ASEAN (2007): 'ASEAN Economic Community Blueprint' (http://www.asean.org/wp-content/uploads/archive/5187-10.pdf).
18. ASEAN (2007): 'The ASEAN Charter' (http://www.asean.org/storage/images/ASEAN_RTK_2014/ASEAN_Charter.pdf).
19. ASEAN (2006): 'Report of the Eminent Persons Group on the ASEAN Charter' (http://www.asean.org/storage/images/archive/19247.pdf).
20. ASEAN (2004): 'ASEAN Protocol of Enhanced Dispute Settlement Mechanism' (agreement.asean.org/media/download/20140119110714.pdf).
21. ASEAN (2010): 'Protocol to the ASEAN Charter on Dispute Settlement Mechanisms' (agreement.asean.org/media/download/20131229165853.pdf).

REFERENCES

Acharya, A. (1999). Realism, Institutionalism, and the Asian Economic Crisis. *Contemporary Southeast Asia, 21*, 1–29.

Acharya, A. (2001). *Constructing a Security Community in Southeast Asia: ASEAN and the Problem of Regional Order*. London: Routledge.

Acharya, A. (2011). The Future of ASEAN: Obsolescent or Resilient? In L. Y. Yoong (Ed.), *ASEAN Matters! Reflecting on the Association of Southeast Asian Nations* (pp. 283–288). Singapore: World Scientific Publishing.

Ariff, M. (1994). *AFTA = Another Futile Trade Area?* Kuala Lumpur: Universiti Malaya.

Ariff, M. (1996). From ASEAN-Six to ASEAN-Ten: Issues and Prospects. In J. L. H. Tan (Ed.), *AFTA in the Changing International Economy* (pp. 66–75). Singapore: Institute of Southeast Asian Studies.

Athukorala, P.-C., & Menon, J. (1996). Foreign Direct Investments: Can AFTA Make a Difference? In J. L. H. Tan (Ed.), *AFTA in the Changing International Economy* (pp. 76–92). Singapore: Institute of Southeast Asian Studies.

Ba, A. D. (2003). China and ASEAN: Renavigating Relations for a 21st-Century Asia. *Asian Survey, 43*, 622–647.

Baldwin, R. E. (2006). Multilateralising Regionalism: Spaghetti Bowls as Building Blocs on the Path to Global Free Trade. *The World Economy, 29*, 1451–1518.

Baldwin, R. E., & Seghezza, E. (2010). Are Trade Blocs Building or Stumbling Blocs? *Journal of Economic Integration, 25*, 276–297.

Bhagwati, J. N. (1988). Export-Promoting Trade Strategy. *World Bank Research Observer, 3*, 27–57.

Bowles, P. (1997). ASEAN, AFTA and the "New Regionalism". *Pacific Affairs, 10*, 219–233.

Bowles, P. (2002). Asia's Post-Crisis Regionalism: Bringing the State Back in, Keeping the (United) States Out. *Review of International Political Economy, 9*, 244–270.

Cai, K. G. (2003). The ASEAN-China Free Trade Agreement and East Asian Regional Grouping. *Contemporary Southeast Asia, 25*, 387–404.

Capie, D., & Evans, P. (2002). The ASEAN Way. In D. Capie & P. Evans (Eds.), *The Asia-Pacific Security Lexicon*. Singapore: Institute of Southeast Asian Studies.

Capling, A., & Ravenhill, J. (2011). Multilateralising Regionalism: What Role for the Trans-Pacific Partnership Agreement? *The Pacific Review, 24*, 553–575.

Chalermpalanupap, T. (2009). In Defence of the ASEAN Charter. In T. Koh, R. G. Manalo, & W. Woon (Eds.), *The Making of the ASEAN Charter* (pp. 117–135). Singapore: World Scientific Publishing.

Chirathivat, S. (1996). ASEAN Economic Integration with the World through AFTA. In J. L. H. Tan (Ed.), *AFTA in the Changing International Economy* (pp. 21–41). Singapore: Institute of Southeast Asian Studies.

Chirathivat, S. (2006). *ASEAN's Role and Interests in the Formation of East Asian Regionalism* (Working Paper).

Corning, G. P. (2009). Between Bilateralism and Regionalism in East Asia: The ASEAN-Japan Comprehensive Economic Partnership. *The Pacific Review, 22*, 639–665.

Cuyvers, L., De Lombaerde, P., & Verherstraeten, S. (2005). *From AFTA Towards an ASEAN Economic Community ... and Beyond* (CAS Discussion Paper No 46).

Cuyvers, L., & Pupphavesa, W. (1996). *From ASEAN to AFTA* (CAS Discussion Paper No 6).

Dieter, H. (2008). ASEAN and the Emerging Monetary Regionalism: A Case of Limited Contribution. *The Pacific Review, 21*, 489–506.

Dieter, H., & Higgott, R. (2003). Exploring Alternative Theories of Economic Regionalism: From Trade to Finance in Asian Co-operation? *Review of International Political Economy, 10*, 430–454.

Dosch, J. (1997). *Die ASEAN: Bilanz eines Erfolges*. Hamburg: Abera Verlag.

Dosch, J. (2008). ASEAN's Reluctant Liberal Turn and the Thorny Road to Democracy Promotion. *The Pacific Review, 21*, 527–545.

Emmers, R. (2014). Indonesia's Role in ASEAN: A Case of Incomplete and Sectorial Leadership. *The Pacific Review, 27*, 543–562.

Freistein, K. (2013). "A Living Document": Promises of the ASEAN Charter. *The Pacific Review, 26*, 407–429.

Garcia, M. (2013). From Idealism to Realism? EU Preferential Trade Agreement Policy. *Journal of Contemporary European Research, 9*, 521–541.

Gilson, J. (2004). Complex Regional Multilateralism: "Strategising" Japan's Responses to Southeast Asia. *The Pacific Review, 17*, 71–94.

Gilson, J. (2006). Region Building in East Asia: ASEAN Plus Three and Beyond. In P. J. J. Welfens, F. Knipping, S. Chirathivat, & C. Ryan (Eds.), *Integration*

in Asia and Europe: Historical Dynamics, Political Issues, and Economic Perspectives (pp. 217–234). Heidelberg: Springer.
Grimes, W. W. (2011a). The Asian Monetary Fund Reborn? Implications of Chiang Mai Initiative Multilateralization. Asia Policy, 11, 79–104.
Grimes, W. W. (2011b). The Future of Regional Liquidity Arrangements in East Asia: Lessons from the Global Financial Crisis. The Pacific Review, 24, 291–310.
Grimes, W. W. (2015). East Asian Financial Regionalism: Why Economic Enhancements Undermine Political Sustainability. Contemporary Politics, 21, 145–160.
Hayakawa, K., Hiratsuka, D., Shiino, K., & Sukegawa, S. (2013). Who Uses Free Trade Agreements? Asian Economic Journal, 27, 245–264.
Henning, C. R. (2002). East Asian Financial Cooperation (Policy Analyses in International Economics 68). Washington, DC: Peterson Institute for International Economics.
Igusa, K., & Shimada, H. (1996). AFTA and Japan. In J. L. H. Tan (Ed.), AFTA in the Changing International Economy (pp. 139–163). Singapore: Institute of Southeast Asian Studies.
Ikenberry, G. J. (2008). The Rise of China and the Future of the West: Can the Liberal System Survive? Foreign Affairs, 87, 23–37.
Jetschke, A., & Murray, P. (2012). Diffusing Regional Integration: The EU and Southeast Asia. West European Politics, 35, 174–191.
Jetschke, A., & Rüland, J. (2009). Decoupling Rhetoric and Practice: The Cultural Limits of ASEAN Cooperation. The Pacific Review, 22, 179–203.
Jiang, Y. (2010). Response and Responsibility: China in East Asian Financial Cooperation. The Pacific Review, 23, 603–623.
Jones, D. M. (2008). Security and Democracy: The ASEAN Charter and the Dilemma of Regionalism in Southeast Asia. International Affairs, 84, 735–756.
Katzenstein, P. J. (2000). Regionalism and Asia. New Political Economy, 5, 353–368.
Kingdon, J. W. (1995). Agendas, Alternatives, and Public Policies. New York: Pearson.
Koga, K. (2014). Institutional Transformation of ASEAN: ZOPFAN, TAC, and the Bali Concord I in 1968-1976. The Pacific Review, 27, 729–753.
Koh, T. (2009). The Negotiating Process. In T. Koh, R. G. Manalo, & W. Woon (Eds.), The Making of the ASEAN Charter (pp. 47–68). Singapore: World Scientific Publishing.
Krapohl, S. (2015). Financial Crises as Catalysts for Regional Cooperation? Chances and Obstacles for Financial Integration in ASEAN+3, MERCOSUR and the Eurozone. Contemporary Politics, 21, 161–178.
Krapohl, S., & Fink, S. (2013). Different Paths of Regional Integration: Trade Networks and Regional Institution-Building in Europe, Southeast Asia and Southern Africa. Journal of Common Market Studies, 51, 472–488.

Krueger, A. O. (1997). Trade Policy and Economic Development: How We Learn. *American Economic Review, 87*, 1–22.
Leviter, L. (2010). The ASEAN Charter: ASEAN Failure or Member Failure? *NYU Journal of International Law and Politics, 43*, 159–210.
MacIntyre, A. (2001). Institutions and Investors: The Politics of the Economic Crisis in Southeast Asia. *International Organization, 55*, 81–122.
Mansfield, E. D., & Milner, H. V. (1999). The New Wave of Regionalism. *International Organization, 53*, 589–627.
Menon, J. (1998). The Expansion of AFTA: Widening and Deepening. *Asian-Pacific Economic Literature, 12*.
Nair, D. (2008). Regionalism in the Asia Pacific/East Asia: A Frustrated Regionalism? *Contemporary Southeast Asia, 31*, 110–142.
Narine, S. (2008). Forty Years of ASEAN: A Historical Review. *The Pacific Review, 21*, 411–429.
Nesadurai, H. E. S. (2001). Cooperation and Institutional Transformation in ASEAN: Insights from the AFTA Project. In A. T. H. Tan & J. D. K. Boutin (Eds.), *Non-Traditional Security Issues in Southeast Asia* (pp. 197–226). Singapore: Institute of Defence and Strategic Studies/Select Publishing.
Obermeier, A. (2013). *Mechanismen institutioneller Dynamiken: Eine vergleichende Prozessanalyse der Entwicklung des ASEAN Handelsregimes*. Bamberg: University of Bamberg Press.
Pangestu, M., Soesastro, H., & Ahmand, M. (1992). A New Look at Intra-ASEAN Economic Co-operation. *ASEAN Economic Bulletin, 8*, 344–352.
Park, I. (2009). Regional Trade Agreements in East Asia: Will they be Sustainable? *Asian Economic Journal, 23*, 169–194.
Petri, P. A., Plummer, M. G., & Zhai, F. (2012). ASEAN Economic Community: A General Equilibrium Analysis. *Asian Economic Journal, 26*, 93–118.
Radelet, S., & Sachs, J. D. (1998). *The East Asian Financial Crisis: Diagnosis, Remedies, Prospects* (Brooking Papers on Economic Activity 1:1998).
Ravenhill, J. (1995). Economic Cooperation in Southeast Asia: Changing Incentives. *Asian Survey, 35*, 850–866.
Ravenhill, J. (2008). Fighting Irrelevance: An Economic Community "with ASEAN Characteristics". *The Pacific Review, 21*, 469–488.
Rüland, J. (2000). ASEAN and the Asian Crisis: Theoretical Implications and Practical Consequences for Southeast Asian Regionalism. *The Pacific Review, 13*, 421–451.
Simon, S. (2008). ASEAN and Multilateralism: The Long, Bumpy Road to Community. *Contemporary Southeast Asia, 30*, 264–292.
Stiglitz, J. (2003). What I Learned at the World Economic Crisis. In W. Driscoll & J. Lark (Eds.), *Globalization and the Poor: Exploitation or Equalizer?* (pp. 195–206). New York: The International Debate Education Association.
Stubbs, R. (2000). Signing on to Liberalization: AFTA and the Politics of Regional Economic Cooperation. *The Pacific Review, 13*, 297–318.

Stubbs, R. (2002). ASEAN Plus Three: Emerging East Asian Regionalism? *Asian Survey, 42*, 440–455.

Stubbs, R. (2014). ASEAN's Leadership in East Asian Region-Building: Strength in Weakness. *The Pacific Review, 27*, 523–541.

Tay, S. (2010). The ASEAN Charter: Between National Sovereignty and the Region's Constitutional Moment. *Singapore Yearbook of International Law, 12*, 151–170.

Terada, T. (2010). The Origins of ASEAN+6 and Japan's Initiatives: China's Rise and the Agent-Structure Analysis. *The Pacific Review, 23*, 71–92.

Thompson, E. C. (2006). Singaporean Exceptionalism and Its Implications for ASEAN Regionalism. *Contemporary Southeast Asia, 28*, 183–206.

Webber, D. (2001). Two Funerals and a Wedding? The Ups and Downs of Regionalism in East Asia and Asia-Pacific after the Asian Crisis. *The Pacific Review, 14*, 339–372.

Webber, D. (2010). The Regional Integration that Didn't Happen: Cooperation without Integration in Early Twenty-First Century East Asia. *The Pacific Review, 23*, 313–333.

Wesley, M. (1999). The Asian Crisis and the Adequacy of Regional Institutions. *Contemporary Southeast Asia, 21*, 54–73.

Williamson, J. (1993). Democracy and the "Washington Consensus". *World Development, 21*, 1329–1336.

Wong, J. (1989). The ASEAN Model of Regional Cooperation. In S. Naya, M. Urrutia, S. Mark, & A. Fuentes (Eds.), *Lessons in Development: A Comparative Study of Asia and Latin America* (pp. 121–141). San Francisco, CA: International Center for Economic Growth.

Woon, W. (2009). The ASEAN Charter Dispute Settlement Mechanisms. In T. Koh, R. G. Manalo, & W. Woon (Eds.), *The Making of the ASEAN Charter* (pp. 69–77). Singapore: World Scientific Publishing.

Yoshimatsu, H. (2006). Collective Action Problems and Regional Integration in ASEAN. *Contemporary Southeast Asia, 28*, 115–140.

Yuan, L. T. (1994). The ASEAN Free Trade Area: The Search for a Common Prosperity. *Asian-Pacific Economic Literature, 8*, 1–7.

Yue, C. S. (1999). Trade, Foreign Direct Investment and Economic Development of Southeast Asia. *The Pacific Review, 12*, 249–270.

Yuen, N. C., & Wagner, N. (1989). Privatization and Deregulation in ASEAN: An Overview. *ASEAN Economic Bulletin, 5*, 209–223.

CHAPTER 6

MERCOSUR

The Ups and Downs of Regional Integration in South America

Katharina L. Meissner

Brazil is one of the rising powers on the global market, and as such it has received growing scholarly attention (e.g. Burges 2013). The country has increasingly engaged in global governance (Hopewell 2013), and it was and still is very active on its own continent (Christensen 2013). Without a doubt, Brazil is the regional power of South America, and its contribution to the Common Market of South America (MERCOSUR) is crucial for the success or failure of regional integration. Brazil is the most important trade and investment partner for its regional neighbours (Chudnovsky and López 2004), but at the same time Brazil is the country in MERCOSUR for which extra-regional economic relations are most important. Brazil occupies the central position in the regional trade network, but its own most important trade links are its external relations with the USA, the EU, and Japan (see Chap. 4). As a result of extra-regional interests, Brazil's behaviour towards MERCOSUR

K.L. Meissner (✉)
Institute for European Integration Research EIF, University of Vienna, Vienna, Austria
e-mail: katharina.meissner@univie.ac.at

© The Author(s) 2017
S. Krapohl (Ed.), *Regional Integration in the Global South*,
International Political Economy Series,
DOI 10.1007/978-3-319-38895-3_6

has been volatile; it shifted from cooperation during the 1990s to non-collaboration and even defection at the turn of the millennium. This chapter explains why Brazil first pushed the establishment of the customs union, but then refused any kind of monetary coordination in the face of the Argentinean crisis in 1999. The regional power's behaviour during that crisis led to long-term problems of regional integration in MERCOSUR, which thus far has not yet regained the dynamic it had during the 1990s.

MERCOSUR's dependence on extra-regional trade (see Chap. 4) and Brazil's asymmetric economic power within the region make regional integration vulnerable (Doctor 2013) to extra-regional influences. The risk of Rambo situations, in which Brazil unilaterally defects rather than cooperates, is particularly high when the regional power faces a trade-off between regional cooperation and extra-regional privileges. In the following, this chapter analyses the impact of extra-regional trade and investment relations on Brazil's behaviour in MERCOSUR. It argues that cooperation was successful as long as Brazil and its neighbours expected commercial benefits from extra-regional economic relations. However, once the region was hit by the consequences of the Asian financial crisis and the Russian debt default, extra-regional actors withdrew their investments, and the regional economies deteriorated. When this happened, Brazil floated its currency unilaterally without even giving notice to its neighbours (Genna and Hiroi 2007: 49). As a result of this beggar-thy-neighbour policy (Kronberger 2002), Brazil recovered quickly from economic turmoil, whereas Argentina entered a devastating crisis and produced one of history's largest defaults. The economic asymmetries resulting from the crisis translated into the external trade agenda of the regional power. Brazil defected from regional cooperation again and signed its bilateral strategic partnership with the EU. In addition, the regional power searched for cooperation outside of MERCOSUR by launching the Union of South American Nations (UNASUR). As a result, trust between MERCOSUR's member states was hurt, and regional integration stagnated. Several attempts to revitalize regional integration—including the reform of MERCOSUR's dispute settlement mechanism, the establishment of the supranational parliament Parlasur, and Venezuela's accession into MERCOSUR—remained largely ineffective.

After providing some background information on MERCOSUR, this chapter starts out with an analysis of Brazil's cooperation during the establishment of the customs union from 1991 to 1994. It demonstrates that Brazil pushed the customs union because the member states could improve their extra-regional economic relations through regional integration. The result was indeed the economic success of MERCOSUR, which deteriorated only when the consequences of the Asian crisis and the Russian default hit the region. Section 2 examines how the following financial turmoil led to increasing competition among MERCOSUR's member states and to Brazil's decision to float the real. Brazil enjoyed an export boom after its unilateral devaluation, whereas its neighbours went into deep recessions. Section 3 demonstrates the devaluation's long-term impacts. Heavy economic asymmetries combined with dependence on extra-regional economic relations led to a growing fragmentation of MERCOSUR, which culminated in the bilateral EU–Brazil strategic partnership. Finally, the conclusion summarizes the results of the case studies and reflects on the hypotheses developed in Chap. 2.

1 THE ESTABLISHMENT OF THE CUSTOMS UNION FROM 1991 TO 1994

In 1991, Brazil, Argentina, Paraguay, and Uruguay set up MERCOSUR, and just three years after that they established the (as yet incompletely implemented) MERCOSUR customs union (MERCOSUR-CU). A project of open regionalism, MERCOSUR was part of a broader liberalization policy initiated by Argentina and Brazil. Neo-liberal economic strategies (Cason 2000: 24) and reforms that were in line with the so-called Washington Consensus—liberalization, privatization, and deregulation—were the guidelines for MERCOSUR's integration. For Brazil, whose needs have driven MERCOSUR (e.g. Cason and Power 2009; Klom 2003; Mecham 2003), regional integration was part of a new development strategy to increasingly open its economy and that of its neighbours to the global market (Grugel and De Almeida Medeiros 1999). This strategy proved successful throughout the early 1990s. Intraregional and extra-regional trade and investment increased so that regional integration was a win-win situation for all members.

Although MERCOSUR's institutional setup was influenced by the example of the European Union (EU, Lenz 2012), it always was and still is strongly intergovernmental. Decisions require consensus among the member states, and the organization lacked any supranational body throughout the 1990s. MERCOSUR's most important bodies—the Common Market Council, the Common Market Group, and the Trade Commission—consist of ministers or representatives of member states' governments. Decision-making by unanimity is the rule, and it takes often place at presidential summits, for which Malamud (2003) invented the term 'interpresidentialism'.

1.1 MERCOSUR's Dependence on Extra-Regional Economic Relations

When the MERCOSUR member states started to integrate their economies, intraregional economic interdependence was particularly low. MERCOSUR's intraregional trade share was at only around 12 per cent at the beginning of the 1990s, and it reached its peak of 23 per cent in 1998. In comparison, the share of intraregional trade ranges between 61 and 67 per cent in the EU and between 41 and 46 per cent in the North American Free Trade Agreement (NAFTA).[1] The size and structure of the regional economies are responsible for this low level of economic interdependence (Mukhamedinov 2007); the member states are relatively poor and less developed, and two of them (Paraguay and Uruguay) constitute very small markets for intraregional trade.

Rather than relying on economic interdependence, the MERCOSUR member states were much more dependent on extra-regional trade and investment partners during the 1990s (see Chap. 4). When MERCOSUR was established in 1991, the overall region's most important trade partners were the EU and the USA.[2] This was also true for the regional power Brazil (see Table 6.1), for which the Argentinean export market ranked only fourth after a wide margin. However, the picture changes when

Table 6.1 The three most important export destinations of the MERCOSUR member states in 1991

	First	Second	Third
Argentina	EU 39 %	Brazil 14 %	USA 11 %
Brazil	EU 36 %	USA 21 %	Japan 9 %
Paraguay	EU 43 %	Brazil 27 %	Chile 7 %
Uruguay	EU 29 %	Brazil 25 %	USA 11 %

Calculation based on the UN Comtrade database (comtrade.un.org)

turning to the smaller member states. Although Argentina's exports mainly addressed the EU, the Brazilian market already ranked second, ahead of the US market, which was in third place. The two smallest member states, Paraguay and Uruguay, are the least significant as addressees of intraregional trade, but they are also the countries for which intraregional trade within MERCOSUR is most important (Nunnenkamp 1999). Although Paraguay and Uruguay wanted to open up the regional market as a first step, they had an equally important interest in improving their standing on the global market. By themselves, Paraguay and Uruguay are not interesting markets for extra-regional investments or trade agreements. Consequently, both countries tried to push interregional trade negotiations between MERCOSUR and the EU during the early 2000s (Vaillant and Bizzozero 2003: 127).

A heavy intraregional asymmetry accompanies the relative dependence of MERCOSUR on extra-regional economic relations. Brazil is by far the region's most important country in economic and political terms. Argentina, Paraguay, and Uruguay target their intraregional exports to Brazil, and so do extra-regional trade partners. Other indicators also point to Brazil's central position in MERCOSUR. In 1991, Brazil's population accounted for nearly 79 per cent of the region's total population and the country contributed 66 per cent to MERCOSUR's gross domestic product (GDP).[3] Brazil's geographical area is more than twice that of Argentina, Paraguay, and Uruguay together. At the same time, Brazil is the one member state of MERCOSUR for which extra-regional economic relations are most important. About 57 per cent of Brazil's exports addressed the EU and the USA (see Table 6.1), whereas less than 10 per cent addressed its regional neighbour Argentina. Given Brazil's economic dominance in South America, its behaviour was decisive for regional cooperation within MERCOSUR. And while the region was dependent on its regional power, Brazil's own motivation to engage within the region was driven by its extra-regional interests.

1.2 Converging Interests during the Early 1990s

Despite limited intraregional economic interdependence, the MERCOSUR member states started regional cooperation in 1991, and it was most of all Brazil that had a strong interest in the MERCOSUR-CU. The interest of the regional power in the

MERCOSUR-CU is surprising, given Brazil's limited trade with its regional neighbours and its focus on economic relations with extra-regional partners. But for Brazil, the benefits of MERCOSUR were twofold. Firstly, the Brazilian government aimed at increasing its global visibility and at boosting its bargaining power on the international stage (Bandeira 2006: 12–21; Varas 2008). This fact was emphasized repeatedly by Brazilian officials. In 1995, the ambassador Sebastião do Rego Barros highlighted the importance of MERCOSUR for Brazil's external credibility and international presence.[4] And secondly, MERCOSUR was an instrument to make trade and investment between the region and extra-regional actors more dynamic. The Southern Cone served as a credible commitment to the liberal policy of opening up the Brazilian market. In this respect, Sebastião do Rego Barro identified two benefits for Brazil: MERCOSUR is a factor for opening up new export markets both intra- and extra-regionally, and it is an instrument to attract investments.[5] In sum, Brazil needed the integration scheme for extra-regional purposes rather than for intraregional trade and investments.

Regional integration in MERCOSUR started out as a bilateral agreement between Argentina and Brazil (Baer 2008; Cason 2000). As a result of the deep economic crisis that Latin America witnessed during the 1980s, the two countries committed themselves to an outward-oriented integration. MERCOSUR was a means to free trade with other partners within and outside the region. Paraguay and Uruguay only joined MERCOSUR later and adapted to the principles laid out by the two bigger member states (González 2009). The two smaller member states shared the guidelines and the goals of the integration scheme in the sense that they needed access to foreign markets anyway. Their preference for open economies became particularly obvious in their active support for interregional negotiations with MERCOSUR's extra-regional partners.[6] Paraguay's and Uruguay's interest in the size effects of regional integration and Argentina's and Brazil's interest in the stability effects of regional integration support the theoretical argument developed in Chap. 2. Regarding size effects, Paraguay and Uruguay teamed up with their bigger neighbours in order to make their tiny markets visible on the global stage. Regarding stability effects, Argentina and Brazil locked in liberal economic policies through MERCOSUR's regional integration, which was supposed to make their markets more attractive to extra-regional trade and investment partners (Schirm 2002).

Nevertheless, regional cooperation in MERCOSUR did not only take place in order to achieve extra-regional economic gains; other factors supported regional integration as well. Firstly, MERCOSUR's integration was driven by political considerations. Argentina and Brazil aimed to improve their relationship through regional integration in order to ensure security and democracy in South America after rather tense relations during the 1970s (Manzetti 1994). The building of regional security and trust among the countries was also of crucial importance for Paraguay (Doctor 2013: 519). And secondly, MERCOSUR also aimed to produce intraregional economic gains, especially for the smaller member states. Although regional integration served to trigger trade and investments with extra-regional partners, it also enhanced intraregional economic interdependence. Especially Paraguay and Uruguay tried to push towards more internal liberalization in trade, investments, and services. And it was important for Argentina to gain access to the Brazilian market and to retrieve more investments from the regional power (Bouzas 2009).

1.3 Regional Cooperation in the Case of the Customs Union

Brazilian leadership in South America is controversial (De Lima and Hirst 2006; Gomes Saraiva 2010; Malamud 2008, 2011; Maniam et al. 2003; Sennes et al. 2006), but the country is nevertheless the crucial player for regional integration in MERCOSUR. Brazil paid extraordinary attention to regional integration during the 1990s and made the MERCOSUR-CU a top foreign policy priority (Baer 2008; Bandeira 2006; De Lima and Hirst 2006). From 1991 to 1994, Brazil strongly insisted on the timetable of the CU as it had been laid down in the Treaty of Asunción (Fidler 1992). Regional tariff barriers were scheduled to disappear by the end of 1994 with a common external tariff to be implemented at the same time. The other member states were committed to MERCOSUR as well and cooperated with Brazil. Argentina, Paraguay, and Uruguay favoured the establishment of the CU in general terms, and especially the two smallest member states appreciated it as a step towards free trade within the region that could produce economic growth in their countries.

The smaller MERCOSUR member states and Brazil differed over the actual form of the MERCOSUR-CU and MERCOSUR's institutional structure. While Paraguay and Uruguay wanted to implement the MERCOSUR-CU as perfectly and as quickly as possible, Brazil took unilateral measures during the implementation process that were not in line with MERCOSUR's principles. MERCOSUR reports from that time are full of stories about Brazil's non-cooperative behaviour. Fundamental to these unilateral breaches of MERCOSUR law was Brazil's 'big country sense and confidence' (Klom 2003), and its leeway resulting from that. In addition, the smaller member states favoured supranational institutions and the delegation of competencies to MERCOSUR bodies (de Almeida 1998; Gomes Saraiva 2012). In contrast, Brazil insisted on MERCOSUR being a union of nation-states with decisions taken by consensus. In the end, MERCOSUR's institutional design favoured Brazil's position; the Common Market Group, the Common Market Council, and the Trade Commission are strictly intergovernmental and decide by unanimity (Bouzas and Soltz 2001; Bajo 2005).

Despite these diverging preferences over MERCOSUR's institutional architecture, all member states anticipated economic benefits from regional integration, and shared the common goal of making the region more attractive to extra-regional partners. Smoothing distributional conflicts, Brazil facilitated successful regional cooperation and provided soft regional leadership. In 1992, for instance, Argentina applied a series of protectionist measures and imposed anti-dumping duties, safeguard measures and an import tax against imports from Brazil (Eichengreen 1998). Although Brazil regarded these measures as being incompatible with MERCOSUR law, it encouraged Argentina's commitment to MERCOSUR by buying oil and larger amounts of wheat from Argentina, which reduced bilateral trade imbalances between the two countries (Bouzas 2001; Cason 2000; Baer et al. 2002).

Regional integration was so dynamic during the early 1990s that Argentina and Brazil even tried to initiate some form of macroeconomic cooperation. They set up a high-level working group in 1993 to discuss different proposals for monetary integration. Brazil's proposal favoured the monitoring of exchange rate movements and the setting of maximum bands for fluctuations (Kronberger 2002; Pelufo 2004). In contrast, Argentina suggested the harmonization of regional exchange rates on the basis of fixed rates relative to the US dollar. Because Argentina and Brazil were not able to agree on either of the two positions, monetary integration failed to take off in MERCOSUR at that time (Pelufo 2004). This failure paved the way for Brazil's unilateral devaluation and the Argentine crisis at the turn of the millennium.

1.4 MERCOSUR's Initial Success during the 1990s

As hoped by the MERCOSUR member states, structural reforms—including liberalization and macroeconomic stabilization—improved the region's economic competitiveness (Chudnovsky and López 2004). Extra-regional actors rewarded these developments so that every MERCOSUR member state benefited from a boom in trade and investment. Firstly, MERCOSUR's total exports grew by more than 40 per cent between 1991 and 1998.[7] The most important addressees were the EU and the USA, to which exports rose by around 10 and 20 per cent, respectively, between 1991 and 1998. Secondly, the MERCOSUR member states increased their intraregional economic interdependence (see Chap. 4), which made regional integration a positive-sum game (Cason 2010: 68). The intraregional trade share climbed from 13 per cent in 1991 to its peak of 23 per cent in 1998.[8] This was particularly important for Argentina, Paraguay, and Uruguay, which were successful in increasing their trade with Brazil. Finally, MERCOSUR witnessed an investment boom until 1999 with increasing foreign direct investment (FDI) inflows from less than 1 per cent of the GDP in 1991 to a maximum of nearly 6 per cent in 1999 (Chudnovsky and López 2004; Costa Vaz 2003; Eden 2007; Ffrench-Davis and Studart 2003; Kehoe 2005; Malamud 2005a, b; Saxton 2003).

Brazil came out as the main beneficiary of MERCOSUR's positive economic development. The country became the region's leading market so that in 1996 almost 70 per cent of MERCOSUR's exports were Brazilian.[9] By the mid-1990s, Brazil was the hub of regional commerce and extremely important for its neighbours as an export destination. Further on, Brazil intensified its trade with the EU and the USA. In 1992, these extra-regional trade relations were four times more important for Brazil than intraregional ones; Brazil's extra-regional trade was at 82 per cent, compared to 18 per cent trade with Argentina, Paraguay, and Uruguay put together. The inflow of FDI into Brazil rose immensely as well. From the mid-1990s onwards, Brazil took the lead in the attraction of extra-regional investments, and it received more than 70 per cent of the region's investment inflows.[10] Investment inflows into Brazil increased from US$1 billion in 1991 to more than US$30 billion in 1998.

MERCOSUR reached its initial goals successfully; the region enhanced its competitiveness on the global market, attracted investments, and boosted its exports during the early 1990s. All member states benefited from this success, but Brazil came out as the main beneficiary by absorbing the majority of investments and by boosting its exports to the EU and the USA. Argentina, Paraguay, and Uruguay benefited from access to the Brazilian market and from extra-regional economic relations alike; without doubt this smoothed regional cooperation.

2 Brazil as a Regional Rambo during the Late 1990s

Regional integration stalled when South America was hit by the consequences of the East Asian financial crisis of 1997 and the Russian debt default in 1998. Due to these currency crises international investors became cautious about their investments in developing countries in general, and this affected MERCOSUR starting in 1998 (Carranza 2003). The impact was extreme because MERCOSUR's asymmetric economic structure had not changed fundamentally despite slightly increasing intraregional interdependence. The region still depended on extra-regional economic relations, and Brazil's predominant position had been intensified rather than reduced. Because Brazil feared losing its privileged position as the main economic partner for extra-regional actors, it fiercely competed for these benefits by sacrificing regional cooperation.

2.1 Brazil's Privileged Position in MERCOSUR

In 1998, MERCOSUR's intraregional trade share peaked at around 23 per cent. Nevertheless, economic interdependence was still much lower than in industrialized regions, and most intraregional trade addressed Brazil (see Chap. 4). There was a heavy asymmetry in the countries' dependence on the regional market. Brazil's economy became vital for Argentina, Paraguay, and Uruguay (see Table 6.2). For example, Argentina's exports

Table 6.2 The three most important export destinations of the MERCOSUR member states in 1998

	First	Second	Third
Argentina	Brazil 32 %	EU 19 %	USA 9 %
Brazil	EU 31 %	USA 20 %	Argentina 14 %
Paraguay	Brazil 28 %	Argentina 27 %	EU 24 %
Uruguay	Brazil 35 %	Argentina 17 %	EU 16 %

Calculation based on the UN Comtrade database (comtrade.un.org)

to Brazil more than tripled between 1991 and 1998, and manufactured exports of the three smaller member states were directed to South America rather than to other regions (Burges 2005). The press invented the expressions Brazil- or Merco-dependence for this (Belivaqua et al. 2001).

In contrast, the regional market was nearly irrelevant for Brazil itself. In 1998, the regional power's most important trade partners were the EU and the USA, well ahead of Argentina, Paraguay, and Uruguay (see Table 6.2). China's increasing economic importance to Brazil complemented the significance of extra-regional trade partners (see Chap. 4). Besides, the Brazilian economy steadily enhanced its attractiveness to extra-regional investors so that both foreign direct and indirect investments increased until 1997.[11] In 1998, European investors poured more than US$19 billion into the Brazilian economy, which marked a peak for the entire decade. MERCOSUR was important for the smaller member states to get access to the Brazilian market, while Brazil used it to 'recruit FDI flows' (Burges 2005). The privileged position Brazil enjoyed in MERCOSUR became a danger for regional integration in the late 1990s when financial turmoil hit the region.

2.2 MERCOSUR's Economic Deterioration during the Late 1990s

The Asian financial crisis and the Russian default[12] had profound, negative effects on foreign capital, trade volumes, product prices, and international interest rates[13] in South America. The negative impact on extra-regional trade was particularly intense in the export of metals and of primary commodities, especially agricultural products. A negative effect on the export of manufactured products was also expected because East Asian countries boosted their exports through currency devaluations, deflation, and low domestic demand.[14] The sudden decline of extra-regional trade was felt in 1999 when MERCOSUR's exports to the EU declined by almost 6 per cent as compared to 1997. Economic growth in Brazil deteriorated from almost 6 per cent to nearly minus 2 per cent between 1997 and 1999. From there, the crisis spread to the other MERCOSUR member states, which were highly dependent on exports to the Brazilian market. Thus, the Argentinean economy declined by almost 7 per cent in 1999; in comparison, its growth was at 6 per cent in 1997.[15]

Due to the crises in Asia and Russia, international investors panicked and withdrew capital from developing countries all over the world (Faucher and Armijo 2003). This trend affected mainly portfolio investments in MERCOSUR (Amann and Baer 2003; Kehoe 2005; Saxton 2003), and the value of these investments turned negative in 1998, compared to a positive US$7 billion in 1997.[16] The impact on FDI set in somewhat later, when inflows into MERCOSUR fell by almost 20 per cent in 2000[17] after having peaked at US$827 billion in 1999.[18] In the case of the regional power Brazil, investors massively withdrew capital and even speculated against the Brazilian real. Portfolio investment inflows dropped from positive US$5 billion in 1997 into negative territory in 1998. The Brazilian central bank had to uphold high interest rates in order to keep the fixed exchange rate to the US dollar even though the country faced increasing public debt at this time (Amann and Baer 2003).

2.3 Brazil's Unilateral Devaluation

Due to massive outflows of portfolio investments, Brazil could not keep its exchange rate fixed to the US dollar any longer, and the government floated its currency in January 1999 (Faucher and Armijo 2003: 27). After this decision, the value of the Brazilian real dropped by more than 30 per cent. The fact that this decision was domestically contested (Bulmer-Thomas 1999) proves that Brazil had other options, such as widening the exchange rate band. The central bank's governor suggested the latter and had to resign for that reason. Immediately after Arminio Fraga took on the position, he announced the floating of the currency (Bulmer-Thomas 1999). Brazil's 'beggar-thy-neighbour' policy (Kronberger 2002) of devaluing the real made the Brazilian economy more competitive in comparison to that of its regional neighbours (Bearce and Tirone 2010; Eden 2007: 98). Brazil's devaluation can be regarded as Rambo behaviour (see Chap. 2), because the decision was taken unilaterally and in secret. The regional power did not inform its regional neighbours, which learned about the devaluation from the news (Kronberger 2002; Genna and Hiroi 2007). After January 1999, the exchange rates of the MERCOSUR member states floated against each other, which is the exact opposite of regional monetary integration (Pelufo 2004). Although there was no common macroeconomic or monetary policy in MERCOSUR, Brazil defected from regional cooperation in the sense that it refused any kind of cooperation ex ante.

Before the crisis hit South America, Brazil repeatedly rejected proposals for monetary cooperation from its neighbours. From 1997 to 1998, Argentina suggested monetary coordination and discussed the possibility of a common currency at a seminar in Buenos Aires and at MERCOSUR's presidential summits (Eichengreen 1998; Giambiagi 1999; Yeyati and Sturzenegger 2000). Argentina perceived Brazil's unilateral monetary policy as a major threat (De Pavia Abreu 1997; Heymann and Ramos 2005), but Brazil was unwilling to compromise on monetary coordination (Yeyati and Sturzenegger 2000). Brazil ignored its neighbours' complaints (Carranza 2003) and adopted safeguards and defensive measures for its own economy rather than cooperate with Argentina, Paraguay, and Uruguay. The smaller MERCOSUR member states demanded 'more MERCOSUR' (Genna and Hiroi 2007). Argentina even suggested the implementation of a currency board and a debt conversion plan, which Brazil dismissed immediately (Kronberger 2002).

2.4 The Argentinean Crisis

Brazil's unilateral devaluation had a huge impact on the country's economic competitiveness on global and regional markets. Because of declining exchange rates, Brazilian exports became cheaper, and Argentinean, Uruguayan, and Paraguayan exports became more expensive in comparison. As a consequence, the three smaller MERCOSUR member states went into recessions (Carranza 2003; Maniam et al. 2003; Saxton 2003; Stiglitz 2002). While the crisis was reaching a 'scale of a veritable disaster'[19] in Argentina, Paraguay and Uruguay, Brazil was economically prospering. It attracted new investments, increased its exports, and became one of the world's most dynamic emerging markets.

In respect to direct investment inflows, Brazil was quickly back at its peak at US$32 billion in 2000, which was even 3 per cent higher than its

FDI inflows in 1998. Throughout the Argentinean crisis, Brazil steadily attracted more than US$10 billion in FDI per year, whereas Argentina's FDI inflows declined to only US$1 billion in 2003 (in comparison, the difference between FDI inflows to Brazil and Argentina was at only 18 per cent in 1999). Between 1991 and 2000, direct investment inflows from the EU into Brazil climbed 20-fold from less than US$1 billion to nearly US$20 billion, and inflows from the USA tripled from less than US$1 billion to US$3 billion. Brazil's enhanced competitiveness can be observed best in its trade performance. Between 1999 and 2004, Brazil expanded its exports to the EU and the USA by almost 50 per cent.[20] At the end of 2000, Brazil's economy entered an 'expansionary cycle',[21] whereas the other regional economies suffered from recessions.

Brazil's devaluation was particularly severe for Argentina, which entered a deep crisis (Bouzas 2001; O'Connell 2002; Saxton 2003). Argentina perceived the devaluation as a material attack,[22] and the minister of economic affairs explicitly blamed the Brazilians, saying, 'Those who devalue their currency are stealing their neighbour's house' (as cited by Baer et al. 2002: 277). Argentina's intraregional exports dropped by nearly 45 per cent between 1998 and 2003.[23] In particular, Argentinean exports to Brazil declined; this was most obvious in the automobile sector, where exports decreased by 71 per cent from 1998 to 1999 (Belivaqua et al. 2001). The Brazilian devaluation produced a flood of Brazilian imports to Argentina and made bilateral trade extremely asymmetrical (Carranza 2003). At the same time, the amount of FDI inflows into Argentina decreased by more than 95 per cent between 1999 and 2003.[24] As was the case for trade, the impact of Brazil's devaluation on Argentina's FDI inflows was most obvious in the automobile sector, where Argentinean exports became much more expensive after January 1999. Consequently, companies transferred their production to Brazil and concentrated their investments there.[25] In general, Argentina witnessed a massive outflow of capital, and investors withdrew more than US$13 billion in the years 1999 and 2000, which amounted to more than half of foreign investments in the country.[26]

Argentina entered a 'great depression' (Kehoe 2005) in the years after the Brazilian devaluation. The country suffered its worst crisis since the 1980s, and the government desperately tried to find a way out of it or at least measures to relieve the immediate consequences (Saxton 2003). The crisis led to exploding public debt, increasing unemployment and most of all an overvaluation of the Argentinean peso (Perry and Servén 2003). There were two reasons why Argentina did not devalue its peso immediately after the Brazilian devaluation. Firstly, Argentina wanted to ensure fiscal stability by trying to keep the so-called Convertibility Plan in place (Kehoe 2005). And secondly, the government faced domestic resistance so that the devaluation could only come into play in 2002.

In 2001, Argentina started to raise tariffs on imports from countries not belonging to MERCOSUR, took anti-dumping measures, and increased export reimbursements (Lederman and Sanguinetti 2003). However, this was not enough to compensate for the economic effects of the Brazilian devaluation. Other options like cutting spending or a new tax policy were politically not feasible (Saxton 2003). The idea to change the Convertibility Plan and to give up fixed exchange rates to the US dollar was proposed by the minister of economic affairs in 2001. The newly appointed minister, Cavallo, suggested to peg the peso not solely to the US dollar, but to a half–half combination of the US dollar and the euro. Extra-regional partners interpreted this as the beginning of a devaluation, which caused further mistrust among investors (Murphy et al. 2006). Thereafter, the economic and political situation in Argentina worsened, and inflation increased dramatically, which made Argentina's exports and its market for investments unattractive. The International Monetary Fund (IMF) put pressure on the Argentinean government, which decided to get rid of the Convertibility Plan in January 2002. This meant a massive devaluation of the Argentinean peso and a default on the country's public debt (Saxton 2003). Nevertheless, the devaluation came far too late and did not make the Argentinean economy more attractive. On the contrary, it led to fiscal instability and to mistrust among investors and trade partners. The economy worsened, unemployment increased further, and Argentina faced massive liquidity problems (Saxton 2003). A slight reprieve came only at the end of 2002, when the economy began to recover slowly.

The Argentinean crisis was a direct consequence of the fact that the regional power Brazil acted like a regional Rambo instead of providing regional leadership. The economic pressure after the Asian crisis and the Russian default affected the whole MERCOSUR. Regional leadership would have required Brazil to assemble the region behind itself and find a regional answer to the crisis. Instead, Brazil took unilateral advantage of the situation. By floating its currency, the regional power improved the competitiveness of its economy in comparison to those of its regional neighbours. This 'beggar-thy-neighbour' strategy was the death blow to the Argentinean economy, which consequently entered the infamous Argentinean crisis. Brazil's action had devastating consequences for its relationship with Argentina in particular and for the dynamic of regional integration in MERCOSUR in general.

3   Brazil's Turning Away from MERCOSUR

As a consequence of Brazil's unilateral devaluation and the Argentinean crisis, tensions between the two countries culminated in a trade war. Argentina implemented protectionist measures and imposed a surcharge on imports of Brazilian iron, quotas for imports of textiles (Carranza 2003; Lapper 1999), and an instrument of previous permission on 1200 Brazilian imports (Kronberger 2002). Brazil responded by taking countermeasures such as prior licences for foodstuff and border sanitary controls on Argentine products (Carranza 2003). Additionally, the regional power launched an investigation into Argentine dairy products and readopted domestic price subsidies for respective producers (Lapper 1999). Finally, Brazil suspended all pending negotiations with Argentina in July 1999, and it thereby threatened to get rid of MERCOSUR altogether (Carranza 2003). The conflict had a lasting impact on regional cooperation and integration in MERCOSUR (Bouzas 2001; Carranza 2003; Costa Vaz 2003). Although Brazil's behaviour changed in the beginning of the new millennium through the assistance of Argentina with safeguard measures and an investment fund (Baer et al. 2002: 276, Genna and Hiroi 2007: 50), MERCOSUR's regional integration never reached the dynamics of the 1990s again. Rather, regional integration stagnated, and tensions between the member states spilled over from the intraregional to the extra-regional trade agenda. This culminated in attempts by Brazil to search for cooperation outside of MERCOSUR when it launched UNASUR in 2004 and signed a bilateral strategic partnership with the EU in 2007.

3.1   Increasingly Asymmetric Trade and Investment Relations

At the turn of the millennium, MERCOSUR's level of intraregional interdependence remained low, and its member states depended on extra-regional economic relations with the EU, the USA and, then also more recently, China. Although intraregional trade in MERCOSUR rose in 2006 due to Brazilian purchases from its neighbours,[27] the intraregional trade share in that year was only back at 13 per cent, which was a decline by nearly 57 per cent since 1998.[28] Dependence on extra-regional economic relations was higher than by the end of the 1990s. Only Paraguay had dominant trade links with a MERCOSUR member state (Argentina, at 24 per cent, ranked as Paraguay's first trade partner), while the EU was the top export destination for Argentina, Brazil, and Uruguay with shares above 20 per cent (see Table 6.3). The majority of Brazilian exports (54 per cent) addressed extra-regional partners. Between 1991 and 2006, Argentinean and Brazilian exports to the Chinese market grew 25-fold.[29]

Growing economic asymmetries accompanied this dependence on extra-regional economic relations. This materialized above all in trade relations among MERCOSUR's member states. Brazil came out as the big winner of the economic crisis in 1999 and became a crucial export market for Argentina with 17 per cent, for Paraguay with 14 per cent, and for Uruguay with 14 per cent (see Table 6.3). Investment relations between MERCOSUR and extra-regional actors complemented the economic asymmetry among the member states. Although there was an overall increase of 23 per cent of FDI inflows in 2006 compared to 2005, this was still only at around 50 per cent of the high point during the 1990s.[31] With nearly 73 per cent, Brazil absorbed by far the largest amount of FDI inflows.[32] Because of Brazil's growing and internationalizing firms, FDI outflows outweighed FDI inflows for the first time in MERCOSUR's history in 2006.[33] A heavy gap in investment inflows between Paraguay and Uruguay on the one hand and Argentina on the other hand complemented this economic asymmetry. Between 2005 and 2006, Paraguay's FDI inflows grew 26-fold and Uruguay's by 82 per cent. In contrast, Argentina's FDI inflows grew by only 5 per cent.[34] The discrepancy in FDI inflows between Argentina and Uruguay was due to the construction of a pulp mill in Uruguay,[35] which resulted in an intense dispute that was taken to the International Court of Justice (ICJ) in 2006. The heavy economic asymmetries within MERCOSUR led to a number of complaints by the smaller member states,[36] and spilled over into the bloc's external trade agenda by the early 2000s.

Table 6.3 The three most important export destinations of the MERCOSUR member states in 2006

	First	Second	Third
Argentina	EU 20 %	Brazil 17 %	Chile 9 %
Brazil	EU 25 %	USA 20 %	China 9 %
Paraguay	Argentina 24 %	EU 18 %	Brazil 14 %
Uruguay	EU 21 %	Brazil 14 %	USA 12 %

Calculation based on the UN Comtrade database (comtrade.un.org)

3.2 Divergent Preferences Regarding the External Trade Agenda

The long-term result of Brazil's devaluation was a fragmentation of MERCOSUR, which materialized in multiple dimensions: the resolution of trade disputes, a lack of solidarity in international institutions and the member states' trade preferences. Firstly, although the relative amount of trade disputes from 2000 to 2006 did not increase compared to the 1990s,[37] the intensity of conflicts grew. After 2000, three disputes reached the stage of escalation and were brought to the International Court of Justice (ICJ) and the World Trade Organization's (WTO) dispute settlement mechanism. This was a sharp contrast to the 1990s, when no dispute was brought to a third dispute settlement body outside of MERCOSUR.[38] Using the level at which conflict resolution occurred as the measure of the intensity of conflicts—that is, moving from bilateral resolution, to ad hoc arbitration, to MERCOSUR's Permanent Review Tribunal and then to third bodies outside of MERCOSUR—disputes among Argentina, Brazil, Paraguay, and Uruguay have become more intense.

Secondly, MERCOSUR's member states lacked solidarity and rejected Brazil's demands to lead on the global stage several times. In 2005, Brazil's bid for a permanent seat in the UN Security Council received no support from its regional neighbours and Argentina even opposed Brazil's application openly (Christensen 2013: 277, Malamud 2011). Further, Brazil and Uruguay both proposed candidates for the position of director general of the WTO. Uruguay's candidate made it to the last round, while Brazil's candidate was rejected after the very first round (Malamud 2011: 9). In the Inter-American Development Bank, Brazil applied for a leadership position in competition with Colombia; Argentina, Paraguay, and Uruguay supported the Colombian candidate instead of the Brazilian one (Malamud 2011: 10).

And thirdly, Brazil's claim for regional leadership on the one hand and the diverging interests of its regional neighbours on the other hand spilled over into MERCOSUR's external trade agenda, in which member states' interests diverged. Argentina, Paraguay, and Uruguay wanted broader and deeper macroeconomic cooperation in order to quickly advance negotiations with the EU and the USA.[39] In contrast, Brazil favoured a wait-and-see approach and did only a minimum to satisfy its neighbours' demands (Carranza 2003). Confident of its economic potential and its bargaining leverage, Brazil increasingly followed a pro-liberalization agenda on manufactured goods (Christensen 2013: 276) and lacked interest in a free trade agreement that would not meet its demands regarding agriculture.[40] The increasingly divergent trade preferences (Christensen 2013: 275) culminated in a request from Argentina and Uruguay to allow bilateral negotiations with extra-regional partners[41]—which Brazil denied.

3.3 UNASUR and the Strategic Partnership

In this situation of MERCOSUR's increasing fragmentation, Brazil was no longer willing to lead the group in international affairs such as interregional trade negotiations with the EU and the USA.[42] This is why the regional power circumvented MERCOSUR by launching UNASUR in 2004 and its bilateral strategic partnership with the EU in 2007. Brazil's absence of leadership and its divergent preferences regarding the external trade agenda led to an inability of MERCOSUR to appear as a coherent group on the global stage.[43] This led to a loss of interest in interregional negotiations with the EU[44] and political cooperation with third actors through MERCOSUR.

A first attempt by Brazil to cooperate internationally outside of MERCOSUR was the establishment of UNASUR. MERCOSUR's member states together with Bolivia, Chile, Colombia, Ecuador, Guyana, Peru, Suriname, and Venezuela established UNASUR in 2004 and finalized it with the Constitutive Treaty signed in 2008. UNASUR was a Brazilian initiative (Luchetti 2015: 96), and it accommodated the regional power's foreign policy objective to create South American cooperation through which Brazil could secure regional and global influence (Gratius and Gomes Saraiva 2013: 218, Espinosa 2014: 40). Whereas MERCOSUR was supposed to serve economic integration, UNASUR was deemed to be a venue for political cooperation and integration of infrastructure (Gratius and Gomes Saraiva 2013: 227). UNASUR is organizationally independent of MERCOSUR, which leads to overlapping regionalism in South America. There are two potential impacts of UNASUR on MERCOSUR (Peña 2012: 10). Either UNASUR will complement MERCOSUR or UNASUR will lead to a dissolution of MERCOSUR by substituting its political outreach. Regardless of the eventual result, the establishment of UNASUR meant that Brazil set up political cooperation independent of MERCOSUR, and shifted its attention towards a new regional organization.

Another instance of deviating from MERCOSUR and shifting priorities to cooperation beyond the regional organization was that of bilateral discussions that materialized in 2007 between Brazil and the EU for their strategic partnership (Carlos Lessa 2010: 128). The strategic partnership was not a preferential trade agreement, but it included only issues that were not in conflict with the MERCOSUR-CU.[45] It addressed political dialogues, economic matters (particularly non-tariff trade barriers), sustainable development, bi-regional cooperation, science and technology, and cultural aspects.[46] Nevertheless, the strategic partnership can be viewed as a defection from regional integration for two reasons. Firstly, Brazil took the decision to launch the strategic partnership with the EU without consulting its regional neighbours and the strategic partnership harmed relations within the region. An anecdotal fact that illustrates MERCOSUR's fragmentation in 2007 is that Argentina, Paraguay, and Uruguay asked EU diplomats—and not Brazilian diplomats—for information about the strategic partnership.[47] And secondly, the strategic partnership can have potentially negative effects on interregional trade negotiations with the EU (Gomes Saraiva 2010: 164).[48] The newly established bilateralism between the EU and Brazil stirred up worries among MERCOSUR's member states that Brazil could negotiate a bilateral trade agreement with the EU[49]—an option that Brazil had rejected for its neighbours.[50] These concerns were not completely unrealistic. Although there is no formal linkage between the strategic partnership and the interregional negotiations, bilateralism was an immediate consequence of the stagnation in interregional negotiations (Van Loon 2015: 142).[51] One interviewee pointed out that the EU and Brazil would not have launched the strategic partnership if an interregional agreement had been concluded in the first place.[52] The strategic partnership, therefore, provides two options for the EU and Brazil to move forward on a trade agreement. Either Brazil and the EU pre-negotiate controversial issues bilaterally before taking them to the interregional table, or the strategic partnership smoothes the way for a bilateral agreement. The latter would be fatal for regional integration in MERCOSUR.

UNASUR and the strategic partnership with the EU are not such clear-cut cases of Rambo behaviour as the unilateral devaluation of 1999, but Brazil nevertheless sidelined MERCOSUR when setting up these two initiatives. The regional power actively searched for cooperation independent of MERCOSUR, and it shifted priorities away from economic integration with its neighbours. Particularly the strategic partnership with the EU has brought about concerns among Argentina, Paraguay, and Uruguay. Although there is no sign yet that Brazil and the EU could iron out a bilateral trade deal given the relaunched interregional negotiations since

2010, the strategic partnership has added to a growing fragmentation of MERCOSUR. Brazil stopped leading the regional group in international negotiations and shifted to bilateralism without consulting its neighbours. This justifies the assessment that Brazil behaved like a regional Rambo even after the Argentinean crisis (see Chap. 2).

3.4 Stagnating Regional Integration in MERCOSUR

Although MERCOSUR's member states tried to revitalize regional integration several times, these attempts were mostly ineffective and controversial. This ineffectiveness was not a direct consequence of Brazil's cooperation outside of MERCOSUR, but it indicates that regional integration has stagnated more or less since 1999 (see also Gómez-Mera 2015). Three examples of formal regional cooperation, commonly perceived as achievements of MERCOSUR, shall be depicted in order to demonstrate the de facto stalemate of integration: the reform of MERCOSUR's dispute settlement mechanism, the establishment of the parliamentary body Parlasur and MERCOSUR's enlargement with Venezuela.

MERCOSUR's member states took a significant step towards judicial integration in 2002 by enacting the Permanent Review Tribunal (Arnold and Rittberger 2013), which, however, has lacked relevant effects until today. The Protocol of Olivos reformed MERCOSUR's dispute settlement mechanism from bilateral, interstate resolution of conflicts and ad hoc arbitration, to a permanent tribunal modelled on the WTO's dispute settlement procedure (Lenz 2012). Although the creation of a permanent third body to settle disputes was a substantial reform, the tribunal's competences are restricted (see Alter 2013) and access to dispute settlement has remained limited to states only. This excluded private parties from using MERCOSUR's judicial review against their own states (Alter 2013; Malamud 2005a, b). The relatively low level of judicial integration in MERCOSUR (Krapohl et al. 2010) finds expression in the negligible usage of the Permanent Review Tribunal, which has pronounced only six awards and six resolutions since it has started working in 2005.[53] If one compares this number with the European Court of Justice's (ECJ) hundreds of resolutions, MERCOSUR's Permanent Review Tribunal has remained on the whole irrelevant to its member states. And even when the member states applied MERCOSUR's dispute settlement procedure, they sometimes ignored the tribunal's decisions. During the dispute about the construction of a pulp mill by Finnish investors in Uruguay (Pakkasvirta 2008), the first and the second instances of MERCOSUR's dispute settlement mechanism decided that a road blockade by Argentinean protesters violated MERCOSUR law. However, the rulings were ignored by Argentina.

In 2006, the MERCOSUR member states established the regional parliament Parlasur as a successor of the previous Joint Parliamentary Commission. Next to MERCOSUR's Permanent Review Tribunal,[54] Parlasur has been the only supranational body of the regional organization. Despite making a step towards supranationalization and enhanced legitimacy, Parlasur was and still is an ineffective parliament whose only competence is to issue recommendations (Gómez-Mera 2015: 2, Malamud 2015: 171). For more than a decade, the previous Joint Parliamentary Commission met only twice a year (Dri and Ventura 2013: 70), and it took until 2011 to mandate direct elections for the first time. However, direct elections only took place in Paraguay, whereas the other MERCOSUR member states still send representatives from their national parliaments (Malamud 2015: 171).

MERCOSUR's enlargement with Venezuela in 2012 was extremely controversial and raises questions as to the region's commitment to democracy. Venezuela announced its intention to become a full member of MERCOSUR in 2006, but it took until 2012 to approve its membership (Rivera 2014). While Argentina and Brazil appreciated the enlargement (Rivera 2014: 238), Paraguay and Uruguay were extremely sceptical[55] and feared negative political effects if Venezuela were allowed into MERCOSUR (Rivera 2014: 237). Paraguay especially did not want to approve Venezuela's membership (Malamud 2012: 224) and blocked enlargement for quite some time. The events which finally enabled the accession of Venezuela came unexpectedly. It was Paraguay's suspension from its MERCOSUR functions that made Venezuela's membership possible (Mühlich 2014: 199, Rivera 2014: 240). On 15 June 2012, Paraguay witnessed 17 deaths after a clash between the police and protestors. This resulted in the impeachment of president Lugo, which in turn resulted in a temporary suspension of Paraguay from MERCOSUR (Rivera 2014: 240). Thus, Argentina, Brazil, and Uruguay were finally able to approve Venezuela's accession without the consent of Paraguay.

These three steps—the establishment of the Permanent Review Tribunal and Parlasur, as well as Venezuela's accession—at a first glance seem to be major achievements towards judicial integration, supranationalization, and enlargement. Upon a closer look, however, Parlasur and the Permanent Review Tribunal have performed ineffectively, and MERCOSUR's enlargement with Venezuela could not have been any more controversial. The fact that the accession of Venezuela required the temporary suspension of Paraguay from MERCOSUR reflects poorly on the member states' ability to cooperate.

4 Conclusion

The motivation for Brazil's volatile behaviour towards MERCOSUR can be found in the country's extra-regional interests. Between 1991 and 1994, all MERCOSUR member states, including the regional power Brazil, benefited from successful regional integration, which led to increasing investments from and exports to the EU and the USA. Because regional cooperation was in line with Brazil's extra-regional interests, the regional power provided regional leadership and pushed the customs union. This changed when the impact of the Asian and Russian currency crises hit the region and led to a competition for extra-regional investment inflows among the MERCOSUR member states. In 1999, Brazil devaluated its currency unilaterally in order to get a competitive advantage in comparison to its smaller neighbours. In the short run, Brazil's devaluation led to a severe crisis in Argentina, and in the long run, regional integration in MERCOSUR became stalled. Heavy economic asymmetries and dependence on extra-regional commercial relations fragmented MERCOSUR and gave rise to increasingly divergent preferences towards extra-regional partners. Facing these tensions, Brazil began to act outside of MERCOSUR by establishing UNASUR and launching the strategic partnership with the EU.

The three cases of regional cooperation and defection in MERCOSUR allow us to draw conclusions in respect to the theoretical framework of this book (see Chap. 2). Firstly, Brazil's cooperation during the establishment of the MERCOSUR-CU confirms Hypothesis 1. During the early 1990s, regional integration was a positive-sum game from which Brazil benefited the most. The member states cooperated within a battle of the sexes, and the regional power Brazil pushed cooperation. Although MERCOSUR's member states had different preferences regarding MERCOSUR's institutional design, they cooperated and established the customs union. Brazil reinforced Argentina's commitment to MERCOSUR by granting some side payments. The early 1990s were a huge success for MERCOSUR, generating a large regional market and locking in structural reforms whereby the member states attracted increasing extra-regional investments and enhanced their intra- and extra-regional trade.

Secondly, Brazil's unilateral decision to float the real confirms Hypothesis 2. When the impact of the Asian financial crisis of 1997 and the Russian moratorium of 1998 hit South America, MERCOSUR's member states started to compete for declining extra-regional investment inflows. The effects were intense for Brazil, which lost portfolio investments due to the panic of international investors. To ease the effects, Brazil floated its currency in January 1999. The regional power did nothing to inform its partners and rejected any type of monetary coordination. Thereby, Brazil became a regional Rambo, which improved its international economic competitiveness at a cost to its neighbours. Unable to compete with its bigger neighbour, Argentina entered a deep recession, while Brazil's economy recovered quickly. By defecting from regional integration, Brazil managed to maintain its privileged position in the Southern Cone.

And thirdly, Brazil's behaviour after the Argentinean crisis partly confirms Hypothesis 2. Brazil's unilateral devaluation had a profound impact on MERCOSUR and set the region back to 1991's level of intraregional interdependence and increasing economic asymmetries among the member states. These two factors combined led to increasing tensions among MERCOSUR's member states, including competition for investment flows, escalating trade disputes and complaints about economic and political asymmetries. Because of the stalemate within MERCOSUR, the regional power Brazil looked for international cooperation outside of the regional organization. The regional power pushed the establishment of UNASUR, which is compatible with MERCOSUR, but which nevertheless indicates a shift of priorities away from MERCOSUR. Even more critically, Brazil put cooperation with its neighbours on interregional trade negotiations with the EU temporarily on ice and launched the bilateral strategic partnership with the EU—thereby defecting from regional integration. However, it should be acknowledged that the interest in interregional negotiations through MERCOSUR also declined in Argentina, Paraguay, and Uruguay.

Having demonstrated the crucial impact of extra-regional economic relations on MERCOSUR and Brazil's behaviour therein, it shall be highlighted that South America contains more than the extra-regional logic of integration. For Brazil, MERCOSUR is not just an instrument for opening up extra-regional markets and attracting investments. More than that, regional integration boosts Brazil's presence on the global stage, and the regional power made use of MERCOSUR in international negotiations. And for the smaller member states, MERCOSUR is not just an instrument for improving extra-regional economic relations, but also for opening up the Brazilian market. Argentina, Paraguay, and Uruguay increased their exports to Brazil during the successful period of regional integration in the early 1990s. However, Brazil's unilateral devaluation in 1999 interrupted the growing intraregional investment and trade relations. This regional Rambo behaviour had severe consequences for Argentina, Paraguay, and Uruguay precisely because the Brazilian market had become important during the 1990s.

NOTES

1. These numbers are taken from RIKS, an internet database published by the United Nations University Institute on Comparative Regional Integration Studies (www.cris.unu.edu/riks/web).
2. Calculation based on the UN Comtrade database (comtrade.un.org).
3. Calculation based on World Bank data (data.worldbank.org).
4. Do Rego Barros, S. (1995): 'Pronunciamento do Senhor Secretário-Geral das Relações Exteriores: "O Nordeste e o Mercosul", Recife, 8 de agosto de 1995', in: Resenha De Política Exterior Do Brasil 79 (Brasília).
5. Do Rego Barros, S. (1996): 'Encontro do Norte sobre o Mercosul, Manaus, 12 de abril de 1996', in: Resenha De Política Exterior Do Brasil 79 (Brasília).
6. Interview with the Brazilian embassy in Brussels, Belgium, on 4 April 2014.
7. Calculation based on the UN Comtrade database (comtrade.un.org).
8. These numbers are taken from RIKS, an internet database published by the United Nations University Institute on Comparative Regional Integration Studies (www.cris.unu.edu/riks/web).
9. MERCOSUR (1997): 'Report MERCOSUR N° 3: July–December 1997' (Buenos Aires).
10. MERCOSUR (1998): 'Report MERCOSUR N° 4: January–June 1998' (Buenos Aires).
11. Calculation based on World Bank data (data.worldbank.org).
12. MERCOSUR (1999): 'Report MERCOSUR N° 5: 1998–1999' (Buenos Aires).
13. World Bank (1998): 'What Effect Will East Asia's Crisis Have on Developing Countries?' (PremNotes Economic Policy, March 1998, Number 1).
14. CEPAL (1998): 'Impact of the Asian Crisis on Latin America' (www.cepal.org/publicaciones/xml/3/4693/lcg2026i.pdf).
15. WITS (2014): 'World Integrated Trade Solution: Country Profile' (http://wits.worldbank.org/CountryProfile/en/Country/ARG/Year/1997/Summary).

16. Calculation based on World Bank Data (data.worldbank.org).
17. MERCOSUR (2000): 'Report MERCOSUR N° 6: 1999–2000' (Buenos Aires).
18. MERCOSUR (1999): 'Report MERCOSUR N° 5: 1998–1999' (Buenos Aires).
19. MERCOSUR (2003): 'Report MERCOSUR N° 8: 2001–2002' (Buenos Aires).
20. Calculation based on the UN Comtrade database (comtrade.un.org).
21. MERCOSUR (2001): 'Report MERCOSUR N° 7: 2000–2001' (Buenos Aires).
22. MERCOSUR (2000): 'Report MERCOSUR N° 6: 1999–2000' (Buenos Aires).
23. Calculation based on the UN Comtrade database (comtrade.un.org).
24. Calculation based on World Bank Data (data.worldbank.org).
25. MERCOSUR (1999): 'Report MERCOSUR N° 5: 1998–1999' (Buenos Aires).
26. Calculation based on World Bank Data (data.worldbank.org).
27. MERCOSUR (2008): 'MERCOSUR Report No. 12 2006–2007' (Buenos Aires).
28. Calculation based on the UN Comtrade database (comtrade.un.org).
29. MERCOSUR (2008): 'MERCOSUR Report No. 12 2006–2007' (Buenos Aires).
30. MERCOSUR (2008): 'MERCOSUR Report No. 12 2006–2007' (Buenos Aires).
31. Calculation based on World Bank Data (data.worldbank.org).
32. Calculation based on World Bank Data (data.worldbank.org).
33. MERCOSUR (2008): 'MERCOSUR Report No. 12 2006–2007' (Buenos Aires).
34. Calculation based on World Bank Data (data.worldbank.org).
35. MERCOSUR (2008): 'MERCOSUR Report No. 12 2006–2007' (Buenos Aires).
36. MERCOSUR (2008): 'MERCOSUR Report No. 12 2006–2007' (Buenos Aires).
37. Calculation based on the Integrated Database of Trade Disputes (idatd.cepal.org).
38. Calculation based on the Integrated Database of Trade Disputes (idatd.cepal.org).
39. FAZ (2001): 'Streit um Währungspolitik im Mercosur: Argentinien fordert Kurskontrolle des Real/Brasilien protestiert', in: Frankfurter Allgemeine Zeitung 215: 18.
40. Interview with the Friedrich Ebert Foundation in Montevideo, Uruguay, on 18 August 2014.
41. Mercopress (2006): 'Mercosur "rebel" member' (en.mercopress.com/2006/01/19/mercosur-rebel-member-seen-from-buenos-aires).

42. Mercopress (2006): 'US/Uruguay free trade accord "not in the agenda"' (en.mercopress.com/2006/02/04/us-uruguay-free-trade-accord-not-in-the-agenda).
43. Mercopress (2008): 'Mercosur is virtually fractured' (en.mercopress.com/2008/12/10/mercosur-is-virtually-fractured-uruguay-admits-openly).
44. MERCOSUR (2007): 'Mercosur Report No. 11 2005–2006' (Buenos Aires): 140.
45. Interview with the European Commission in Brussels, Belgium, on 18 March 2014.
46. EU (2011): 'Factsheet: EU-Brazil Summit: EU Strategic Partnership with Brazil' (www.consilium.europa.eu/uedocs/cms_data/docs/pressdata/EN/foraff/124831.pdf).
47. Mercopress (2007): 'Brazil to become a strategic partner of the European Union' (en.mercopress.com/2007/07/04/brazil-to-become-a-strategic-partner-of-the-european-union).
48. Interregional negotiations on an Association Agreement between the EU and MERCOSUR took place between 1999 and 2004. They were officially resumed in 2010 after six years of stagnation and are still ongoing at the time of this writing in February 2016.
49. Interview with an expert at UDELAR in Montevideo, Uruguay, on 08 August, 2014.
50. Interview with the Brazilian embassy in Brussels, Belgium, on 04 April, 2014.
51. Interview with the European Commission in Brussels, Belgium, on 08 April, 2014.
52. Interview with the European External Action Service in Brussels, Belgium, on 20 March 2014.
53. Tribunal Permanente de Revisión (2016): 'Solución de Controversias' (www.tprmercosur.org/es/sol_controversias.htm).
54. MERCOSUR (2002): 'Protocol of Olivos' (www.sice.oas.org/Trade/MRCSR/olivos/polivos_s.asp).
55. Interview with a former Uruguayan diplomat in Montevideo, Uruguay, on 08 August 2014.

REFERENCES

Alter, K. (2013). The Multiple Roles of International Courts and Tribunals: Enforcement, Dispute Settlement, Constitutional and Administrative Review. In J. L. Dunoff & M. A. Pollack (Eds.), *International Law and International Relations: Introducing an Interdisciplinary Dialogue* (pp. 345–370). New York: Cambridge University Press.

Amann, E., & Baer, W. (2003). Anchors Away: The Cost and Benefits of Brazil's Devaluation. *World Development, 31*, 1033–1046.

Arnold, C., & Rittberger, B. (2013). The Legalization of Dispute Resolution in Mercosur. *Journal of Politics in Latin America*, 5, 97–132.
Baer, W. (2008). *The Brazilian Economy: Growth and Development* (6th ed.). Boulder, CO: Lynne Rienner Publishers.
Baer, W., Cavalcanti, T., & Silva, P. (2002). Economic Integration without Policy Coordination: The Case of Mercosur. *Emerging Markets Review*, 3, 269–291.
Bajo Sanchez, C. (2005). The European Union and Mercosur: A Case of Interregionalism. *Third World Quarterly*, 20, 927–941.
Bandeira, L. A. M. (2006). Brazil as a Regional Power and Its Relations with the United States. *Latin American Perspectives*, 33, 12–27.
Bearce, D. H., & Tirone, D. C. (2010). Foreign Aid Effectiveness and the Strategic Goals of Donor Governments. *The Journal of Politics*, 72, 837.
Belivaqua, A., Catena, M., & Talvi, E. (2001). Integration, Interdependence and Regional Goods: An Application to Mercosur. *Economia*, 2, 153–207.
Bouzas, R. (2001). *Mercosur Ten Years After: Learning Process or Deja-vu?* www.netamericas.net/Researchpapers/Documents/Bouzas/Bouzas2.pdf
Bouzas, R. (2009). *Apuntes sobre el estado de la integración regional en America Latina* (Documento de trabajo, 1-2010, Red Mercosur).
Bouzas, R., & Soltz, H. (2001). Institutions and Regional Integration: The Case of MERCOSUR. In Bulmer-Thomas, V. (Ed.), *Regional Integration in Latin America and the Caribbean: The Political Economy of Open Regionalism* (pp. 95–118). London: Biddles Ltd.
Bulmer-Thomas, V. (1999). The Brazilian Devaluation: National Responses and International Consequences. *International Affairs*, 75, 729–741.
Burges, S. W. (2005). Bounded by the Reality of Trade: Practical Limits to a South American Region. *Cambridge Review of International Affairs*, 18, 437–454.
Burges, S. W. (2013). Brazil as a Bridge between Old and New Powers? *International Affairs*, 89, 577–594.
Carlos Lessa, A. (2010). Brazil's Strategic Partnerships: An Assessment of the Lula Era (2003-2010). *Revista Brasileira de Politica Internacional*, 53, 115–131.
Carranza, M. (2003). Can MERCOSUR Survive? Domestic and International Constraints on MERCOSUR. *Latin American Politics and Society*, 45, 67–103.
Cason, J. W. (2000). On the Road to Southern Cone Economic Integration. *Journal of Interamerican Studies and World Affairs*, 42, 23–42.
Cason, J. W. (2010). *The Political Economy of Integration: The Experience of Mercosur*. Hoboken, NJ: Routledge.
Cason, J. W., & Power, J. (2009). Presidentialization, Pluralization, and the Rollback of Itamaraty: Explaining Change in Brazilian Foreign Policymaking in the Cardoso-Lula Era. *International Political Science Review*, 30, 117–140.
Christensen, S. F. (2013). Brazil's Foreign Policy Priorities. *Third World Quarterly*, 34, 271–286.
Chudnovsky, D., & López, A. (2004). Transnational Corporations' Strategies and Foreign Trade Patterns in MERCOSUR Countries in the 1990s. *Cambridge Journal of Economics*, 28, 635–652.

Costa Vaz, A. (2003). *Trade Strategies in the Context of Economic Regionalism: The Case of Mercosur* (CLAS Working Papers 4).
De Almeida, P. R. (1998). Brazil and the Future of Mercosur: Dilemmas and Options. *Integration and Trade, 2,* 59–74.
De Lima, M. R. S., & Hirst, M. (2006). Brazil as an Intermediate State and Regional Power: Action, Choice and Responsibilities. *International Affairs, 82,* 21–40.
De Pavia Abreu, M. (1997). Financial Integration in MERCOSUR Countries. *Integration and Trade, 1,* 79–94.
Doctor, M. (2013). Prospects for Deepening MERCOSUR Integration: Economic Asymmetry and Institutional Deficits. *Review of International Political Economy, 20,* 515–540.
Dri, C., & Ventura, D. (2013). The MERCOSUR Parliament: A Challenging Position between Late Institutionalization and Early Statement. In O. Costa, C. Dri, & S. Stavridis (Eds.), *Parliamentary Dimensions of Regionalization and Globalization: The Role of Inter-Parliamentary Institutions* (pp. 70–89). New York: Palgrave Macmillan.
Eden, L. (2007). Multinationals, Foreign Direct Investment and the New Regionalism in the Americas. *Integration and Trade, 11,* 97–123.
Eichengreen, B. (1998). *Does Mercosur Need a Single Currency?* Center for International and Development Economics Research, Institute of Business and Economic Research, UC Berkeley.
Espinosa, C. (2014). The Origins of the Union of South American Nations: A Multicausal Account of South American Regionalism. In E. Vivares (Ed.), *Exploring the New South American Regionalism (NSAR)* (pp. 29–49). Farnham: Ashgate.
Faucher, P., & Armijo, L. E. (2003). *Currency Crisis and Decision-making Frameworks: The Politics of Bouncing Back in Argentina and Brazil.* citeseerx.ist.psu.edu/viewdoc/download?doi=10.1.1.197.6786&rep=rep1&type=pdf
Ffrench-Davis, R., & Studart, R. (2003). The Regional Fallout of Argentina's Crisis. In J. J. Teunissen & A. Akkerman (Eds.), *The Crisis That Was Not Prevented: Argentina, the IMF, and Globalisation.* The Hague: FONDAD.
Fidler, S. (1992). Brazilian Economy Paces Mercosur's Tariffs Timetable. *The Financial Times, 31,* 791: 3.
Genna, G. M., & Hiroi, T. (2007). Brazilian Regional Power in the Development of Mercosul. *Latin American Perspectives, 34,* 43–57.
Giambiagi, F. (1999). MERCOSUR: Why Does Monetary Union Make Sense in the Long-term? *Integration and Trade, 3,* 59–81.
Gomes Saraiva, M. (2010). Brazilian Foreign Policy Towards South America During the Lula Administration: Caught between South America and Mercosur. *Revista Brasileira de Política Internacional, 53,* 151–168.
Gomes Saraiva, M. (2012). Procesos de integración de América del Sur y el papel de Brasil: los casos del Mercosur y la Unasur. *Revista CIDOB d'Afers Internacionals, 97/98,* 87–100.

Gómez-Mera, L. (2015). *Power and Regionalism in Latin America: The Politics of MERCOSUR*. Notre Dame: University of Notre Dame Press.
González Guyer, F. (2009). *Uruguay El país de los fisiócratas: Auge y decadencia del "Uruguay feliz"*. Montevideo: Ediciones de la Banda Oriental.
Gratius, S., & Gomes Saraiva, M. (2013). Continental Regionalism: Brazil's Prominent Role in the Americas. In M. Emerson & R. Flores (Eds.), *Enhancing the Brazil-EU Strategic Partnership: From the Bilateral and Regional to the Global* (pp. 218–237). Brussels: CEPS.
Grugel, J. B., & De Almeida Medeiros, M. (1999). Brazil and MERCOSUR. In J. B. Grugel & W. Hout (Eds.), *Regionalism Across the North-South Divide: State Strategies and Globalization* (pp. 43–56). London: Routledge.
Heymann, D., & Ramos, A. (2005). *MERCOSUR in Transition: Macroeconomic Perspectives* (ECLAC Project Document). Santiago: United Nations.
Hopewell, K. (2013). New Protagonists in Global Economic Governance: Brazilian Agribusiness at the WTO. *New Political Economy, 18*, 603–623.
Kehoe, T. J. (2005). What Can We Learn from the Current Crisis in Argentina? *Scottish Journal of Political Economy, 50*, 609–633.
Klom, A. (2003). Mercosur and Brazil: A European Perspective. *International Affairs, 79*, 351–368.
Krapohl, S., Faude, B., & Dinkel, J. (2010). Judicial Integration in the Americas? A Comparison of Dispute Settlement in NAFTA and MERCOSUR. In F. Laursen (Ed.), *Comparative Regional Integration: Europe and Beyond* (pp. 169–192). Abingdon: Ashgate.
Kronberger, R. (2002). A Cost-Benefit Analysis of a Monetary Union for MERCOSUR with Particular Emphasis on the Optimum Currency Area Theory. *Integration and Trade, 6*, 29–93.
Lapper, R. (1999). Common Market Weathers the Disputes. *The Financial Times*, 34, 054: V.
Lederman, D., & Sanguinetti, P. (2003). Trade Policy Options for Argentina in the Short and Long Run. *Integration and Trade, 19*, 99–133.
Lenz, T. (2012). Spurred Emulation: The EU and Regional Integration in MERCOSUR and SADC. *West European Politics, 35*, 155–173.
Luchetti, J. F. (2015). Political Dialogue in South America: The Role of South-American Nations Union. In S. Dosenrode (Ed.), *Limits to Regional Integration* (pp. 95–109). Farnham: Ashgate.
Malamud, A. (2003). Presidentialism and Mercosur: A Hidden Cause for a Successful Experience. In F. Laursen (Ed.), *Comparative Regional Integration: Theoretical Perspectives* (pp. 53–73). Aldershot: Ashgate.
Malamud, A. (2005a). Presidential Diplomacy and the Institutional Underpinnings of Mercosur: An Empirical Examination. *Latin American Research Review, 40*, 138–164.
Malamud, A. (2005b). Mercosur Turns 15: Between Rising Rhetoric and Declining Achievement. *Cambridge Review of International Affairs, 18*, 421–436.

Malamud, A. (2008). *The Internal Agenda of Mercosur: Interdependence, Leadership and Institutionalization.* www.ics.ul.pt/rdonweb-docs/Andr%C3%A9s%20 Malamud%20-%20Publica%C3%A7%C3%B5es%202008%20n%C2%BA5.pdf
Malamud, A. (2011). A Leader without Followers? The Growing Divergence between the Regional and Global Performance of Brazilian Foreign Policy. *Latin American Politics and Society, 53*, 1–24.
Malamud, A. (2012). La Unión Europea, del interregionalismo con América Latina a la asociación estratégica con Brasil. *Revista CIDOB d'Afers Internacionals, 97/98*, 219–230.
Malamud, A. (2015). Interdependence, Leadership and Institutionalization: The Triple Deficit and Fading Prospects of Mercosur. In S. Dosenrode (Ed.), *Limits to Regional Integration* (pp. 163–179). Farnham: Ashgate.
Maniam, B., Leavell, H., & Mehrens, D. (2003). Free Trade Area or Customs Union? The Case of the South American Trade Bloc Mercosur. *Journal of International Business Research, 2*, 23–34.
Manzetti, L. (1994). The Political Economy of Mercosur. *Journal of Interamerican Studies and World Affairs, 35*, 101–141.
Mecham, M. (2003). Mercosur: A Failing Development Project? *International Affairs, 79*, 369–387.
Mühlich, L. (2014). *Advancing Regional Monetary Cooperation: The Case of Fragile Financial Markets.* New York: Palgrave Macmillan.
Mukhamedinov, M. (2007). Mercosur and the European Union: Variation Among the Factors of Regional Cohesion. *Cooperation and Conflict, 42*, 207–228.
Murphy, R. L., Artana, D., & Navajas, F. (2006). The Argentine Economic Crisis. *Cato Journal, 23*, 23–28.
Nunnenkamp, P. (1999). *Latin America after the Currency Crash in Brazil: Why the Optimists may be Wrong* (Kieler Diskussionsbeiträge 337).
O'Connell, A. (2002, September). *The Recent Crisis of the Argentine Economy: Some Elements and Background.* Paper Presented at the METU Conference in Ankara, Turkey.
Pakkasvirta, J. (2008). From Pulp to Fiction? Fray Bentos Pulp Investment Conflict through the Finish Media. *Cooperation and Conflict, 43*, 421–446.
Pelufo, J. I. G. (2004). *MERCOSUR's Insertion into a Globalized World* (Working Paper, Special Initiative on Trade and Integration 6).
Peña, F. (2012). *Mercosur as a Regional and Global Protagonist* (EUI Policy Papers RSCAS 2012/01).
Perry, G., & Servén, L. (2003). *The Anatomy of a Multiple Crisis: Why Was Argentina Special and What Can We Learn from It?* (World Bank Policy Research Working Paper 3081).
Rivera, S. (2014). *Latin American Unification: A History of Political and Economic Integration Efforts.* Jefferson, NC: McFarland.
Saxton, J. (2003). *Argentina's Economic Crisis: Causes and Cures.* Washington: Joint Economic Committee United States Congress. www.hacer.org/pdf/Schuler.pdf.

Schirm, S. A. (2002). *Globalization and the New Regionalism: Global Markets, Domestic Politics and Regional Cooperation*. Cambridge: Polity Press.
Sennes, R., Onuki, J., & De Oliveira, A. J. (2006). The Brazilian Foreign Policy and the Hemispheric Security. *Revista Fuerzas Armadas y Sociedad, 1*, 1–16.
Stiglitz, J. E. (2002). *Argentina, Short-changed: Why the Nation that Followed the Rules Fell to Pieces*. www.yorku.ca/drache/talks/2002/stiglitz_argentina.pdf
Vaillant, M., & Bizzozero, L. (2003). *Association Agreement between European Union and Mercosur: A Slow and Long Negotiation* (MPRA, 47249). Munich.
Van Loon, A. (2015). From Interregionalism to Bilateralism: Power and Interests in EU-Brazil Trade Cooperation. In M. Rewizorski (Ed.), *The European Union and the BRICS: Complex Relations in the Era of Global Governance* (pp. 141–161). Cham: Springer.
Varas, A. (2008). *Brazil in South America: From Indifference to Hegemony*. www.fride.org/download/COM_Brazil_Sudamerican_ENG.pdf
Yeyati, E. L., & Sturzenegger, F. (2000). Is EMU a Blueprint for Mercosur? *Cuadernos de Economia, 37*, 63–99.

CHAPTER 7

SADC

Extra-Regional Trade Relations Constrain Deeper Market Integration

Johannes Muntschick

The Southern African Development Community (SADC) counts as one of the most realistic, stable, and promising examples of the new regionalism in Africa (Weiland 2006; Adelmann 2012). SADC consists of 15 member states[1] that cover an area of almost 10 million square kilometres with a population of about 300 million inhabitants. Most of the organisation's member states—with the exception of Botswana, Mauritius, the Seychelles, and South Africa—are classified as least or less-developed countries (Oosthuizen 2006). The South African economy is by far the biggest and most industrialised in the region, since Zimbabwe under President Robert Mugabe has experienced political turmoil and a devastating economic crisis for almost two decades now (MacLean 2005; Alden and Schoeman 2013). South Africa occupies a central role in SADC's regional trade network (see Chap. 4). Thus, South Africa qualifies as Southern Africa's regional power, whose cooperation is key for all regional

J. Muntschick (✉)
Department of Political Science/International Relations,
Johannes Gutenberg-University of Mainz, Mainz, Germany
e-mail: muntschick@uni-mainz.de

© The Author(s) 2017
S. Krapohl (ed.), *Regional Integration in the Global South*,
International Political Economy Series,
DOI 10.1007/978-3-319-38895-3_7

integration efforts of SADC. At the same time, the entire region and most of its member states are economically dependent on extra-regional actors, most notably from Europe. The European Union (EU) is Southern Africa's most important trading partner, which gives it some leverage to influence regional integration in SADC (Muntschick 2012).

Initially, regional integration in Southern Africa was not a phenomenon of the new regionalism. SADC's predecessor, the Southern African Development Coordination Conference (SADCC), had been established by black majority-ruled countries back in 1980 in order to coordinate the inflow of European development aid and to reduce economic dependence on apartheid South Africa (Mufune 1993). This objective of the old SADCC became obsolete with the end of apartheid in South Africa during the early 1990s. The transformation from SADCC to SADC in 1992 meant not only an institutional reorganisation, but also a realignment of its policies and integration agenda. In this course, SADC changed its character from a primarily protectionist organisation of the 'old regionalism' towards an open and globally oriented organisation of the 'new regionalism'. It put a focus on regional market integration and economic block building as a major strategy to advance socio-economic development and to face the challenges of globalisation (Oosthuizen 2006; Vogt 2007). In 1994, majority-ruled South Africa under President Nelson Mandela joined SADC; this marked the final step in ending the old cleavage between minority- and majority-ruled Southern African countries.

SADC has shown considerable progress in market integration during the past two decades, but this dynamic has stopped recently. The member states' main objectives of economic integration are outlined in the SADC Treaty, the Protocol on Trade and the Regional Indicative Strategic Development Plan (RISDP). The Protocol on Trade of 1999 committed the member states to set up the SADC free trade area (SADC-FTA) and this goal was achieved on time in August 2008.[2] According to the RISDP, the process of regional market integration should then have deepened with the creation of an SADC customs union (SADC-CU) in 2010 as a next step on the road towards a common market.[3] While the SADC-FTA can be seen as a successful example of regional cooperation, the organisation's further agenda on deepening economic integration has been obstructed. SADC did not only fail to comply with its own schedule to establish the SADC-CU in 2010, but it is probably also unable to accomplish this goal in the near future (Khumalo and Phiri 2009; Muntschick 2013b).

This pattern of success and failure of regional cooperation is puzzling, because the political situation and economic environment within Southern Africa was virtually the same prior to the formation of the SADC-FTA as well as in the run-up to the scheduled SADC-CU. This chapter aims to address the question of which factors explain the ups and downs of regional integration in Southern Africa. The argument unfolds in two case studies about the SADC-FTA and the SADC-CU. The analysis explores whether the causal mechanisms established in Chap. 3 are able to explain the two decision-making processes. Finally, the conclusion provides a summary of the empirical findings and reflects on the hypotheses of the theoretical argument (see Chap. 2).

1 THE FORMATION OF THE SADC-FTA FROM 1996 TO 2008

The new formation of SADC in 1992 went hand in hand with a paradigm shift in the region's approach towards regional economic integration. Instead of focusing on reducing economic dependence on South Africa, import substitution, and economically isolating the region from the global market, the SADC member states increasingly followed a strategy of trade liberalisation, open regionalism, and integration into the global market. The member states aimed to integrate the regional market incrementally into the global market in order to improve the region's economic standing in trade relations with other regions and—most importantly— to receive more foreign direct investments (FDI) (Weeks 1996). SADC also used regional integration in order to attract foreign development aid, because the member states had realised—not least from the times of the old SADCC—that regional cooperation was rewarded with significant external funding, especially by the EU (Solomon 2004). Hence, the extra-regional stimulus for regional market integration in SADC rooted to a large degree in the region's structural dependence on extra-regional investments and development aid from Europe.

Although the share of intraregional trade in SADC was comparably low, there was nevertheless a significant potential for increasing intraregional trade flows in view of existing comparative cost advantages in the SADC region (Cleary 1999: 7; Chauvin and Gaulier 2002: 24–25). Moreover, some share of the large amount of informal trade in the region could be directed into formal channels by means of tariff reduction and trade liberalisation (Holden 1996: 25). The most promising prospect for exploiting intraregional comparative cost advantages existed between the smaller, developing SADC member states with their natural resources and labour-intensive products on the one hand and the fairly developed and industrialised South Africa with its comparably capital-intensive goods on the other hand (Qualmann 2003: 141–143). According to experts, there was a realistic chance for increasing the share of intraregional trade to up to 20–35 per cent by establishing a SADC-FTA (Chauvin and Gaulier 2002: 12–14).

1.1 Extra- and Intraregional Economic Relations of the SADC Member States

Southern Africa is highly dependent on extra-regional economic relations, whereas the share of formal intraregional trade has always been low—of course in comparison to well-developed regions like the EU or the North American Free Trade Agreement (NAFTA), but also in comparison to ASEAN and MERCOSUR (see Chaps. 5 and 6). During the mid-1990s, intraregional trade in Southern Africa oscillated between only 4 and 7 per cent of the member states' international trade (excluding informal and unrecorded trade).[4] In contrast, about 30 per cent of SADC's total exports were destined for the EU during the mid-1990s, which made Europe the most important trade partner for Southern Africa. More specifically, the EU was also the most important trade partner for 6 of the 12 SADC members in 1995, and the USA constituted an important extra-regional export destination as well (Table 7.1). These figures are not surprising, because they reflect the notoriously asymmetric relationship between former colonial masters in the Global North and their economic dependencies in the Global South (Axline 1977; Hout and Meijerink 1996). The SADC trade network of the year 1995 confirms these facts as it depicts strong and asymmetric ties between about half of SADC member states, including South Africa, and the EU as an extra-regional actor (see Chap. 4).

The dependence of extra-regional actors in respect to export outflows was (and still is) mirrored by a similar dependence on extra-regional investment and development aid inflows (Sidiropoulos 2002; Oosthuizen 2006: 155–159). SADC as a whole was to a significant degree reliant on investment inflows from Europe. But whereas the regional power South Africa received nearly all investments from overseas, most of the other SADC member states were dependent on investment inflows from South Africa (Goldstein 2004: 45; Grobbelaar 2004: 93–95). In respect to development aid, which can also be interpreted as a form of 'investment'

Table 7.1 The three most important export destinations of the SADC member states in 1995

	First	Second	Third
Angola	USA 66 %	EU 17 %	China 4 %
Botswana[a]	No data		
DR Congo[b]	USA 18 %	EU 16 %	South Africa 7 %
Lesotho[a]	No data		
Madagascar[b]	EU 65 %	USA 9 %	Japan 5 %
Malawi	EU 41 %	South Africa 14 %	Japan 12 %
Mauritius	EU 71 %	USA 15 %	Réunion 2 %
Mozambique	EU 36 %	Japan 13 %	South Africa 13 %
Namibia[a]	No data		
Seychelles[b]	EU 45 %	Thailand 32 %	USA 5 %
South Africa	EU 30 %	USA 12 %	Japan 11 %
Swaziland[a]	No data		
Tanzania	EU 36 %	India 14 %	Japan 10 %
Zambia	Japan 20 %	Saudi Arabia 15 %	Thailand 14 %
Zimbabwe	EU 38 %	South Africa 16 %	Japan 11 %

Figures based on the UN Comtrade database (comtrade.un.org).

It is important to keep in mind that trade data on most SADC countries is often to some degree underreported, inconsistent and does not cover informal trade flows. In order to keep consistency with the rest of the book, the author uses the available trade data from the Comtrade database. Trade databases and experts from the SADC region, however, provide slightly different figures that indicate stronger intraregional trade flows—with South Africa as a more important trade partner (Muntschick 2015: 113–115).

[a]Botswana, Lesotho, Namibia, and Swaziland form the Southern African Customs Union (SACU) together with South Africa. According to the Comtrade database, they have not reported trade data independently from South Africa for 1995.

[b]The DR Congo, Madagascar, and the Seychelles were not yet SADC member states in 1995.

(Sachs 2005), SADC has experienced a long tradition of extra-regional dependence as well. Southern Africa got most of its aid from the EU, and the regional organisation SADC financed about 80 per cent of its projects by these financial means during the mid-1990s.[5] The EU's Seventh European Development Fund (EDF), for example, provided a multimillion euro envelope for trade promotion and regional capacity building in SADC for the period from 1990 to 1995.[6]

In the shadow of this pattern of extra-regional economic dependence existed another pattern of asymmetrical intraregional interdependence within Southern Africa. The fairly industrialised South Africa had been the regional economic power since colonial times. The country was the most important trade hub in Southern Africa, and its economy covered about 70 per cent of SADC's total GDP (Oosthuizen 2006: 261). The regional power was among the three most important export destinations of Malawi, Mozambique, and Zimbabwe (see Table 7.1). The South African market was probably even more important for Pretoria's direct neighbours Botswana, Lesotho, Namibia, and Swaziland (the so-called BLNS countries), which constitute the Southern African Customs Union (SACU) together with South Africa. While they did not report any trade data independently from South Africa back in 1995, it is almost certain (and supported by trade data of later years) that South Africa was a very important export destination for the BLNS countries. In contrast, only 10 per cent of South Africa's exports were traded within SADC, and none of the SADC member states was among South Africa's three most important trade partners (see Table 7.1). The regional power traded mainly with extra-regional partners in the EU and the USA. Nevertheless, about 30 per cent of South Africa's exports from the manufacturing sector remained within the region, which highlights the importance of the regional market for these kinds of goods (Qualmann 2003: 29; Draper et al. 2006: 73–81).

The pattern of intraregional investment flows resembled the trade pattern of asymmetric economic interdependence. The majority of the SADC member states had already been dependent on South African investments for decades, and the regional power was the top foreign investor in seven SADC member states between 1994 and 2003. The share of South African FDI has been particularly important for Lesotho (86 per cent), Malawi (80 per cent), Swaziland (71 per cent), the DR Congo (71 per cent), Botswana (58 per cent), Tanzania (35 per cent), Mozambique (31 per cent), and Zambia (29 per cent) during this time period under observation (Grobbelaar 2004: 91–103; Page and te Velde 2004: 22–26). South African FDI is especially valuable for its smaller neighbours, because it is more wide ranging (in terms of investment targets and business sectors) than comparable investments from overseas (Dahl 2002; Tleane 2006).

1.2 Member States' Interest in the SADC-FTA

The prevailing pattern of intraregional economic relations in the SADC region during the mid-1990s was highly asymmetric and resembled a 'hub-and-spoke' (McCarthy 1998: 79) with the regional power South Africa holding the centre position. This corresponds to the picture that has been illustrated earlier by means of trade networks (see Chap. 4). On the one hand, the smaller SADC member states exported a significant amount of primary goods to South Africa, whereas the regional power exported to a large degree manufactured goods to its smaller neighbours. On the other hand, this intraregional interdependence was overshadowed by an overall dependence on extra-regional economic relations. Although South Africa had an interest in a privileged access to the regional market, this was outweighed by an even stronger dependency on access to the European market, to which South Africa exported around three times as much as to the SADC market. The situation in SADC resembled that of MERCOSUR insofar as the smaller member states were dependent on access to the regional powers' market, whereas the latter depended strongly on extra-regional trade relations (see Chap. 6).

Due to the size of its economy and due to the pattern of asymmetric extra- and intraregional economic interdependence, South Africa was (and still is) in a key position in the SADC region. The regional power is expected to play the most decisive role with regard to the emergence and progress of any economic integration project in SADC. However, since South Africa, several other SADC member states and the entire SADC as a whole are dependent on economic relations with the EU as the most important extra-regional actor, regional economic integration is likely to proceed only as long as its extra-regional effects do not play against it (Muntschick 2015: 128). The extra-regional economic interests of South Africa in particular are a likely constraint for regional cooperation within SADC (see Chap. 2).

A free trade area like the SADC-FTA is not mutually exclusive with divergent extra-regional economic interests of the member states. Establishing a free trade area does not require an agreement on common tariffs against external actors, and the member states are still able to set up different trade regimes for the outside world (Viner 1950). Thus, although positive extra-regional effects of regional integration have been one motive for setting up the SADC-FTA, the negotiations between the member states focussed very much on the intraregional dimension of regional integration. Hereby, the member states had different interests in respect to the time schedule of liberalisation, to the different goods for which trade should be liberalised and to special agreements on sensitive products. The less-developed member states wanted to protect their domestic markets for as long as possible against the imports of manufactured goods from South Africa in order not to endanger their own small industries (Erasmus et al. 2006: 7). In contrast, the regional power South

Africa aimed for a quick and wide-ranging trade liberalisation in order to get a stable regional market particularly for products from its manufacturing industry, which were not competitive on a global scale (Flatters 2004: 55; Brenton et al. 2005: 15–27).

Within the SADC-FTA, the instrument to protect the regional markets against imports from extra-regional competitors are the rules of origin. If all trade within SADC was liberalised, extra-regional exporters could take advantage of the different customs rules of the member states. Extra-regional exporters would ship their goods in the member state with the lowest trade barriers and thereafter distribute them on the whole Southern African market. The result would be a de facto harmonisation of the member states' external trade regimes at the lowest level of protection. To prevent this, rules of origin prescribe which goods count as domestically or regionally produced goods that can be traded freely on the SADC market (Erasmus et al. 2006). This is a relatively simple task for agricultural products and raw materials, which are entirely produced within one of the SADC member states. The task is much more difficult in respect to manufactured goods, which are imported from extra-regional sources or which are processed to some degree out of imports from extra-regional sources. Here, especially the regional power South Africa had an interest in restrictive rules of origin in order to protect its manufacturing industry against the inflow of cheaper manufactured goods from extra-regional countries like China (Brenton et al. 2005: 27; Draper et al. 2006: 78–82).

1.3 Regional Trade Negotiations, the Protocol on Trade, and the SADC-FTA

The Protocol on Trade provides the legal foundation for the SADC-FTA. According to the World Trade Organization's (WTO) standards, at least 85 per cent of the member states' intraregional trade had to be liberalised from any customs duties in order to constitute a free trade area.[7] A preliminary version of the protocol was signed in 1996, but it took another 4 years and 19 rounds of negotiations until the final version was passed, ratified, and entered into force in August 2000 (Lee 2003: 112). The Protocol on Trade obliged the SADC member states (excluding Angola and the DR Congo) to phase out existing tariffs and to establish the SADC-FTA within eight years after its ratification. The Protocol's general content mirrors the member states' ambition of open regionalism. It contains visionary statements and rather non-specific provisions that aim for regional block building in order to achieve extra-regional economic gains on the global market.[8]

In contrast to the very general statements on the extra-regional effects of the SADC-FTA, the more detailed rules of the Protocol on Trade reflect conflicting intraregional preferences of the member states in respect to the obligation, pace, and scope of trade liberalisation. Here, South Africa dominated the negotiations with its particular interests. The regional power set the agenda of the negotiations, pushed the other member states to agree on disputed topics, and insisted on setting up binding rules and provisions. This dominance reflected South Africa's position in the region and the readiness of the economically weaker SADC member states to accept the regional power's economic agenda (Flatters 2001; Vogt 2007: 199). However, South Africa also provided constructive regional leadership and granted the least developed SADC member states a time-related advantage to implement the tariff reduction schedule. This concession to the least developed member states allowed for a prolonged protection of their markets against competition with South Africa's merchandise exports (Lee 2003: 116–119; Erasmus et al. 2006: 7).

The agreed tariff reduction schedule consisted of a linear approach to tariff reduction in combination with an asymmetrical strategy in respect to the different member states. Firstly, products were divided into four categories (A, B, C, and E), of which A was subject to immediate and B to gradual liberalisation. Category C concerned 'sensitive products' (with liberalisation set for more than eight years after the Protocol coming into force) and category E was an exclusion list.[9] And secondly, the negotiators agreed to group the member states that signed the protocol into three categories. Category I comprised relatively well-developed countries like South Africa and the BLNS countries, category II included developing countries like Mauritius and Zimbabwe, and category III consisted of least developed countries (LDCs) like Malawi, Mozambique, and Zambia. This compromise acknowledged the differences in economic strength and development between the SADC member states. It prescribed that SACU countries (with comparably stronger economies) would reduce tariffs within eight years (front-loading) and countries of categories II and III would respectively start their liberalisation processes within four to eight years (mid-loading) and six to eight years (back-loading) after the Protocol came into force.[10]

The negotiated rules of origin reflected as well the conflicting economic preferences of the SADC member states. Nearly all member states aimed to protect their sensitive industries against imports from extra-regional sources, and thus, they pushed for exceptions to free trade and for restrictive rules of origin in their individually affected sectors. Especially the regional power South Africa (and in fact SACU as a whole) demanded particularly restrictive rules of origin in order to protect its regionally export-oriented manufacturing industry from the inflow of competing products (e.g. from China) via non-SACU SADC members (Brenton et al. 2005: 27). Products and components of the vehicle and motor industry became subject to rules of origin; restrictive rules of origin were imposed on primary goods like coffee, tea, spices, tobacco, and several products of the milling industry[11]; and the most restrictive rules of origin were in the textile and garments sector (Flatters 2004: 55; Hentz 2005). In general, the rules of origin were particularly strict in those sectors where South Africa perceived the most competition at the time of negotiation. The same applied for sensitive sectors (especially sugar and textiles), for which the SADC member states agreed in two supplements to pro-South African provisions (Erasmus et al. 2006). In sum, the design of the rules of origin—a vital part of the Protocol on Trade and the SADC-FTA—reflect most of all the interests of the regional power South Africa (Brenton et al. 2005; Hentz 2005).

The dependence of Southern Africa on extra-regional economic relations with the EU had no negative impact on the formation of the SADC-FTA, because the member states' external trade regimes did not need to be harmonised (Viner 1950; Muntschick 2015: 171–172). On the contrary, the EU and some of its member states supported regional market integration in SADC, and have provided inter alia 490 million euro for regional development in Southern Africa through the European Development Funds (EDFs) since 1976. Besides, the EU improved the interregional dialogue with SADC by means of the Berlin Declaration in 1994 (Mills 2002).[12] It was especially regional integration and trade liberalisation that were a focal point of development assistance (Jakobeit et al. 2005: 30). Thus, the impact of extra-regional actors was supportive of rather than indifferent or destructive to the establishment of the SADC-FTA.

1.4   *The Moderate Effects of the SADC-FTA*

The SADC-FTA came into force in August 2008 after the member states had implemented the provisions of the Protocol on Trade and liberalised 85 per cent of all intraregional trade. In general, the effects of the

SADC-FTA on intraregional trade have not been spectacular, but visible. The amount of intraregional exports of most member states has grown, and SADC's share of intraregional trade increased from 6.8 per cent in 1996 to 15.7 per cent in 2012.[13] This indicates that existing comparative cost advantages within the region are increasingly being exploited. Of particular importance is the fact that South Africa is increasingly sourcing imports from the region. The intraregional imports of the regional power quintupled in absolute terms since 1999 and are of significant importance for the economically weaker regional neighbours (Muntschick 2015: 144–145). Besides these effects, there is consensus that the impact of the SADC-FTA on intraregional trade shares would have been more significant if the Zimbabwean economy had not collapsed during the last 20 years under the rule of President Mugabe (Kurz et al. 2008).[14]

The establishment of a larger and more stable regional market in Southern Africa seemed also to have a positive effect on the inflow of extra-regional investments. Surveys indicate that market size is the major motivation for investors to locate their assets and investments in Southern Africa (Jenkins and Thomas 2002: 28). Other studies found a significant positive correlation between the growth of SADC's trade and an increase of investment inflows (Bezuidenhout and Naudé 2008). Altogether, data on FDI inflows to SADC member states shows an increase from US$4 billion in 1998 to more than US$10 billion in 2009 during the time of the implementation of the Protocol on Trade (Muntschick 2015: 147).

In sum, the regional power South Africa most prominently demanded, designed, and benefitted—and actually still benefits –from regional economic integration and the establishment of the SADC-FTA. The extra-regional interests of the SADC member states did not interfere with regional cooperation, because the establishment of a free trade area did not require the harmonisation of external trade regimes. On the contrary, the EU fuelled regional economic integration in SADC with contributions from its EDF, which supported a regional agreement by slightly lowering the administrative and implementation costs for the member states and SADC itself.

2 THE SADC CUSTOMS UNION AND THE ECONOMIC PARTNERSHIP AGREEMENTS

After the SADC-FTA was successfully established in 2008, the SADC-CU should have been the next step towards deeper regional economic integration.[15] The RISDP referred to this project in its chapter on economic integration and stipulated that the customs union should be achieved by the year 2010.[16] Further steps of regional integration included a common market in 2015, an economic union in 2016, and a monetary union in 2018. A number of state leaders, SADC officials, and governmental documents repeatedly expressed the need for a regional customs union in order to simplify intraregional trade and offer extra-regional investors a larger and more stable regional market for doing business. Especially the SADC secretariat advocated market integration as part of an outward-oriented, open regionalism in order to enhance regional development.[17]

The EU often claims to support regional integration in developing regions, but the recent negotiations about Economic Partnership Agreements (EPAs) between African states and the EU split SADC into different negotiation groupings and prevented the establishment of the SADC-CU. Brussels was and still is a key player for regional integration in Southern Africa, because the EU is the most important extra-regional trade partner, investor and aid donor if one looks at SADC as a whole. Previously, the EU had generally supported regional integration in developing regions, because Europe had always been keen to spread its own model of prosperity through regionalism (Farell 2007; Börzel and Risse 2009). In keeping with this, the tenth EDF programme provided 116 million euro for Southern Africa of which 85 million euro were explicitly dedicated to regional economic integration.[18] This support raised incentives for the SADC member states to engage in further regional integration, because it reduced the administrative costs of implementation. However, whereas the EU's development policy supported regional integration in Southern Africa, the EU's external trade policy proved to be a serious obstacle for deeper integration. The EPA negotiations split the SADC member states in different groups with different external trade regimes towards the EU. As a result, the SADC member states were unable to harmonise their external trade policies in order to establish the SADC-CU (Muntschick 2013a).

2.1 The Ongoing Dominance of Extra-Regional Economic Dependence

The economic structure of SADC changed only slightly between the 1990s, when the SADC-FTA was negotiated, and the late 2000s, when the SADC-CU should have been set up. The SADC trade network remained dominated by the regional power South Africa and the EU as extra-regional actor (see Chap. 4). Thus, South Africa was still the key actor for regional integration in Southern Africa, and it remained likely that the regional power's behaviour was constrained by its extra-regional interests towards the European market. Within this picture of continuity, one can observe only two minor variations in SADC's trade network between the 1990s and the 2000s. One small change occurred in SADC's intraregional economic interdependence, and the other concerns SADC's most important extra-regional trade partners.

The establishment of the SADC-FTA has led to a moderate increase in intraregional trade, and this trade was still concentrated on South Africa. During the period when the SADC-FTA was negotiated and implemented, intraregional trade in SADC increased—from 6.8 per cent in 1996 to 15.7 per cent in 2012.[19] It is estimated that informal trade flows (especially agricultural products and electronic devices) added a significant amount of intraregional trade to the formal trade figures reported within the region (Sandrey 2012). South Africa remained the most important market within the region and was among the three most important trade partners of three SADC member states (Malawi, Mozambique, and Zimbabwe) in 2008 (see Table 7.2). The rest of intraregional trade took place mainly between pairs of directly neighbouring countries like Malawi and Mozambique. Thus, despite the moderate growth of intraregional trade, the structure of the intraregional network has changed only marginally.

In respect to extra-regional trade, the rise of China during the 2000s increased the importance of the Chinese market for Southern Africa's exports, but not so much as to significantly reduce Southern Africa's dependence on the European market. Whereas China was only a significant export destination for Angola in 1995, it became the most important export market for Angola and the DR Congo, as well as an important market for Madagascar, South Africa, and Zimbabwe in 2008. China improved its standing within Southern Africa mainly at the cost of Japan, but not at the cost of the EU (Hess 2010). Thus, the increasing exports from Southern Africa to China did not really endanger the dominance

Table 7.2 The three most important export destinations of the SADC member states in 2008

	First	Second	Third
Angola	China 34 %	USA 30 %	EU 17 %
Botswana	Norway 26 %	EU 25 %	Zimbabwe 9 %
DR Congo	China 42 %	EU 30 %	Zambia 14 %
Lesotho	USA 58 %	EU 37 %	Madagascar 1 %
Madagascar	EU 56 %	USA 25 %	China 5 %
Malawi	EU 37 %	South Africa 15 %	USA 9 %
Mauritius	EU 70 %	USA 8 %	Madagascar 4 %
Mozambique	EU 50 %	Malawi 15 %	South Africa 14 %
Namibia	EU 36 %	Angola 21 %	USA 15 %
Seychelles	EU 63 %	Japan 8 %	Mauritius 5 %
South Africa	EU 32 %	USA 10 %	China 9 %
Swaziland	EU 20 %	USA 13 %	Kuwait 8 %
Tanzania	EU 27 %	India 11 %	Japan 7 %
Zambia	EU 17 %	Saudi Arabia 16 %	Egypt 16 %
Zimbabwe	South Africa 34 %	EU 22 %	China 7 %

Figures based on the UN Comtrade database (comtrade.un.org). See the comment on trade data in Table 7.1 as well.

of the EU, which remained the most important export market for most SADC member states, for the regional power South Africa, and for the region as a whole.

To conclude, SADC's economic structure still followed the 'hub-And-Spoke' pattern (McCarthy 1998: 79), with South Africa as the most important intraregional market and the EU as the most important extra-regional market. The economically weaker SADC member states still had an interest in gaining access to the South African market, whereas the regional power continued to trade a large share of the products from its manufacturing industry within the SADC region. However, this intraregional economic interdependence was overshadowed by the region's overall dependence on extra-regional export markets—most notably on the European and increasingly on the Chinese markets. Intraregional trade within SADC was already liberalised to some degree by the SADC-FTA, whereas a SADC-CU with a common external trade regime would have had a much stronger impact on the member states' extra-regional economic relations.

2.2 Conflicting Extra-Regional Interests

In contrast to the SADC-FTA, the SADC-CU would have required the harmonisation of the external trade regimes of the member states towards extra-regional trade partners like the EU. This would have meant that all SADC member states would have had to agree on a common external trade regime first, and thereafter have presented one single offer to external partners when entering trade negotiations. Such a unified approach could have improved SADC's bargaining position in relation to extra-regional trade partners by utilising the size and stability effects of regional integration. However, the external trade regimes of the SADC member states differed significantly and the formulation of a common position in interregional trade negotiations seemed unlikely (Jakobeit et al. 2005: 20–25; Bilal and Stevens 2009).

Although most SADC member states were dependent on extra-regional trade with the EU, the actual composition of their exports revealed a distinct degree of specialisation. While natural resources from the primary sector generally dominated SADC's extra-regional exports to the EU, several SADC member states had different export baskets; there were countries specialising in crude oil (Angola), fish and beef (Namibia and Botswana), sugar (Swaziland), aluminium and copper products (Mozambique and Zambia), precious stones and metals (Botswana, Lesotho and Namibia), machines, manufactures, and industrial products (South Africa) and other light manufactures, consumer goods, and foodstuffs (Lesotho, Malawi, Zimbabwe, and South Africa) during the 2000s (Muntschick 2015: 167).[20] Consequently, the character of the member states' dependence on the European market was not exactly uniform because different countries regarded different arrays of products and commodities as crucial in respect to their exports to the EU. It was therefore very difficult to agree upon a unified SADC bargaining position, because the member states often favoured free access to the European market for certain various product categories, whereas they were keen to protect different national industries with exception clauses at the same time.

After the year 2000, the EU and the SADC member states had to reorganise their trade relations, because the previous Lomé Convention, which granted the African, Caribbean, and Pacific (ACP) countries privileged and non-reciprocal access to the European market, was judged to violate WTO-Law. The new Cotonou Agreement[21] redefined the trade relationship between the ACP countries and the EU, and demanded preferential market access on the basis of reciprocity. In order to cushion the possibly negative effects of trade liberalisation for the weaker partners, it allowed the negotiation of EPAs as accompanying frameworks (Keck and Piermartini 2008: 86). Most SADC member states were affected by this realignment of North–South trade (Bilal and Stevens 2009), and they had to sign an EPA in order to safeguard their privileged access to the European market. If the Southern African countries and the EU could not have agreed on EPAs, the EU market would have been closed for the reluctant states insofar as they would have faced high protective tariffs and serious barriers to their most important export destination (Stevens and Kennan 2006: 75–77; Oosthuizen 2007: 156–158). Only the LDCs[22] of Southern Africa would still have had privileged access to the European market under the everything-but-arms (EBA)[23] initiative if the EPA negotiations had failed.

The regional power South Africa did not necessarily need an EPA, because it already enjoyed privileged trade relations with the EU due to the Trade, Development and Cooperation Agreement (TDCA) of 1999. This particular North–South trade regime had been concluded in the aftermath of apartheid at the turn of the millennium, and provided South Africa with privileged access to the European market. The TDCA contains very advantageous provisions and even unilateral benefits for South Africa that resulted from the supportive attitude of Europe towards South Africa under President Nelson Mandela at a time shortly after the peaceful transformation from the apartheid regime to democratic rule (Olympio et al. 2006). Thus, the TDCA constituted a privileged position for SADC's regional power, because only South Africa was receiving stable access to its most important extra-regional export destination. This privilege may have been a major obstacle to the planned SADC-CU, because it predetermined South Africa's external trade regime towards the EU without taking care of other member states' extra-regional trade interests (Krapohl et al. 2014: 890).

The privileged position of the regional power South Africa towards its most important trade partner, the EU, brought the risk of a Rambo constellation within SADC. Regional economic integration in form of the SADC-CU could have only proceeded if this had not put the extra-regional privileges of South Africa into question (see Chap. 2). While the regional power had officially advocated the formation of the SADC-CU, it had no interest in compromising its TDCA for the sake of a common SADC position towards the EU. Instead of providing regional leadership as it had during the setup of the SADC-FTA, South Africa may have been tempted to protect its own extra-regional economic privileges during the negotiations towards the SADC-CU.

2.3 The Division into Different EPA Groups

The need to reorganise their extra-regional trade relations with the EU put considerable pressure on the SADC member states, which were afraid of losing access to the European market. Due to SADC's dependence on the European export market, the EU was in a dominant position and able to determine the 'rules of the game' and to follow a 'carrot-and-stick' strategy (Muntschick 2013b). The EU insistently demanded from the SADC member states that reciprocal trade liberalisation be implemented as soon as possible, and that at least provisional Interim EPAs be signed and implemented by 1 January 2014 (Stevens and Kennan 2006: 75–77; Bilal and Stevens 2009). The EPAs were not explicitly linked to particular existing regional organisations so that the member states of SADC could be split in different negotiation groups. However, the EU did not only put the SADC member states under pressure, but it also provided positive incentives for signing EPAs. Development aid and Aid-for-Trade policies[24] enhanced the attractiveness of the EPAs by reducing the implementation costs for the SADC member states.[25]

The SADC member states did not negotiate as one group for EPAs with the EU, but instead split into four different groupings in order to pursue and protect different extra-regional trade interests. The character of the SADC member states' extra-regional economic relations with the EU differed due to their varying export baskets. Consequently, several SADC countries had different interests with regard to the design and specific contents of a trade regime with Europe (Meyn 2010). SADC as a regional organisation was not in a position to compel its member states to stick to the RISPD and refrain from signing different EPAs. Membership in the regional organisation did not mean that the member states had given up their sovereignty to negotiate trade agreements with third parties. Therefore, neither SADC nor its secretariat had the power to command its members to negotiate as one group with the EU (Tjønneland 2005; Oosthuizen 2006: 201). This situation in SADC was not conducive to establishing a customs union and a unified EPA negotiation group. SADC became disunited and its member states split into the following four EPA groups, which all aimed to negotiate different and separate trade agreements with the EU (Muntschick 2015: 177):

- SADC-EPA group: Angola, Botswana, Lesotho, Mozambique, Namibia, Swaziland, South Africa
- ESA-EPA group (Eastern and Southern Africa): Madagascar, Malawi, Mauritius, the Seychelles, Zambia, Zimbabwe
- EAC-EPA group (East African Community): Tanzania
- CEMAC-EPA group (Economic and Monetary Community of Central Africa): DR Congo

Actually, Angola, the DR Congo, Lesotho, Madagascar, Malawi, Mozambique, Tanzania, and Zambia did not need to join any EPA group, because they are LDCs and enjoyed access to the European market under the EBA initiative. However, they all decided to participate in EPA negotiations in order to avoid being sidestepped by their regional neighbours and so as to be able to articulate their interests in these important interregional negotiations with the EU.

The EU's strategy of negotiating mutual trade liberalisation with developing countries by using the instrument of EPAs has been strongly criticised and met with resistance in several countries in Southern Africa. The negotiations were very cumbersome and often delayed (Holland and Doidge 2012: 87). As of the year 2015, the EU has not been able to sign a final agreement with any group of Southern African states, and instead only several Interim EPAs have been adopted. These Interim EPAs guarantee continued preferential access to the European market, but they are only provisional.

From the SADC-EPA group, only Botswana, Lesotho, Mozambique, and Swaziland have signed an Interim EPA (Walker 2009). Namibia rejected the EU's latest offer and privileged regional trade relations with SADC and COMESA over that with the EU—despite the fact that the EU is Windhoek's most important trade partner and receives 36 per cent of Namibian exports (see Table 7.2). The deputy minister of finance of Namibia stated that 'it will be better to utilise these opportunities [SADC and COMESA] than to lock ourselves into a bad EPA that prevents us from utilising these markets'.[26] He argued that SADC member states like Angola, the DRC, and South Africa offered growing market opportunities for Namibia's beef exports, and emphasised that the country was about to diversify its fruit exports to trading destinations beyond the EU as well. South Africa initially had only an observer status during the EPA negotiations because it enjoyed privileged access to the European market under the TDCA,[27] but the regional power finally joined the SADC-EPA group in

2007. Nevertheless, South Africa refrained from signing the Interim EPA because the TDCA was an attractive fallback option. As members of the ESA-EPA group, Madagascar, Mauritius, the Seychelles, and Zimbabwe had already signed an Interim EPA in August 2009 that was different to the one that was signed by the SADC-EPA group.[28] Tanzania signed yet another Interim EPA as member of the EAC-EPA group in 2007.[29]

South Africa was not solely responsible for the split of SADC member states into different EPA groups. Although the regional power still enjoyed its extra-regional privileges under the TDCA, it was several other SADC countries that decided to participate in different negotiation groups. In fact, all SADC member states outside the SADC-EPA group acted as regional Rambos (Muntschick 2012: 14), privileging their particular extra-regional interests at the cost of regional cooperation. Nevertheless, the regional power South Africa did not provide the regional leadership that would have been necessary to keep the region together as one block within the EPA negotiations. As a benevolent regional hegemon (Mattli 1999), South Africa would have needed to take the lead during the negotiations and to compensate the smaller member states for possible losses. It appeared only very recently that at least the SADC-EPA group is unifying around the regional power. In 2010, the process of ratifying the Interim EPA had been stalled by Botswana, Lesotho, and Swaziland.[30] It was forseeable at that time that the intended EPA of the SADC-EPA group had to be harmonised with the TDCA's trade chapter due to pressure from the SACU member states (Muntschick 2013b: 706). Following this, the SADC-EPA group and the EU signed a full EPA in June 2016. But this new unity is only among the SACU member states plus Mozambique (Angola may join the EPA later), and not among those SADC member states that participate in other EPA groups. Thus, SADC remains split in respect to its extra-regional trade relations with the EU.

2.4 Widening Instead of Deepening Regional Integration

The signing of the Interim EPAs was a clear step on the road towards an irreversible institutionalisation of North–South trade liberalisation between the EU and several groups of SADC member states instead of one single grouping of SADC as a whole. This prevented the establishment of the SADC-CU in 2010, and it will most certainly also prevent a customs union among all 15 SADC member states in the future. If full EPAs were implemented, SADC would consist of at least three groups of member states with varying trade regimes towards the region's most important trade partner, the EU. This scenario is likely to materialise because the EU does not seem to be changing its negotiating strategy and is keeping the opportunity open for different EPA groups for the SADC member states (Stevens and Kennan 2006: 76–77; Bilal and Stevens 2009). Under these circumstances, a SADC-CU could only be formed among the members of the SADC-EPA group and would then look like an extended SACU; it would very likely exclude the other SADC member states, which participate in other EPA groups.

The different external trade regimes towards the EU are not in direct conflict with the SADC-FTA, but they are a problem for the SADC-CU. As long as SADC does not stick to its plan to establish a customs union, the situation is perhaps awkward, but will not jeopardise the region's integrity. The SADC-FTA is compatible with different external trade regimes, as proved by the examples of the TDCA and the partial overlap of the SADC-FTA with the COMESA-FTA (Olivier 2006: 62–83). However, according to the RISDP, SADC regards deeper regional integration towards a customs union, a common market, an economic union, and a monetary union as a cornerstone to socio-economic development. Deeper regional integration is not possible if the member states cannot even agree on the SADC-CU. This leads to a conflict between SADC's self-conception as a dynamically integrating region on the one hand and the reality of interfering extra-regional trade regimes on the other hand.

Instead of deepening regional economic integration within SADC, the member states of several regional organisations in Africa started to engage in widening integration by planning a Tripartite Free Trade Area (TFTA). Regionalism in Africa is distinguished by a fragmentation into different regional organisations which often partly overlap in terms of territory and member states. This means that some countries have double memberships (Braude 2008). Three of these partly overlapping regional organisations are COMESA, EAC, and SADC. Already in 2008, the member states of these three organisations had decided to establish a free trade area among themselves. The respective negotiations started in 2011, and the so-called TFTA should be established by 2018. The TFTA is a very ambitious project as it would fulfil an old dream of free trade from 'Cape to Cairo' (Kalenga 2011). It cannot yet be assessed whether the TFTA will really be set in place on time and whether it will be effective, or whether it will only add another layer to Africa's spaghetti bowl of preferential trade agreements. What can be assessed, however, is the fact that this widening of rather superficial regional cooperation replaces the much more ambitious plans of deeper economic integration in SADC.

3 Conclusion

The Southern African countries were able to establish the SADC-FTA in 2008 because free trade areas do not require harmonising the external trade regimes of the member states. Although regional integration in Southern Africa in general and the establishment of the SADC-FTA in particular happened to some degree in order to improve the region's position on the global market, the negotiations for the SADC-FTA were strongly influenced by the different intraregional interests of the member states. Thus, Hypothesis 1 (see Chap. 2) is only partly supported. The extra-regional economic effects of regional integration are not the only purpose of the SADC-FTA. The positive effects on intraregional trade and investment also motivated the SADC member states, including the regional power South Africa, to cooperate with each other and to establish a free trade area. It is difficult to weigh the relative importance of the extra-regional and intraregional gains from regional integration against each other, but the least one can say is that the intraregional effects are not negligible. The negotiations for and the design of the SADC-FTA were clearly dominated by the interests of South Africa. The regional power had an interest in the regional exportation of its manufacturing products, which face difficulties in competition on the global market. At the same time, it wanted to protect its manufacturing industry against extra-regional competition. The result was that South Africa provided some regional leadership by granting generous transition periods for the smaller member states, but it also insisted on very protective rules of origin within the SADC-FTA. The EU as the most important extra-regional actor in Southern Africa did not interfere with the setup of the SADC-FTA because the external trade regimes of the member states were not at stake. On the contrary, the EU supported regional integration with development aid from the EDF.

In contrast, the SADC member states could not agree to harmonise their external trade regimes towards the EU, and this prevented the establishment of the SADC-CU in 2010. Although the economic preconditions for regional integration were very similar to those in the case of the SADC-FTA, the case of the SADC-CU developed fundamentally differently because customs unions require a common trade regime to the outside world. Because the SADC member states had different interests in their trade relations with the EU, they could not form a single SADC group in the EPA negotiations, but rather split into four different groups, and the regional power South Africa relied on its privileged position under the bilateral TDCA for quite some time. South Africa acted as a regional Rambo and did not provide the necessary regional leadership for establishing a single SADC-EPA group and the SADC-CU—but also, in fact, most of the other member states likewise followed their own extra-regional interests at the cost of regional integration (Muntschick 2012). Hypothesis 2 (see Chap. 2) is generally supported by the case of the SADC-CU: When important extra-regional interests were at stake, the regional power (and also the other member states) defected from regional cooperation. Due to the impact of the EPA negotiations and South Africa's interest in preserving its special extra-regional trading conditions under the TDCA, the creation of a customs union comprising all 15 SADC member states has become highly unlikely for the near future.

Like in MERCOSUR, the intraregional gains of regional integration were certainly one motive for member states' cooperation in SADC, but this cooperation always remained constrained by the extra-regional interests of several member states. Developing regions in general, and Southern Africa as one of the least developed regions in particular, are still highly dependent on trade with their traditional partners in Europe. Even if regional economies profit from comparative cost advantages and economies of scale through intraregional trade and investment, the regional member states still give priority to their extra-regional interests as soon as these are in conflict with regional cooperation. This has been very well illustrated by the two cases of the SADC-FTA and the SADC-CU. The SADC-FTA produced intraregional (and extra-regional) economic gains and did not conflict with the member states' extra-regional interests. Regional cooperation under the lead of the regional power South Africa was therefore possible. In contrast, the SADC-CU may also have brought such economic benefits, but it was not compatible with the member states' extra-regional interests during the EPA negotiations. The regional power South Africa in particular protected its extra-regional interests and relied on the bilateral TDCA instead of providing regional leadership in order to form an all-encompassing SADC-EPA group.

NOTES

1. These are Angola, Botswana, the Democratic Republic of the Congo (DRC), Lesotho, Madagascar, Malawi, Mauritius, Mozambique, Namibia, the Seychelles, South Africa, Swaziland, Tanzania, Zambia, and Zimbabwe.
2. SADC (2008): 'SADC Free Trade Area Handbook: Growth, Development and Wealth Creation' (Gaborone), 2.
3. SADC (2004): 'Regional Indicative Strategic Development Plan' (www.sadc.int/files/5713/5292/8372/Regional_Indicative_Strategic_Development_Plan.pdf).
4. These numbers are taken from RIKS, an internet database published by the United Nations University Institute on Comparative Regional Integration Studies (www.cris.unu.edu/riks/web).
5. SADC (1996): 'Annual Report: June 1995–July 1996' (Gaborone).
6. SADC-European Community (2002): 'Regional Strategy Paper and Regional Indicative Development Programme: For the Period 2002–2007' (Gaborone).
7. SADC (2008): 'SADC Free Trade Area Handbook: Growth, Development and Wealth Creation' (Gaborone), 5.
8. SADC (2000): 'Protocol on Trade' (www.sadc.int/files/4613/5292/8370/Protocol_on_Trade1996.pdf).
9. The exclusion list contains goods like firearms and ammunition, which are rather irrelevant for intraregional trade.
10. SADC (2008): 'SADC Free Trade Area Handbook: Growth, Development and Wealth Creation' (Gaborone), 7–8.
11. SADC (2000): 'Protocol on Trade: Appendix I to Annex I' (www.mcci.org/media/1285/sadc_protocol_annex_i.pdf).
12. Declaration of the EU-Southern African Ministerial Conference of 5th and 6th September 1994 in Berlin (www.dfa.gov.za/foreign/Multilateral/africa/sadcberlin.htm).
13. These numbers are taken from the database of the Regional Integration Knowledge System (RIKS) of the United Nations University Institute on Comparative Regional Integration Studies (UNU-CRIS), (www.cris.unu.edu/riks/web/data) and the International Trade Centre Database (www.trademap.org).
14. Interview with a Senior Regional Trade Integration Programme Manager at the SADC Headquarters (15 September 2011).
15. The SADC-CU should not be confused with the Southern African Customs Union (SACU). The SACU has existed since 1910 and today comprises Botswana, Lesotho, Namibia, South Africa, and Swaziland.

16. SADC (2004): 'Regional Indicative Strategic Development Plan' (www.sadc.int/files/5713/5292/8372/Regional_Indicative_Strategic_Development_Plan.pdf).
17. SADC (2006): 'Sub-Theme on Trade, Economic Liberalization and Development: Prepared for the SADC Consultative Conference Windhoek, Namibia, April 26–27, 2006' (Gaborone).
18. European Community—Southern African Region (2008): 'Regional Strategy Paper and Regional Indicative Programme 2008–2013' (aei.pitt.edu/45273/1/South_africa_2008_1.pdf).
19. These numbers are taken from the database of the Regional Integration Knowledge System (RIKS) of the United Nations University Institute on Comparative Regional Integration Studies (UNU-CRIS), (www.cris.unu.edu/riks/web/data) and the International Trade Centre Database (www.trademap.org).
20. Data on commodity flows and export baskets obtained from the UN Comtrade database (comtrade.un.org).
21. European Community (2000): 'Partnership agreement between the members of the African, Caribbean and Pacific Group of States of the one part, and the European Community and its Member States of the other part, signed in Cotonou on 23 June 2000' (eur-lex.europa.eu/LexUriServ/LexUriServ.do?uri=CELEX:22000A1215%2801 %29:EN:NOT).
22. The LDCs of SADC are: Angola, DR Congo, Lesotho, Madagascar, Malawi, Mozambique, Tanzania, and Zambia.
23. European Union (2005): 'Council Regulation (EC) No. 980/2005 of 27 June 2005 applying a scheme of generalised tariff preferences' (everything-but-arms initiative). (eur-lex.europa.eu/LexUriServ/LexUriServ.do?uri=OJ:L:2005:169:0001:0043:EN:PDF).
24. Council of the EU (2007): 'Conclusions of the Council and of the Representatives of the Governments of the Member States meeting within the Council: EU Strategy on Aid for Trade: Enhancing EU support for trade-related needs in developing countries' (trade.ec.europa.eu/doclib/docs/2008/November/tradoc_141470.pdf).
25. EU-ACP (2010): 'Second Revision of the Cotonou Agreement—Agreed Consolidated Text' (http://eeas.europa.eu/delegations/burkina_faso/documents/eu_burkina_faso/second_rev_cotonou_agreement_20100311_en.pdf).
26. Interview with Calle Schlettwein (deputy minister of finance of Namibia) in: Namibia Economist, October 2011.
27. European Commission (2011): 'Fact Sheet on the Economic Partnership Agreements: SADC EPA Group, November 2011' (http://trade.ec.europa.eu/doclib/docs/2009/January/tradoc_142189.pdf).

28. European Commission (2012): 'Fact Sheet on the Economic Partnership Agreements: Eastern and Southern Africa (ESA)' (trade.ec.europa.eu/doclib/docs/2012/march/tradoc_149213.pdf).
29. European Commission (2012): 'Fact Sheet on the Economic Partnership Agreements: The Eastern African Community (EAC)' (http://trade.ec.europa.eu/doclib/docs/2009/January/tradoc_142194.pdf).
30. European Commission (2011): 'Fact Sheet on the Economic Partnership Agreements. SADC EPA Group, November 2011' (http://trade.ec.europa.eu/doclib/docs/2009/January/tradoc_142189.pdf).

REFERENCES

Adelmann, M. (2012). *SADC—An Actor in International Relations? The External Relations of the Southern African Development Community*. Freiburg: University of Freiburg.
Alden, C., & Schoeman, M. (2013). South Africa's Search for Leadership in a Transforming Global Order. *International Affairs, 89*, 110–129.
Axline, W. A. (1977). Underdevelopment, Dependence, and Integration: The Politics of Regionalism in the Third World. *International Organization, 31*, 83–105.
Bezuidenhout, H., & Naudé, W. (2008). *Foreign Direct Investment and Trade in the Southern African Development Community*. Helsinki: UNU-WIDER.
Bilal, S., & Stevens, C. (2009). *The Interim Economic Partnership Agreements between the EU and African States. Contents, Challenges and Prospects*. Maastricht: ECDPM.
Börzel, T., & Risse, T. (2009). *Diffusing (Inter-)Regionalism. The EU as a Model of Regional Integration* (KFG Working Paper 7). Berlin: Freie Universität Berlin.
Braude, W. (2008). *SADC, COMESA and the EAC: Conflicting Regional and Trade Agendas*. Johannesburg: Institute for Global Dialogue.
Brenton, P., Flatters, F., & Kalenga, P. (2005). *Rules of Origin and SADC: The Case for Change in the Mid Term Review of the Trade Protocol* (Africa Region Working Paper Series).
Chauvin, S., & Gaulier, G. (2002). Prospects for Increasing Trade Among SADC Countries. In D. Hansohm, C. Peters-Berries, W. Breytenbach, et al. (Eds.), *Monitoring Regional Integration in Southern Africa Yearbook* (pp. 21–42). Windhoek: NEPRU.
Cleary, S. (1999). Regional Integration and the Southern African Development Community. *Journal of Public and International Affairs, 10*, 1–15.
Dahl, J. (2002). Regional Integration and Foreign Direct Investment: The Case of SADC. In D. Hansohm, C. Peters-Berries, W. Breytenbach, T. Hartzenberg,

W. Maier, & P. Meyns (Eds.), *Monitoring Regional Integration in Southern Africa Yearbook* (pp. 59–82). Windhoek: NEPRU.

Draper, P., Alves, P., & Kalaba, M. (2006). *South Africa's International Trade Diplomacy: Implications for Regional Integration*. Gaborone: Friedrich Ebert Foundation.

Erasmus, H., Flatters, F., & Kirk, R. (2006). Rules of Origin as Tools for Development? Some Lessons from SADC. In O. Cadot, A. Estevadeordal, A. Suwa-Eisenmann, & T. Verdier (Eds.), *The Origin of Goods. Rules of Origin in Regional Trade Agreements* (pp. 259–294). Oxford: Oxford University Press.

Farell, M. (2007). From EU Model to External Policy? Promoting Regional Integration in the Rest of the World. In S. Meunier & K. R. McNamara (Eds.), *Making History: European Integration and Institutional Change at Fifty* (pp. 299–315). Oxford: Oxford University Press.

Flatters, F. (2001). *The SADC Trade Protocol: Impacts, Issues and the Way Ahead*. qed.econ.queensu.ca/faculty/flatters/writings/ff_sadc_impacts.pdf

Flatters, F. (2004). SADC Rules of Origin in Textiles and Garments: Barriers to Regional Trade and Global Integration. In R. Grynberg (Ed.), *The Impact of Preferential Rules of Origin in the Textile and Clothing Sector in Africa* (pp. 41–66). London: Commonwealth Secretariat.

Goldstein, A. (2004). *Regional Integration, FDI and Competitiveness in Southern Africa*. Paris: OECD Publishing.

Grobbelaar, N. (2004). Can South African Business Drive Regional Integration on the Continent? *South African Journal of International Affairs, 11*, 91–106.

Hentz, J. J. (2005). *South Africa and the Logic of Regional Cooperation. Bloomington*. Indianapolis, IN: Indiana University Press.

Hess, N. M. (2010). Südafrika—Begehrter Partner Externer Akteure am Beispiel der USA, China und der EU. In F. Stehnken, A. Daniel, H. Asche, & R. Öhlgeschläger (Eds.), *Afrika und externe Akteure—Partner auf Augenhöhe?* (pp. 177–200). Baden-Baden: Nomos Verlagsgesellschaft.

Holden, M. (1996). *Economic and Trade Liberalization in Southern Africa. Is There a Role for South Africa?* Washington, DC: World Bank.

Holland, M., & Doidge, M. (2012). *Development Policy of the European Union*. Basingstoke: Palgrave Macmillan.

Hout, W., & Meijerink, F. (1996). Structures in the International Political Economy: World System Theory and Unequal Development. *European Journal of International Relations, 2*, 47–76.

Jakobeit, C., Hartzenberg, T., & Charalambides, N. (2005). *Overlapping Membership in COMESA, EAC, SACU and SADC: Trade Policy Options for the Region and for EPA Negotiations*. Eschborn: GIZ.

Jenkins, C., & Thomas, L. (2002). *Foreign Direct Investment in Southern Africa: Determinants, Characteristics and Implications for Economic Growth and Poverty Alleviation.* Oxford: University of Oxford.

Kalenga, P. (2011). Making the Tripartite FTA Work. In T. Hartzenberg (Ed.), *Cape to Cairo. Making the Tripartite Free Trade Area Work* (pp. 1–23). Stellenbosch: Trade Law Centre for Southern Africa.

Keck, A., & Piermartini, R. (2008). The Impact of Economic Partnership Agreements in Countries of the Southern African Development Community. *Journal of African Economies, 17,* 85–130.

Khumalo, N., & Phiri, D. S. (2009). Economic Partnership Agreements between the Southern African Customs Union and the European Union: The Implications for Regional Integration in Southern Africa. In T. Wheeler (Ed.), *South African Yearbook of International Affairs 2008/9* (pp. 21–30). Johannesburg: South African Institute of International Affairs.

Krapohl, S., Meißner, K. L., & Muntschick, J. (2014). Regional Powers as Leaders or Rambos of Regional Integration? Unilateral Actions of Brazil and South Africa and Their Negative Effects on MERCOSUR and SADC. *Journal of Common Market Studies, 52,* 879–895.

Kurz, S., Otter, T., & Povel, F. (2008). SADC Trade Integration—The Effect of Trade Facilitation on Sectoral Trade: A Quantitative Analysis. In A. Bösl, W. Breytenbach, T. Hartzenberg, C. McCarthy, & K. Schade (Eds.), *Monitoring Regional Integration in Southern Africa: Yearbook* (8th ed., pp. 55–73). Stellenbosch: Trade Law Centre for Southern Africa.

Lee, M. C. (2003). *The Political Economy of Regionalism in Southern Africa. Lansdowne.* Boulder, CO: Lynne Rienner Publishers.

MacLean, S. J. (2005). Discordant Discourses: South(ern) African Narratives on Zimbabwe's Crisis. In M. Bøås, M. H. Marchand, & T. M. Shaw (Eds.), *The Political Economy of Regions and Regionalisms* (pp. 129–146). Basingstoke: Palgrave Macmillan.

Mattli, W. (1999). *The Logic of Regional Integration: Europe and Beyond.* Cambridge: Cambridge University Press.

McCarthy, C. (1998). South African Trade and Industrial Policy in a Regional Context. In L. Petersson (Ed.), *Post-Apartheid Southern Africa: Economic Challenges and Policies for the Future* (pp. 64–86). London: Routledge.

Meyn, M. (2010). Die Wirtschaftspartnerschaftsabkommen der Europäischen Union—Was war, was ist und was kommen muss. In F. Stehnken, A. Daniel, H. Asche, & R. Öhlgeschläger (Eds.), *Afrika und externe akteure—Partner auf Augenhöhe?* (pp. 75–89). Baden-Baden: Nomos Verlagsgesellschaft.

Mills, G. (2002). From Berlin to Today: Looking Back and Forward on SADC-EU Relations. In E. Sidiropoulos, D. Games, P. Fabriciuset, et al. (Eds.), *SADC-EU Relations: Looking Back and Moving Ahead* (pp. 129–154). Copenhagen: Royal Danish Ministry of Foreign Affairs.

Mufune, P. (1993). The Future of Southern African Development Coordination Conference (SADCC). *Pula—Botswana Journal of African Studies*, 7, 14–34.

Muntschick, J. (2012). *Theorising Regionalism and External Influence: A Situation-Structural Approach* (Mainz Papers on International and European Politics 2012/2). Mainz: Johannes Gutenberg University of Mainz.

Muntschick, J. (2013a). Explaining the Influence of Extra-Regional Actors on Regional Economic Integration in Southern Africa: The EU's Interfering Impact on SADC and SACU. In U. Lorenz-Carl & M. Rempe (Eds.), *Mapping Agency: Comparing Regionalisms in Africa* (pp. 77–95). Farnham: Ashgate.

Muntschick, J. (2013b). Regionalismus und Externer Einfluss: Stört die Europäische Union die Regionale Marktintegration im südlichen Afrika? *Politische Vierteljahresschrift*, 54, 686–713.

Muntschick, J. (2015). Regionalism and External Influence: The Southern African Development Community (SADC) and the Ambivalent Impact of the EU on Regional Integration (PhD Thesis, University of Bamberg).

Olivier, G. (2006). *South Africa and the European Union: Self-Interest, Ideology and Altruism*. Pretoria: Protea Boekhuis.

Olympio, J., Robinson, P., & Cocks, M. (2006). The TDCA and SADC EPA: Is the Risk of Giving South Africa Duty-Free Access Alongside that Offered to the Rest of Southern African Countries Perceived or Real? In T. Bertelsmann-Scott & P. Draper (Eds.), *Regional Integration and Economic Partnership Agreements. Southern Africa at the Crossroads* (pp. 97–137). Johannesburg: South African Institute of International Affairs.

Oosthuizen, G. H. (2006). *The Southern African Development Community: The Organisation, Its Policies and Prospects*. Midrand: The Institute for Global Dialogue.

Oosthuizen, G. H. (2007). The Future of the Southern African Development Community. In E. Sidiropoulos (Ed.), *South African Yearbook 2006/7* (pp. 87–98). Johannesburg: South African Institute for International Affairs.

Page, S., & te Velde, D. W. (2004, November). *Foreign Direct Investment by African Countries*. Paper Prepared for InWent/UNCTAD meeting on FDI in Africa, Addis Ababa, Ethiopia.

Qualmann, R. (2003). South Africa's Reintegration into World and Regional Markets. Trade Liberalisation and Emerging Patterns of Specialisation in the Post-Apartheid Era (PhD Thesis, University of Leipzig).

Sachs, J. D. (2005). *Investing in Development: A Practical Plan to Achieve the Millennium Development Goals*. New York: Earthscan.

Sandrey, R. (2012). Foreign Direct Investment in South Africa. In T. Hartzenberg, G. Erasmus, & A. du Pisani (Eds.), *Monitoring Regional Integration in Southern Africa: Yearbook 2011* (pp. 188–213). Stellenbosch: Trade Law Centre for Southern Africa.

Sidiropoulos, E. (2002). SADC and the EU: A Brief Overview. In E. Sidiropoulos, D. Games, P. Fabriciuset, R. Herbert, T. Hughes, R. Gibb, & G. Mills (Eds.), *SADC-EU Relations: Looking Back and Moving Ahead* (pp. 7–23). Copenhagen: Royal Danish Ministry of Foreign Affairs.

Solomon, H. (2004). The Southern African Development Community: Regional Imperatives and Donor Assistance. In M. Muller & B. de Gaay Fortman (Eds.), *From Warfare to Welfare: Human Security in a Southern African Context* (pp. 73–90). Assen: Royal Van Gorcum.

Stevens, C., & Kennan, J. (2006). What Role for EPAs in Regional Economic Integration? In T. Bertelsmann-Scott & P. Draper (Eds.), *Regional Integration and Economic Partnership Agreements: Southern Africa at the Crossroads* (pp. 73–95). Johannesburg: South African Institute of International Affairs.

Tjønneland, E. N. (2005). Making SADC Work? Revisiting Institutional Reform. In D. Hansohm, W. Breytenbach, T. Hartzenberg, & C. McCarthy (Eds.), *Monitoring Regional Integration in Southern Africa Yearbook* (pp. 166–185). Stellenbosch: Trade Law Centre for Southern Africa.

Tleane, C. (2006). *The Great Trek North. The Expansion of South African Media and ICT Companies into the SADC Region.* Braamfontein: Freedom of Expression Institute.

Viner, J. (1950). *The Customs Union Issue.* New York: Carnegie Endowment for International Peace.

Vogt, J. (2007). *Die Regionale Integration des südlichen Afrikas. Unter besonderer Betrachtung der Southern African Development Community (SADC).* Baden-Baden: Nomos Verlagsgesellschaft.

Walker, A. (2009). The EC-SADC EPA: The Moment of Truth for Regional Integration. *Trade Negotiations Insights, 8,* 1–3.

Weeks, J. (1996). Regional Cooperation and Southern African Development. *Journal of Southern African Studies, 22,* 99–117.

Weiland, H. (2006). The European Union and Southern Africa: Interregionalism between Vision and Reality. In H. Hänggi, R. Roloff, & J. Rüland (Eds.), *Interregionalism and International Relations* (pp. 185–198). London: Routledge.

PART IV

Concluding Remarks

CHAPTER 8

Conclusion

Comparing Regional Cooperation and Defection in ASEAN, MERCOSUR and SADC

Sebastian Krapohl

Economic integration efforts within the Association of Southeast Asian Nations (ASEAN), the Common Market of South America (MERCOSUR) and the Southern African Development Community (SADC) are motivated and constrained by the extra-regional effects of regional integration. In the course of the new regionalism (e.g., Breslin et al. 2002; Hettne 1999, 2005; Hettne and Söderbaum 2000; Preusse 2004), MERCOSUR was established in 1991 and ASEAN and SADC were reborn in 1992 in order to help their member states to compete in a rapidly globalising market. As part of the new paradigm of export promotion (Bhagwati 1988; Krueger 1997), developing countries aimed to attract investments from and export goods to Europe, North America and Northeast Asia. Regional integration was supposed to improve their competitiveness in the global struggle for investment and export shares. Regionally integrated markets are necessarily larger than each of their member states' markets, and integrated

S. Krapohl (✉)
University of Amsterdam, Amsterdam, The Netherlands
e-mail: s.krapohl@uva.nl

© The Author(s) 2017
S. Krapohl (ed.), *Regional Integration in the Global South*,
International Political Economy Series,
DOI 10.1007/978-3-319-38895-3_8

regions are more stable in political terms because the regional member states should have friendly relations with each other. Increased market size and regional stability are attractive for investors, who can utilise economies of scale on a regional basis, and who face less risks that their investments be lost due to political turmoil. Besides, large and stable regional markets also increase the bargaining weight of the respective regions in global and interregional trade negotiations.

The extra-regional logic of regional integration in developing regions differs fundamentally from the intraregional logic, which prevails in well-developed regions like Europe. Whereas the intraregional logic of regional integration produces the club good intraregional trade, the extra-regional logic increases the shares of the common pool resources extra-regional exports and investments. This has considerable effects on the cooperation problems between the regional member states. Within the intraregional logic, the member states need to overcome a prisoner's dilemma of trade liberalisation, and they may need to agree on new policies within battles of the sexes. In contrast, the member states of developing regions face battles of the sexes only so long as extra-regional actors reward regional cooperation with growing investment inflows and trade concessions. If extra-regional actors do not systematically reinforce regional cooperation and rather grant privileges to single member states—most importantly, to regional powers—the situation changes fundamentally. The privileged member states then lose any interest in regional integration and become regional Rambos in order to protect their extra-regional privileges at the cost of regional cooperation. Thus, regional powers do not necessarily provide regional leadership, and rather their regional action is constrained by their dominant extra-regional interests.

The prevalence of extra-regional influences on all three regions is striking if one keeps in mind that ASEAN, MERCOSUR and SADC are very diverse with respect to the size of their memberships, the political systems in place in their member states and the cultural homogeneity of their populations. Thus, the three regions constitute dissimilar cases (Przeworski and Teune 1970; Ragin 1987). Whereas SADC has 15 member states, MERCOSUR has only 4 (5 since Venezuela joined the organisation in 2012). MERCOSUR and SADC are dominated by a single regional power, but four important member states balance each other out within ASEAN and none of them is able to dominate the whole region in economic terms. The MERCOSUR member states are all presidential democracies, whereas ASEAN and SADC contain authoritarian and failed states.

MERCOSUR is very homogeneous in cultural terms because Catholicism is the dominating religion in all its member states. In contrast, ASEAN's cultural diversity is striking, and the region contains member states with Buddhist, Christian, Muslim and traditional religion majorities. Despite all these cultural and political differences, the three regions share the commonality that, in their majorities, they consist of developing countries (the only exceptions are Brunei and Singapore in ASEAN). As a result, the share of intraregional investment and trade is low in these regions, and they all depend to a large degree on investments from and exports to other world regions like Europe, North America or Northeast Asia (Hout and Meijerink 1996; Smith and White 1992; Van Rossem 1996). Independently from other cultural or political influences, the dependence on extra-regional economic relations increases the importance of extra-regional gains, which is in contrast to the intraregional logic of regional integration.

Our theoretical approach on regional integration addresses the likelihoods of regional cooperation or defection within the Global South, but it does not preclude that other variables influence the concrete form of regional integration taken. The different institutional designs of regional organisations like ASEAN, the EU, MERCOSUR, North American Free Trade Agreement (NAFTA) and SADC demonstrate that neither the intra- nor the extra-regional logic of regional integration determine which kinds of regional institutions are chosen by their member states. In other words, the intra- and extra-regional logics of regional integration may open or close policy windows (Kingdon 1995) for regional cooperation, but other theoretical concepts are needed in order to explain how open policy windows are used by regional actors. For example, the choices to follow the minimalist approach of NAFTA or extensive harmonisation as with the EU may be dependent on member states' domestic institutions (Duina 2006). In contrast, the fact that many regional organisations resemble in some part the institutional design of the EU may result from the diffusion of the successful European role model of regional integration to other world regions (Börzel and Risse 2012). However, both the path dependency and diffusion arguments only address the *form* of regional integration, and do not explain under which circumstances regional integration succeeds or fails.

1 EMPIRICAL FINDINGS

The findings of the three case studies generally support the two hypotheses that are developed in Chap. 2. Hypothesis 1 addresses the motivation for economic integration in developing regions. Because the intraregional gains of regional integration are low in the Global South, this hypothesis postulates that it is the extra-regional gains of regional integration that motivate member states to cooperate. However, the case studies of MERCOSUR and SADC demonstrate that the intraregional gains of regional integration are not necessarily insignificant, and that they can also motivate regional integration in developing regions to some degree. Nevertheless, this may only happen as long as regional integration is not at odds with important extra-regional economic interests. Hypothesis 2 states that regional cooperation is constrained by the extra-regional interests of the respective regional powers. The MERCOSUR and SADC case studies confirm this hypothesis, because Brazil and South Africa did not cooperate with their regional neighbours on important occasions, but rather acted unilaterally in order to take advantage of extra-regional economic privileges.

1.1 Extra-Regional Motivations for Regional Cooperation

Hypothesis 1: As long as regional integration is systematically rewarded by extra-regional actors, the member states of developing regions cooperate within battles of the sexes.

ASEAN is the most obvious case where economic integration is driven by the extra-regional interests of the member states. At the beginning of the 1990s, the Southeast Asian countries were afraid to lose investment shares to other world regions, most notably to Mexico as a member of NAFTA. The ASEAN member states set up the ASEAN Free Trade Area explicitly in order to become more attractive addressees for extra-regional investments (Bowles 1997; Ravenhill 1995). The more protectionist member states like Indonesia and the more liberal ones like Singapore disagreed about the pace of trade liberalisation and about the exceptions of sensitive product sectors, but they generally agreed on the necessity of economic integration. The situation resembled a battle of the sexes, wherein the contracting parties negotiated for the distributive effects of an agreement. The result was a compromise that included a long implementation period and the possibility for the member states to exclude sensitive products from trade liberalisation (Cuyvers and Pupphavesa 1996; Cuyvers et al. 2005). Despite criticism of AFTA's weakness, this decision heralded some years of dynamic economic development in Southeast Asia until the Asian crisis hit the region in 1997.

The developments in East Asia during the 2000s were a reaction to the Asian crisis of the late 1990s. ASEAN itself was of little help to its member states during the crisis, and many observers expected a decline of the organisation at the turn of the millennium (Rüland 2000; Webber 2001). However, a stable framework of extra-regional cooperation emerged with ASEAN+3, wherein ASEAN cooperated with its neighbours in Northeast Asia (Cai 2003; Dieter and Higgott 2003; Grimes 2011). The Chiang Mai Initiative (CMI) and several trade agreements resulted from that cooperation and brought significant gains for the ASEAN member states. As a result, ASEAN proceeded with regional integration in order to improve its standing in relation to the two regional powers China and Japan. Thus, the ASEAN Economic Community (AEC) and the ASEAN Charter were driven by the extra-regional interests of the member states. The success of this strategy was that ASEAN managed to keep its unity in extra-regional relations.

Like AFTA, the establishment of the MERCOSUR customs union (MERCOSUR-CU) was a project of the new regionalism during the 1990s (Schirm 2002). In the course of a turn towards liberalist economic policies, the two large member states, Argentina and Brazil, wanted to attract extra-regional investment to South America, and they expected that the establishment of a customs union would help them to negotiate en bloc with extra-regional partners for trade agreements. The regional power Brazil in particular had an interest in improving its own influence in global politics by assembling the rest of the region behind itself (Bandeira 2006). The smaller South American states Paraguay and Uruguay joined MERCOSUR not only because of the extra-regional gains of regional integration, but also to profit from free access to the large markets of their regional neighbours (Nunnenkamp 1999). Brazil provided regional leadership during the establishment of the customs union (Malamud 2011). This regional power successfully set the agenda, but it also compensated Argentina for some distributive losses. The customs union marked the beginning of MERCOSUR's most successful period during the 1990s, which was distinguished by an investment boom and increasing intraregional trade.

The different agreements that set up the SADC-FTA and laid out the future path of economic integration in Southern Africa shared the usual rhetoric of the new regionalism. Accordingly, the Southern African countries also aimed to integrate their economies into the global market (Lee 2003). However, SADC is the least developed and competitive of the three regions, and intraregional interests played a more important role than in ASEAN and MERCOSUR. The regional power South Africa needed the regional market in order to sell its manufactured goods, which were not competitive on the global market, and the smaller SADC member states had a strong interest in getting access to the large market of South Africa (Draper et al. 2006; Qualmann 2003). Like Brazil in the case of the MERCOSUR-CU, South Africa provided regional leadership during the establishment of the SADC-FTA. The regional power granted long implementation periods to its smaller neighbours, which allowed for the possible protection of the weaker economies for some time. In return, South Africa dominated the negotiations over very complex rules of origin, the results of which basically protect South African industries against extra-regional imports. The SADC-FTA was implemented rather late (in 2008), but it seemed to go along with slightly increasing intraregional trade and growing extra-regional investments in Southern Africa.

The case studies demonstrate that cooperation within the three developing regions was not dominated by the intraregional interests of the member states. Hypothesis 1 would have been falsified if intraregional interests had dominated the negotiations, and if extra-regional interests had not played a major role. Although the member states of all regions aimed to increase intraregional trade and had different interests with respect to the pace and extent of intraregional trade liberalisation, extra-regional interests clearly pushed new regionalism in developing regions during the 1990s (Schirm 2002). The turn towards export-promoting development strategies made it necessary for developing regions to attract investment and to get access to important export markets. This motivation was most visible in the case of Southeast Asia, where AFTA was explicitly established to improve the region's competitiveness on the global market. In South America, extra-regional investments were important as well, but the regional member states also used MERCOSUR in order to start promising trade negotiations with the EU. Of the three regions, Southern Africa has the least-competitive and least-liberalised economies, but even here South Africa's extra-regional interests dominated the negotiations over SADC's rules of origins.

1.2 Extra-Regional Constraints on Regional Cooperation

Hypothesis 2: As soon as regional integration is at odds with important extra-regional privileges, the regional powers of developing regions become regional Rambos with a dominant strategy of defection.

There exists no regional power in Southeast Asia that dominates ASEAN and enjoys economic privileges in its extra-regional relations. Indonesia, Malaysia, Singapore and Thailand are all important economies within the ASEAN trade network, and they balance each other out so that none of them has a dominant position (see Chap. 4). The lack of regional leadership turned out to be an advantage instead of a disadvantage for regional integration in Southeast Asia. Regional cooperation was never dependent on the goodwill of a single regional power, and no member state needed to protect its privileged position in extra-regional relations. As a result, ASEAN has thus far managed to maintain its unity, and extra-regional cooperation with China, Japan and South Korea within the ASEAN+3 framework has supported rather than disturbed regional integration.

Brazil, the regional power of MERCOSUR, defected from regional cooperation when significant extra-regional economic privileges were at stake. At the turn of the millennium, South America suffered from a loss of investor confidence and capital outflows. With all MERCOSUR member states under pressure, Brazil unilaterally decided to float the real, which consequently lost about 30 per cent of its value (Bulmer-Thomas 1999; Kronberger 2002). This devaluation improved the competitiveness of the Brazilian export industry, and an export boom helped the Brazilian economy to recover quickly. In contrast, the economies of the other South American countries lost competitiveness in comparison with Brazil. Exports of the other MERCOSUR member states declined, and the economic crisis was reinforced. This proved to be the death blow for the Argentinean economy, and the country entered the devastating Argentinean crisis (Kehoe 2005; Saxton 2003). As a result of mistrust between the member states, regional integration in MERCOSUR stagnated after the crisis (Carranza 2003).

Several attempts to restart regional integration in MERCOSUR have not been able to generate the same dynamic as during the 1990s, and the regional power Brazil started to act more outside of the MERCOSUR framework instead. In the 2000s, MERCOSUR's dispute settlement mechanism was strengthened by the establishment of a permanent appellate court (Arnold and Rittberger 2013). And in 2006, the MERCOSUR member states decided to replace the parliamentary commission with a directly elected parliament (Malamud 2015). However, these reforms merely scratched the surface of MERCOSUR's problems, and they did not lead to more regional cooperation or better implementation of regional norms. On the contrary, instead of providing regional leadership within MERCOSUR, the regional power Brazil bypassed the organisation on two occasions. Brazil was the main proponent of the establishment of the Union of South American Nations (UNASUR) in 2004 (Gratius and Gomes Saraiva 2013), and the regional power signed a bilateral Strategic Partnership Agreement with the EU in 2007 (Van Loon 2015). The aims and rules of both agreements do not stand in direct conflict to MERCOSUR, and Brazil did not breach MERCOSUR law in this respect. However, the two agreements are a clear indication that the regional power no longer provides leadership because MERCOSUR is no longer the top priority of its foreign policy.

While South Africa, the regional power of SADC, provided regional leadership during the establishment of the SADC-FTA, it did not push the SADC-CU when this became necessary. South Africa enjoyed its bilateral Trade, Development and Cooperation Agreement (TDCA) with the EU, which granted privileged access to the European market (Frennhoff Larsén 2007; Olympio et al. 2006). In order to establish a customs union, either South Africa would have had to give up its bilateral trade agreement with the EU or the other member states would have needed to adapt to the terms of the TDCA. Instead, the external trade regimes of the SADC member states disintegrated during the negotiations for Economic Partnership Agreements (EPAs) with the EU (Lorenz 2012; Stevens 2008). The SADC negotiation group consisted only of seven SADC member states (including South Africa, which still had the TDCA as an ace up its sleeve), whereas the other eight member states participated in three other negotiation groups. Of course, this heterogeneity prevented the harmonisation of member states' external trade regimes towards a customs union. As the SADC-CU was an important step within a Balassa-like integration plan, the deepening of economic integration within SADC was blocked.

Regional cooperation in MERCOSUR and SADC was clearly constrained by the extra-regional interests of the respective regional powers. Hypothesis 2 would have been falsified if Brazil and South Africa had provided constant regional leadership under unfavourable circumstances within the extra-regional environment. However, the two regional powers fell short of pushing regional integration on important occasions. Firstly, Brazil floated its currency in 1999 without any coordination with its regional neighbours. The result was an export boom in Brazil and a devastating economic crisis in Argentina. Thereafter, MERCOSUR has still not completely recovered, and Brazil has started to bypass the regional organisations in order to follow its own interests. Secondly, South Africa did not need a SADC-EPA because it enjoyed the bilateral TDCA with the EU. Thus, the regional power did not provide regional leadership in order to get all SADC member states into one negotiation group, but rather joined the negotiations only half-heartedly and rather late. As a result, the external trade regime of the SADC member states fell apart and the region has not yet been able to set up the planned customs union.

1.3 From Regional Cooperation to Regional Integration

The analyses of ASEAN, MERCOSUR and SADC address different cases of regional cooperation or defection, but they do not address the whole integration processes. The case studies look at different points in time and investigate whether the economic structures of the respective regions determined member states' interests and the outcome of member states' interactions. The analysed cases of regional cooperation or defection were undoubtedly important for the respective regions and influenced the regional integration process considerably. However, regional integration is the accumulated result of several cases of regional cooperation that together lead to an ever-denser web of regional institutions and commitments (see Chap. 1). In order to grasp regional integration processes as a whole, the different occasions of regional cooperation or defection need to be seen in relation to each other.

The empirical analyses have demonstrated that different cases of regional cooperation and defection within a particular region do not occur independently from each other. The successful experience with AFTA probably motivated the ASEAN member states to pursue further regional cooperation in the critical situation at the beginning of the 2000s. Brazil's unilateral devaluation of the real and the following Argentinean crisis have obviously damaged the regional integration process for some time. And the failure to establish the SADC-CU prevented further steps of economic integration towards a common market in Southern Africa. However, there emerges no clear-cut pattern of how the different cases influence each other. Whereas a regional crisis led to further integration in Southeast

Asia, a similar crisis had devastating effects for regional integration in South America. And regional integration in Southern Africa became stalled without a serious economic crisis at all. Thus, the occurrence or non-occurrence of crises is not a sufficient indicator for predicting the progress of economic integration in developing regions.

The reason for this unpredictability of integration processes in developing regions is the varying influence of external factors, which are treated as an exogenous variable in this book. The MERCOSUR member states were able to establish a customs union; in contrast, the same level of integration already conflicted with the extra-regional interests of the SADC member states. And whereas important external actors (namely, China, Japan and South Korea) supported regional integration in ASEAN, such support was lacking in MERCOSUR and SADC (despite the fact that the EU claims to push regional integration in the Global South). The theoretical concept presented in this book does not attempt to analyse which factors influence the reactions of extra-regional actors towards regional integration efforts in the developing world. In order to analyse the regional responses to extra-regional influences, these external influences were treated as independent variables. In order to analyse the dynamics of regional integration in the Global South, it would be necessary to analyse the interactions between regional cooperation and extra-regional reactions in more detail. The crucial question is under which circumstances successful regional cooperation and positive extra-regional reactions reinforce each other so that something like an extra-regional spillover mechanism emerges. The case of ASEAN and ASEAN+3 demonstrates that this is possible, but much more conceptual work and empirical research needs to be done in order to derive predictive hypotheses.

2 Theoretical Implications

The extra-regional logic of regional integration is neglected by the European integration theories. The reason is of course that these theories were developed to analyse and explain the European case of regional integration. From the very beginning of the European integration process, the European member states were highly developed in economic terms, and the share of intraregional investment and trade was high (see Chap. 4). The intraregional logic dominated European integration, and the extra-regional effects of economic integration were much less important than in developing regions. Thus, scholars concentrated on the intraregional logic and left extra-regional effects aside in order to develop parsimonious theories about European integration. A negative consequence of this development is that the European integration theories cannot really be applied to world regions in the Global South (Söderbaum and Sbragia 2011; Warleigh-Lack and Rosamond 2010; Warleigh-Lack and Van Langenhove 2011). In order to develop comprehensive and widely applicable integration theories, scholars of comparative regionalism need to conceptualise the extra-regional effects of regional integration and include them in existing or newly developed integration theories.

2.1 Intergovernmentalism

Intergovernmentalist approaches (Moravcsik 1993, 1998) can easily broaden their scope in order to grasp the extra-regional interests of regional member states. According to intergovernmentalism, the interests of member states are the driving force of regional integration. Supranational institutions are regarded as having little influence on the path of integration. Intergovernmentalist analyses concentrate on single cases of regional cooperation at certain points in time, which implies that they lose sight of the dynamic character of regional integration. Applied to European integration, intergovernmentalism focuses on the intraregional interests of the regional member states. Applied to developing regions, intergovernmentalist approaches need to take into account as well the extra-regional effects of economic integration and the extra-regional interests of the member states. The fact that supranational institutions do not play an important role in such theories turns out to be an advantage for the analysis of developing regions, where regional institutions are usually much weaker than in Europe. The theory and analyses presented in this book follow in large parts such an intergovernmentalist approach, because they concentrate on the extra-regional interests of the member states, treat regional institutions more as a dependent rather than an independent variable of regional cooperation, and do not explicitly address the dynamics between different cases of regional cooperation or defection.

An intergovernmentalist analysis of economic integration in developing regions needs to consider that the two logics of regional integration do not exclude each other. Regional integration also has extra-regional effects in economically well-developed regions of the Western world. One example of this is the Single European Act of 1986, which of course established the single market and liberalised intraregional trade, but which was also adopted in order to improve Europe's competitiveness in comparison to East Asia and the USA (Moravcsik 1991). And not only the extra- but also the intraregional effects of regional integration play a role in developing regions. One example is the SADC-FTA, wherein the smaller member states wanted to get access to the market of South Africa, and the regional power needed a stable regional market for its manufactured products, which were not competitive on the global market (Muntschick 2013). The two logics of regional integration can reinforce each other, but they can also contradict each other. In the latter case, the important question is which of the two logics determines member states' interests in a particular region at a certain point in time. The more economically developed a region is, the more the potential for intraregional economic interdependence emerges, and the more important the intraregional logic of regional integration becomes, whereas the relative importance of member states' extra-regional interests declines.

2.2 Neofunctionalism

Neofunctionalism faces more problems when conceptualising the extra-regional logic of regional integration. According to neofunctionalism, spillover processes push economic integration forward after it has been started by the member states (Haas 1958; Lindberg and Scheingold 1970; Schmitter 1970). Most important are functional spillovers (Tranholm-Mikkelsen 1991), which heavily rely on interdependence between the member states and between economic sectors. Because of such interdependence, the integration of one sector necessarily leads to functional pressure to also integrate other interdependent sectors in order to not lose out on efficiency gains. This kind of spillover process can only occur within the intraregional (and not within the extra-regional) logic of regional integration. Because there exists no intraregional economic interdependence within the extra-regional logic, the integration of one economic sector does not affect other sectors, thus not causing them to need to be integrated as well. But, within the extra-regional logic, 'external spillovers' may occur in interactions with extra-regional actors. For example, regional cooperation within ASEAN spilled over to successful extra-regional cooperation with China, Japan and South Korea within the ASEAN+3 framework. Then, this successful extra-regional cooperation spilled back over to the regional level, where further steps in economic integration were adopted. Neofunctionalism needs to conceptualise such interactions between the respective regions and the outside world in order to be applicable to developing regions.

There may also emerge spillovers from the extra- to the intraregional logic of regional integration. The relative weights of the intra- and extraregional logics of regional integration are likely to change over time. As long as regions are clearly at a low stage of economic development and dependent on extra-regional economic partners, the extra-regional logic is dominant. However, if the regions concerned successfully attract extra-regional investments, the situation starts to change. Market-seeking investments are attracted if economic integration allows access to the whole regional market, and this necessarily leads to growing intraregional trade. And efficiency-seeking investments may lead to the establishment of regional production networks, which also increases intraregional trade. Generally, the more successful the extra-regional logic of regional integration is, the further economic development proceeds, the more the potential for intraregional economic interdependence emerges, and the more important the intraregional logic becomes. Here again, neofunctionalism needs to be broadened in order to grasp such interactions between the intra- and the extra-regional logics of regional integration.

2.3 Institutionalism

Rational institutionalist approaches to European integration usually deal with questions of institutional design. On the one hand, they ask why the EU member states establish specific supranational institutions like the European Commission, the European Court of Justice or the European Parliament (Pollack 1997, 2003). On the other hand, they analyse the influence of such supranational institutions on the decisions and behaviour of political actors (Tsebelis and Garrett 2001). These questions can of course also be asked for regional organisations in the Global South. However, important differences to the EU exist. Firstly, the member states of developing regions usually refrain from setting up strong supranational institutions. The extra-regional logic of regional integration seems to exude less functional pressure to delegate far-reaching competencies to the regional level than the intraregional logic does. And secondly, even if member states of developing regions decide to establish regional institutions, they often neglect these institutions and do not implement regional agreements. Within the extra-regional logic, regional institutions seem to develop less influence on member states' actual behaviour. In sum, regional institutions do not really seem to commit the member states of regional organisations to cooperate with each other. Rational institutionalism needs to find an answer to the question of why regional institutions in the Global South seem to work fundamentally differently from those in the Western world.

Historical and sociological institutionalisms see European integration as a process of institutional development that is distinguished by path dependency (Pierson 1996). For example, Stone Sweet and others (Fligstein and Stone Sweet 2002; Stone Sweet and Caporaso 1998) argue that the liberalisation of regional trade and the establishment of regional dispute settlement mechanisms start a self-reinforcing virtuous circle of institutional development that the member states can hardly control. Accordingly, trade liberalisation leads to increasing intraregional trade, which necessarily leads to transnational conflicts between trade partners. Dispute settlement mechanisms decide on these conflicts and establish rules, which then liberalise intraregional trade even further. As a result, intraregional trade increases again, and so on. As with neofunctionalism, this feedback mechanism can only unfold within the intraregional logic of regional integration, because trade liberalisation does not immediately lead to more intraregional trade and regional dispute settlement within the extra-regional logic. The question is whether similar feedback mechanisms may also evolve in the extra-regional logic, for example, between regional institutions and extra-regional investors. Historical and sociological institutionalisms need to develop ideas about how path-dependent processes of institutional development unfold in developing regions, where regional institutions are usually weaker and where stakeholders are often located outside of the respective regions.

3 Explaining Some Phenomena of the New Regionalism in the Global South

Economic integration efforts in developing regions seem to be distinguished by some common characteristics that are in stark contrast to European integration and are not yet fully explained by the existing (European) integration theories. Currently, the academic literature mainly (but not exclusively) discusses three different issues: the weakness of regional institutions in the developing world (Acharya and Johnston 2007), the emergence of different and overlapping regional organisations in one particular world region (Malamud 2013) and the prospects for interregional trade negotiations between the EU on the one hand and developing regions on the other hand (Aggarwal and Fogarty 2004; Hänggi 2003). The following sections discuss what insights can be gained into these phenomena if the extra-regional logic of regional integration is taken into account.

3.1 The Weakness of Regional Institutions

Regional institutions in developing regions are usually rather weak and do not effectively commit the member states to common decision-making and the implementation of regional agreements. Firstly, the member states of developing regions are generally very hesitant to delegate far-reaching decision-making competencies to supranational institutions. Of the three regions analysed in this book, MERCOSUR's institutional design comes closest to that of the EU, but all its different decision-making bodies are purely intergovernmental and decide by unanimity (Lenz 2012). One reason behind this may be that differentiated decision-making systems at the regional level do not help the member states of developing regions to deal with possible Rambo situations. The delegation of agenda-setting competencies and the application of majority vote may ensure cooperation within battles of the sexes, in which all member states have an interest in the common good. Within Rambo situations, a majority vote may lead to the overruling of the Rambo, but this does not ensure the Rambo's cooperation. On the contrary, the Rambo would just ignore regional decisions, because it has a dominant interest in defection in order to protect its extra-regional privileges. Such Rambo situations can only be overcome if the member states that are interested in the common good buy the Rambo's cooperation through side payments or through concessions in large package deals. Agenda setting by independent bodies and majority vote do not help to negotiate such highly disputed deals, which need the agreement of highly placed representatives of the member states.

Secondly, even if strong regional institutions like dispute settlement bodies are established, they are rarely used and their decisions are often ignored. MERCOSUR's elaborated dispute settlement mechanism remains very passive (Krapohl et al. 2010), and the one and only ruling of the SADC tribunal was not implemented; the member states decided to abolish the tribunal instead (Cowell 2013). Once again, the possible occurrence of Rambo situations may explain this weakness of judicialisation. Regional dispute settlement mechanisms can support tit-for-tat solutions in iterated prisoners' dilemmas of mutual trade liberalisation (Abbott et al. 2000; Zangl 2008), but they cannot enforce cooperation when regional Rambos protect extra-regional privileges. Within iterated prisoners' dilemmas, the member states all profit from regional cooperation, but they face incentives to free ride on the contributions of others. This gives the other member states some power to enforce the rulings of regional dispute settlement bodies, because defecting member states do not want to lose the gains from regional cooperation in general. However, within a Rambo constellation, the regional Rambo no longer has any interest in any kind of cooperation, because this cooperation would endanger its extra-regional economic privileges. As a result, the rulings of regional dispute settlement mechanisms cannot be enforced by the other member states, and the Rambo just ignores such rulings.

The establishment of more independent and stronger regional institutions does not solve decision-making and implementation problems within the extra-regional logic of regional integration, but rather leads to an increasing gap between political assertions and real action. More independent decision-making is likely to produce more regional rules that are in conflict with the interests of some member states. And independent regional courts are more likely than intergovernmental panels to decide against the particular interests of powerful member states. In order to have an effect on the ground, regional rules and jurisprudence necessarily rely on decentralised enforcement by the member states. This enforcement does not work when regional Rambos want to prevent regional cooperation and ignore rulings against their defections. Rambo constellations may be coated with more intergovernmental decision-making and less independent dispute settlement bodies, because this allows Rambos to influence the rulings beforehand and to not need to breach them openly. Thus, less intergovernmental decision-making and more independent supranational courts can damage the credibility of regional organisations even more than intergovernmental negotiations, because with such courts the gap between regional rulings and a lack of implementation becomes clearly visible.

3.2 Overlapping Regionalism

There exists usually not only one regional organisation within a particular developing region, but rather several organisations competing with each other (Malamud 2013). The three regional organisations analysed in this book are probably the most important and most developed ones in their respective world regions, but they are surely not the only ones. There does not only exist ASEAN in Asia, but also the Asia Pacific Economic Cooperation (APEC) and the South Asian Association for Regional Cooperation (SAARC). Within South America, MERCOSUR competes inter alia with the Andean Community (CAN) and UNASUR. The most regional organisations probably exist in Africa, where SADC is, for example, accompanied by the Common Market for Eastern and Southern Africa (COMESA), the East African Community (EAC) and the Economic Community of West African States (ECOWAS). Membership in these different regional organisations is often not exclusive. All ASEAN member states are also members of APEC, all MERCOSUR member states participate in UNASUR and many of the SADC member states join COMESA or EAC as well. During the history of European integration, the EU also competed with other regional organisations in Europe like the European Free Trade Association (EFTA) (Gstöhl 2002). However, in Europe, the single market developed centripetal forces, and the EU more or less absorbed competing regional organisations. This does not seem to happen in developing regions, where the number of regional organisations seems likelier to grow than to decline.

Within the extra-regional logic of regional integration, regional organisations are signals to extra-regional actors, and it is important for countries to be members of the most successful of these organisations. Regional organisations need to deliver the message that their member states are committing themselves to intraregional market building and the peaceful settlements of disputes. These size and stability advantages attract extra-regional investments and increase the regions' standings in international trade negotiations. However, the regional member states face difficulties in committing themselves credibly to trade liberalisation as long as there is no real potential for intraregional trade. This also means that signalling extra-regional actors remains cheap as long as not much is happening on the ground. Whether trade liberalisation really takes place only becomes visible when extra-regional investments are already made and intraregional trade increases. This brings the incentive for establishing several regional organisations in order to send as many signals as possible to extra-regional actors in the hope that any one of these attempts proves fruitful. Regional countries may decide to spread the risk of failure by joining more than one organisation, and conflicting obligations to the different organisations are not a real issue as long as their implementation is not put to the test by increasing intraregional interdependence.

It may be rational for each country to join as many regional organisations as possible, but the result is likely to be inefficient on a regional level. The more competing regional organisations and agreements that are established, the less convincing these organisations are to extra-regional actors. Conflicting regional obligations lead to legal uncertainties, and extra-regional investors do not know which rules apply and are implemented. The result is an inflationary effect on the value of regional integration. The more regional agreements exist, the less effect each of them has on the calculations of extra-regional actors. If regional integration has no effect anymore and becomes stalled, the regional countries may decide on new regional agreements. Consequently, the number of regional agreements increases, but the value of each single agreement declines further.

3.3 The Failure of Interregionalism

The rise of new regionalism during the 1990s also led to a rise of interregionalism. The EU started interregional negotiations—especially with regions of the Global South—in order to spread its own successful model of regional integration and economic development. For example, the Asia-Europe Meeting (ASEM) between the ASEAN+3 countries and the EU started in 1996 (Hänggi 2003), the EU-MERCOSUR negotiations for an interregional trade agreement began in 1995 (Doctor 2007), and the Cotonou Agreement of 2000 was the starting point for interregional negotiations for EPAs between the EU on the one hand and several regional groups of African, Caribbean and Pacific (ACP) countries on the other hand (Lorenz 2012). The expectation of contemporary observers during the 1990s was that interregionalism should have a positive effect on regionalism in the Global South (Hänggi 2003). Consistent with the theoretical framework of this book, their argument was that developing regions need to integrate in order to improve their standings in interregional negotiations with the EU.

The high hopes in interregionalism have been dashed because none of the interregional trade negotiations has been successfully completed so far. ASEM has not yet produced meaningful agreements, the EU-MERCOSUR negotiations are reanimated from time to time without bringing any results, and the EPA negotiations are highly contested and have proved to be more of an obstacle than a support for regional integration in the Global South (Stevens 2008). Interregional initiatives with the USA (including the NAFTA member states Canada and Mexico) failed as well. APEC seems to be too big and widespread to produce any meaningful results (Webber 2001), and the Free Trade Area of the Americas (FTAA) failed due to the resistance of the South American states, most notably Brazil (Carranza 2004). Due to the failure of interregional negotiations, the EU started to intensify its bilateral relations with the key countries of developing regions. The TDCA between the EU and South Africa from 1999 was the first example of such bilateral agreements (Frennhoff Larsén 2007). In 2007, Brazil and the EU signed a strategic partnership agreement, which, however, excluded the trade issues in order to not endanger the MERCOSUR-CU (Malamud 2011). And the intraregional trade negotiations between ASEAN and the EU, which started in 2007, were replaced by bilateral negotiations between single ASEAN member states and the EU in 2010 (Garcia 2013).

The current failure of interregionalism and the rise of bilateral trade agreements that cut through existing regional organisations are a severe obstacle for regional integration in the Global South. Firstly, if interregional trade agreements are not completed, an important incentive for economic integration in developing regions disappears. The respective regions lose the incentive to speak with one voice in interregional negotiations, and the win-set at the regional level declines. Secondly, bilateral trade agreements constitute privileges for single member states in their extra-regional economic relations. Within the extra-regional logic of regional integration, the respective member states face incentives to protect such important extra-regional privileges at the cost of regional integration. As soon as the bilateral relations are at odds with regional cooperation, the privileged member states lose any interest in cooperation and become regional Rambos.

Due to these two mechanisms—the possibilities of motivating regional integration or of building up further obstacles for regional cooperation—the external trade policies of important global actors like the EU and the USA have a decisive influence on regional integration in the Global South. Unfortunately, developing regions seem to be dependent on the goodwill of the EU and the USA if they want to use regional integration in order to overcome economic marginalisation on the global market. However, it is not necessarily in the interests of the EU and the USA that developing regions become more integrated and stronger in international trade negotiations. Being confronted with stronger negotiation partners means that one needs to make more concessions in order to reach agreements. Thus, it may be at least in the short-term interests of the EU and the USA to follow a divide and conquer strategy in international trade negotiations. As a result of that, the external trade policy of the EU is often in conflict with the official goal of supporting regional integration in the Global South.

4 Outlook

Regional integration is a necessary instrument of developing regions for escaping marginalisation in the global economy. On their own, most developing countries (with the exception of big emerging markets like Brazil, Russia, India, China, and South Africa, or the BRICS) are neither attractive as investment locations, nor do they have any leverage in international trade negotiations. However, investment inflows and market access to well-developed regions in Europe, East Asia and North America are necessary for developing economies in order to create economic growth and welfare. Import substitution widely failed as a developing strategy, and the examples of many East Asian countries demonstrate that export promotion and integration into the globalising world economy are more successful in generating economic development. Globalisation as such is not an obstacle for development, but asymmetric globalisation is a problem if developing regions are left behind in global economic developments. Successful regional integration is one strategy for escaping this marginalisation and creating attractive economic locations for investment, production and export.

Unfortunately, the structural obstacles for regional integration in the Global South are high and they are difficult to overcome. Although the extra-regional logic provides a rationale for regional integration in developing regions, it bears more difficult cooperation problems than the intra-regional logic, which prevails in highly developed regions like Europe. Within the extra-regional logic, regional cooperation depends very much on the reactions of extra-regional actors. As long as regional integration is rewarded with increasing investment inflows and successful international trade negotiations, the member states may relatively easily cooperate within battles of the sexes. However, if extra-regional actors grant one of the member states economic privileges that conflict with regional cooperation, that member state defects from regional integration in order to protect these privileges. Such Rambo constellations are much more difficult to overcome than prisoners' dilemmas or battles of the sexes, because the defecting member states lose any interest in regional cooperation. Then the other member states cannot put pressure on a regional Rambo, but rather need to buy its cooperation with big package deals or side payments.

The importance of regions in international politics is likely to be sustained or even to increase in the future, but the odds for stable and successful regional integration processes in the Global South are low. The trend towards a regionalisation of world politics is unlikely to decline, because '[t]he sovereign nations of the past can no longer solve the problems of the present; they cannot ensure their own progress or control their own future' (the closing words of Jean Monnet's memoirs). This does not only apply to Europe, but even more to developing countries and developing regions. However, due to the structural obstacles for economic integration in developing regions, it is very unlikely that stable regional organisations and integration processes will emerge. The extra-regional influences on developing regions are too strong and too volatile to allow for stable regional orders. It is much more likely that the 'spaghetti bowl' (Baldwin 2006; Baldwin and Seghezza 2010) of bilateral, regional and interregional agreements will persist and become even more complex. This is at least confirmed by the case studies of MERCOSUR and SADC, where the extra-regional interests of the regional powers prevented further regional integration. ASEAN may be an exception from this general pattern, because growing economic interdependence within East Asia—including China, Japan and South Korea—may lead to growing centripetal forces within this world region.

REFERENCES

Abbott, K. W., Keohane, R. O., Moravcsik, A., Slaughter, A.-M., & Snidal, D. (2000). The Concept of Legalization. *International Organization, 54*, 401–419.
Acharya, A., & Johnston, A. J. (Eds.). (2007). *Crafting Cooperation: Regional International Institutions in Comparative Perspective*. Cambridge: Cambridge University Press.
Aggarwal, V. K., & Fogarty, E. A. (Eds.). (2004). *EU Trade Strategies: Between Regionalism and Globalism*. Basingstoke: Palgrave Macmillan.
Arnold, C., & Rittberger, B. (2013). The Legalization of Dispute Resolution in Mercosur. *Journal of Politics in Latin America, 5*, 97–132.
Baldwin, R. E. (2006). Multilateralising Regionalism: Spaghetti Bowls as Building Blocs on the Path to Global Free Trade. *The World Economy, 29*, 1451–1518.
Baldwin, R. E., & Seghezza, E. (2010). Are Trade Blocs Building or Stumbling Blocs? *Journal of Economic Integration, 25*, 276–297.
Bandeira, L. A. M. (2006). Brazil as a Regional Power and Its Relations with the United States. *Latin American Perspectives, 33*, 12–27.
Bhagwati, J. N. (1988). Export-Promoting Trade Strategy. *World Bank Research Observer, 3*, 27–57.
Börzel, T., & Risse, T. (2012). From Europeanisation to Diffusion: An Introduction. *West European Politics, 35*, 1–19.
Bowles, P. (1997). ASEAN, AFTA and the "New Regionalism". *Pacific Affairs, 10*, 219–233.

Breslin, S., Huges, C. W., Phillips, N., & Rosamond, B. (Eds.). (2002). *New Regionalisms in the Global Political Economy: Theories and Cases*. London: Routledge.

Bulmer-Thomas, V. (1999). The Brazilian Devaluation: National Responses and International Consequences. *International Affairs, 75*, 729–741.

Cai, K. G. (2003). The ASEAN-China Free Trade Agreement and East Asian Regional Grouping. *Contemporary Southeast Asia, 25*, 387–404.

Carranza, M. (2003). Can MERCOSUR Survive? Domestic and International Constraints on MERCOSUR. *Latin American Politics and Society, 45*, 67–103.

Carranza, M. (2004). MERCOSUR and the End Game of the FTAA Negotiations: Challenges and Prospects after the Argentine Crisis. *Third World Quarterly, 25*, 319–337.

Cowell, F. (2013). The Death of the Southern African Development Community Tribunal's Human Right Jurisdiction. *Human Rights Law Review, 13*, 153–165.

Cuyvers, L., De Lombaerde, P., & Verherstraeten, S. (2005). *From AFTA Towards an ASEAN Economic Community ... and Beyond* (CAS Discussion Paper No 46).

Cuyvers, L., & Pupphavesa, W. (1996). *From ASEAN to AFTA* (CAS Discussion Paper No 6).

Dieter, H., & Higgott, R. (2003). Exploring Alternative Theories of Economic Regionalism: From Trade to Finance in Asian Co-operation? *Review of International Political Economy, 10*, 430–454.

Doctor, M. (2007). Why Bother with Inter-Regionalism? Negotiations for a European Union-Mercosur Agreement. *Journal of Common Market Studies, 45*, 281–314.

Draper, P., Alves, P., & Kalaba, M. (2006). *South Africa's International Trade Diplomacy: Implications for Regional Integration*. Gaborone: Friedrich Ebert Foundation.

Duina, F. (2006). *The Social Construction of Free Trade: The European Union, NAFTA, and MERCOSUR*. Princeton, NJ: Princeton University Press.

Fligstein, N., & Stone Sweet, A. (2002). Constructing Polities and Markets: An Institutionalist Account of European Integration. *American Journal of Sociology, 107*, 1206–1243.

Frennhoff Larsén, M. (2007). Trade Negotiations between the EU and South Africa: A Three-Level Game. *Journal of Common Market Studies, 45*, 857–881.

Garcia, M. (2013). From Idealism to Realism? EU Preferential Trade Agreement Policy. *Journal of Contemporary European Research, 9*, 521–541.

Gratius, S., & Gomes Saraiva, M. (2013). Continental Regionalism: Brazil's Prominent Role in the Americas. In M. Emerson & R. Flores (Eds.), *Enhancing the Brazil-EU Strategic Partnership: From the Bilateral and Regional to the Global* (pp. 218–237). Brussels: CEPS.

Grimes, W. W. (2011). The Asian Monetary Fund Reborn? Implications of Chiang Mai Initiative Multilateralization. *Asia Policy, 11*, 79–104.

Gstöhl, S. (2002). *Reluctant Europeans: Norway, Sweden, and Switzerland in the Process of Integration*. Boulder, CO: Lynne Rienner Publishers.
Haas, E. B. (1958). *The Uniting of Europe: Political, Social and Economic Forces, 1950-1957*. Stanford, CA: Stanford University Press.
Hänggi, H. (2003). Regionalism through Interregionalism: East Asia and ASEM. In F.-K. Liu & P. Regnier (Eds.), *Regionalism in East Asia: Paradigm Shifting?* (pp. 197–219). London: RoutledgeCurzon.
Hettne, B. (1999). Globalization and the New Regionalism: The Second Great Transformation. In B. Hettne, A. Inotai, & O. Sunkel (Eds.), *Globalism and the New Regionalism* (1st ed., pp. 1–24). Basingstoke: Palgrave Macmillan.
Hettne, B. (2005). Beyond the 'New' Regionalism. *New Political Economy, 10*, 543–571.
Hettne, B., & Söderbaum, F. (2000). Theorising the Rise of Regionness. *New Political Economy, 5*, 457–473.
Hout, W., & Meijerink, F. (1996). Structures in the International Political Economy: World System Theory and Unequal Development. *European Journal of International Relations, 2*, 47–76.
Kehoe, T. J. (2005). What Can We Learn from the Current Crisis in Argentina? *Scottish Journal of Political Economy, 50*, 609–633.
Kingdon, J. W. (1995). *Agendas, Alternatives, and Public Policies*. New York: Pearson.
Krapohl, S., Faude, B., & Dinkel, J. (2010). Judicial Integration in the Americas? A Comparison of Dispute Settlement in NAFTA and MERCOSUR. In F. Laursen (Ed.), *Comparative Regional Integration: Europe and Beyond* (pp. 169–192). Abingdon: Ashgate.
Kronberger, R. (2002). A Cost-Benefit Analysis of a Monetary Union for MERCOSUR with Particular Emphasis on the Optimum Currency Area Theory. *Integration and Trade, 6*, 29–93.
Krueger, A. O. (1997). Trade Policy and Economic Development: How We Learn. *American Economic Review, 87*, 1–22.
Lee, M. C. (2003). *The Political Economy of Regionalism in Southern Africa*. Lansdowne. Boulder, CO: Lynne Rienner Publishers.
Lenz, T. (2012). Spurred Emulation: The EU and Regional Integration in MERCOSUR and SADC. *West European Politics, 35*, 155–173.
Lindberg, L. N., & Scheingold, S. A. (1970). *Europe's Would-Be Polity: Patterns of Change in the European Community*. Englewood, CO: Prentice-Hall.
Lorenz, U. (2012). *Transformations on Whose Terms? Understanding the New EU-ACP Trade Relations from the Outside in* (KFG Workink Paper No. 40). Berlin.
Malamud, A. (2011). A Leader without Followers? The Growing Divergence between the Regional and Global Performance of Brazilian Foreign Policy. *Latin American Politics and Society, 53*, 1–24.

Malamud, A. (2013). *Overlapping Regionalism, No Integration: Conceptual Issues and the Latin American Experiences* (EUI Working Papers RSCAS 2013/20).
Malamud, A. (2015). Interdependence, Leadership and Institutionalization: The Triple Deficit and Fading Prospects of Mercosur. In S. Dosenrode (Ed.), *Limits to Regional Integration* (pp. 163–179). Farnham: Ashgate.
Moravcsik, A. (1991). Negotiating the Single European Act: National Interest and Conventional Statecraft in the European Community. *International Organization, 45*, 19–56.
Moravcsik, A. (1993). Preferences and Power in the European Community: A Liberal Intergovernmentalist Approach. *Journal of Common Market Studies, 31*, 473–524.
Moravcsik, A. (1998). *The Choice for Europe: Social Purpose and State Power from Messina to Maastricht.* Ithaca, NY: Cornell University Press.
Muntschick, J. (2013). Regionalismus und Externer Einfluss: Stört die Europäische Union die Regionale Marktintegration im südlichen Afrika? *Politische Vierteljahresschrift, 54*, 686–713.
Nunnenkamp, P. (1999). *Latin America after the Currency Crash in Brazil: Why the Optimists may be Wrong* (Kieler Diskussionsbeiträge 337).
Olympio, J., Robinson, P., & Cocks, M. (2006). The TDCA and SADC EPA: Is the Risk of Giving South Africa Duty-Free Access Alongside that Offered to the Rest of Southern African Countries Perceived or Real? In T. Bertelsmann-Scott & P. Draper (Eds.), *Regional Integration and Economic Partnership Agreements. Southern Africa at the Crossroads* (pp. 97–137). Johannesburg: South African Institute of International Affairs.
Pierson, P. (1996). The Path to European Political Integration: A Historical Institutionalist Analysis. *Comparative Political Studies, 29*, 123–163.
Pollack, M. A. (1997). Delegation, Agency and Agenda-Setting in the European Community. *International Organization, 51*, 99–134.
Pollack, M. A. (2003). *The Engines of European Integration: Delegation, Agency, and Agenda-Setting in the EU.* Oxford: Oxford University Press.
Preusse, H. G. (2004). *The New American Regionalism.* Cheltenham: Edward Elgar.
Przeworski, A., & Teune, H. (1970). *The Logic of Comparative Social Inquiry.* New York: Krieger Publishing.
Qualmann, R. (2003). South Africa's Reintegration into World and Regional Markets. Trade Liberalisation and Emerging Patterns of Specialisation in the Post-Apartheid Era (PhD Thesis, University of Leipzig).
Ragin, C. C. (1987). *The Comparative Method: Moving Beyond Qualitative and Quantitative Strategies.* Berkeley, CA: University of California Press.
Ravenhill, J. (1995). Economic Cooperation in Southeast Asia: Changing Incentives. *Asian Survey, 35*, 850–866.
Rüland, J. (2000). ASEAN and the Asian Crisis: Theoretical Implications and Practical Consequences for Southeast Asian Regionalism. *The Pacific Review, 13*, 421–451.

Saxton, J. (2003). *Argentina's Economic Crisis: Causes and Cures.* Washington: Joint Economic Committee United States Congress. www.hacer.org/pdf/Schuler.pdf.
Schirm, S. A. (2002). *Globalization and the New Regionalism: Global Markets, Domestic Politics and Regional Cooperation.* Cambridge: Polity Press.
Schmitter, P. C. (1970). A Revised Theory of Regional Integration. *International Organization, 24,* 836–868.
Smith, D. A., & White, D. R. (1992). Structure and Dynamics of the Global Economy: Network Analysis of International Trade 1965–1980. *Social Forces, 70,* 857–893.
Söderbaum, F., & Sbragia, A. (2011). EU Studies and the 'New Regionalism': What can be Gained from Dialogue? *Journal of European Integration, 32,* 563–582.
Stevens, C. (2008). Economic Partnership Agreements: What Can We Learn? *New Political Economy, 13,* 211–223.
Stone Sweet, A., & Caporaso, J. A. (1998). From Free Trade to Supranational Polity: The European Court and Integration. In W. Sandholtz & A. Stone Sweet (Eds.), *European Integration and Supranational Governance* (pp. 92–133). Oxford: Oxford University Press.
Tranholm-Mikkelsen, J. (1991). Neofunctionalism: Obstinate or Obsolete? A Reappraisal in the Light of the New Dynamism of the EC. *Millennium: Journal of International Studies, 20,* 1–22.
Tsebelis, G., & Garrett, G. (2001). The Institutional Foundations of Intergovernmentalism and Supranationalism in the European Union. *International Organization, 55,* 357–390.
Van Loon, A. (2015). From Interregionalism to Bilateralism: Power and Interests in EU-Brazil Trade Cooperation. In M. Rewizorski (Ed.), *The European Union and the BRICS: Complex Relations in the Era of Global Governance* (pp. 141–161). Cham: Springer.
Van Rossem, R. (1996). The World System Paradigm as General Theory of Development: A Cross-National Test. *American Sociological Review, 61,* 508–527.
Warleigh-Lack, A., & Rosamond, B. (2010). Across the EU-Studies-New Regionalism Frontier: Invitation to a Dialogue. *Journal of Common Market Studies, 48,* 993–1013.
Warleigh-Lack, A., & Van Langenhove, L. (2011). Rethinking EU Studies: The Contribution of Comparative Regionalism. *Journal of European Integration, 32,* 541–562.
Webber, D. (2001). Two Funerals and a Wedding? The Ups and Downs of Regionalism in East Asia and Asia-Pacific after the Asian Crisis. *The Pacific Review, 14,* 339–372.
Zangl, B. (2008). Judicialisation Matters! A Comparison of Dispute Settlement Under GATT and the WTO. *International Studies Quarterly, 52,* 825–854.

Index[1]

A
agenda setting, 41, 48, 82, 225
Argentina, 21, 22, 101, 103–5, 148–57, 159–71, 215, 219
Argentine crisis, 69, 105, 155
Asian crisis, 20, 21, 100, 115–17, 123–31, 139, 149, 161, 171n14, 215
Asia-Pacific Economic Cooperation (APEC), 126, 226–8
Association of South East Asian Nations (ASEAN)
 ASEAN+3, 20, 74, 101, 116, 117, 125, 127–34, 136, 138, 139, 141n12, 141n13, 215, 217, 220, 222, 228
 ASEAN Charter, 21, 74, 117, 131–9, 215
 ASEAN Economic Community (AEC), 117, 131–9, 215
 ASEAN Free Trade Area (AFTA), 20, 74, 117–24, 126, 129–31, 134, 137–9, 214–216, 219

ASEAN+1 trade agreements, 21, 129, 133, 139
ASEAN-way, 21, 115, 116, 131, 134

B
background condition, 3, 4, 6, 8, 9
Bangkok Declaration, 117, 134, 135
beggar-thy-neighbour, 22, 148, 158, 161
bilateral
 cooperation, 104
 trade agreement, 10, 16, 23, 44, 48, 54, 66, 129, 130, 166, 218, 229
BLNS countries, 184, 187
Brazil, 21, 22, 71, 72, 74, 93, 101, 103–5, 109, 116, 137, 147–71, 214–19, 228, 229

[1] Note: Page numbers with "n" denote notes.

C

case study
  case selection, 17–19, 63–84, 96
  in-case comparison, 64, 66, 74–5, 83
  most different cases, 18
  universe of cases, 65, 66
  unlikely cases, 18, 64, 66–70
causal mechanism, 75, 78–84, 92, 93, 95, 102, 108, 181
Chiang-Mai-Initiative, 20, 128, 215
Chiang-Mai-Initiative multilateralized, 128
China, 20, 21, 74, 101, 104, 116, 119, 125, 127–34, 136, 138–40, 157, 162, 163, 183, 186, 188, 191, 192, 215, 217, 220, 222, 231
CLMV countries, 119, 123, 129, 135, 136
Cold War, 10, 117, 118, 120, 124, 138
collective action, 39, 46
collective good
  club good, 34, 36–8
  common pool resource, 35, 37, 50
commitment, 5, 8, 9, 42, 43, 121, 123, 134–6, 152, 154, 168, 169, 219
Common Effective Preferential Tariff Scheme (CEPT scheme), 118, 122–4, 141n6, 141n7
common market, 5, 22, 105, 180, 190, 198, 219
Common Market for Eastern and Southern Africa (COMESA), 23, 196, 198, 227
comparability, 5, 17–19, 66, 70, 84n4
comparative cost advantage, 2, 14, 16, 33, 34, 36, 38, 51–3, 55, 57, 63, 67, 96, 99, 138, 181, 182, 189, 200
competition, 10, 14, 15, 38, 45, 46, 50, 67, 120, 121, 123, 125, 134, 138, 149, 164, 169, 170, 187, 188, 199
competitive advantage, 43, 48, 169
compliance, 16, 40, 50, 80, 82, 136
consumption
  (non-)excludability, 37, 44, 45
  (non-)rivalry, 37, 38
controlled comparison, 66, 70, 75, 83
cooperation problem
  battle of the sexes, 15, 34, 212
  prisoner's dilemma, 15, 34, 212
  Rambo constellation, 230
Cotonou Agreement, 193, 202n25, 228
customs union, 5, 24n4, 46, 48, 54, 66, 74, 96, 103, 105, 109n1, 116, 135, 137, 148–56, 169, 180, 184, 190–9, 215, 220

D

deadlocks, 48, 50, 57, 80
delegation, 5, 41, 48–50, 56, 154, 225
demand for regional integration, 17, 34, 51–4, 57
dependency, 185, 213, 224
  theory, 52, 120
devaluation, 74, 125, 149, 155, 158–62, 164, 166, 169–71, 217, 219
developing
  country, 1, 4, 9, 12, 16, 42, 51, 52, 57, 63, 67, 125, 156, 158, 187, 196, 202n24, 211, 213, 230, 231
  region, 1–4, 9–13, 16–18, 42, 50–8, 63–84, 92, 96, 104, 108, 131, 139, 140, 190, 200, 212, 214, 216, 217, 220–31
  world, 1–3, 9, 12, 13, 18, 20, 21, 50, 51, 64, 66–71, 83, 103, 120, 220, 224
development strategy, 11, 12, 16, 42, 52, 57, 63, 67, 68, 101, 102, 124, 149, 216

dispute settlement, 15, 39–41, 49, 50, 56, 82, 134, 136, 137, 148, 164, 167, 217, 224–6
dominant strategy, 16, 17, 35, 47, 48, 55, 64, 107, 217

E
East African Community (EAC), 23, 196, 227
economic
 asymmetry, 19, 80, 83, 95, 104, 105, 107–9, 148, 149, 163, 169, 170
 attractiveness, 44, 120
 development, 5, 17, 20, 51, 52, 56, 69, 116, 120, 134, 140n1 155, 215, 223, 228, 230
 growth, 12, 67, 132, 133, 154, 158, 230
 privileges, 75, 93, 195, 214, 217, 226, 230
 structure, 19, 21, 23, 64, 65, 75, 76, 80, 81, 83, 84, 91–110, 156, 191, 192, 219
Economic Partnership Agreement (EPA), 12, 129, 190–200, 218, 228
SADC EPA, 196–8, 200, 219
economies of scale, 2, 11, 14, 16, 33, 34, 36, 38, 51–3, 55, 57, 63, 67, 96, 99, 138, 200, 212
emerging market, 9, 21, 22, 51, 52, 57, 63, 67, 104, 159, 230
enlargement, 71, 167, 168
Europe, 2–9, 12, 51, 53, 68, 92, 96, 108, 118, 120, 121, 137, 180–2, 190, 194, 195, 200, 211–13, 221, 227, 230, 231
European Community (EC), 6, 91–110, 202n18, 202n21
European Single Market, 12, 23
European Union (EU), 2–4, 6–9, 12, 20–3, 24n2 34–6, 65, 91–110, 149, 180, 183
EU studies, 2–4, 70

exchange rate, 4, 14, 125, 154, 155, 158, 159
 fixed, 158, 161
export
 extra-regional, 12, 16, 43, 44, 53, 57, 82, 126, 182, 192–4, 212
 intraregional, 124, 151, 160, 189
 promotion, 11, 118, 121, 211, 230
external
 tariff, 46, 135–7, 153
 trade regime, 48, 54, 130, 135, 186, 188–90, 192–4, 198, 199, 218, 219
extra-regional
 actor, 2, 11, 13, 15, 16, 19–21, 35, 42, 44–8, 50, 51, 54, 57, 58, 64, 77, 80, 82, 95, 96, 120, 124, 133, 137–40, 148, 152, 153, 155, 156, 163, 180, 182, 185, 188, 191, 199, 212, 214, 220, 222, 227, 228, 230
 agreement, 47, 48, 185, 229
 cooperation, 20, 21, 74, 115–42, 215, 217, 222
 economic partner, 2, 78, 132, 223
 influence, 18, 44, 74, 148, 212, 220, 231
 interests, 21–3, 53, 56, 58, 69, 81, 107, 116, 138, 148, 151, 169, 189, 191, 193–5, 197, 200, 212, 214–16, 218, 220–2, 231
 investment, 11, 12, 14–16, 20, 21, 34, 35, 37, 42–6, 48, 50, 51, 53, 54, 56, 57, 63, 67, 78, 80–3, 117–21, 124, 151, 156, 169, 170, 181,182, 189, 214–16, 223, 227
 privilege, 17, 19, 20, 22, 48, 50, 55, 58, 64, 65, 75, 76, 78, 80–3, 120, 148, 194, 197, 212, 217, 225, 229
 trade, 19–23, 77, 78, 80, 94–6, 99, 101, 103–8, 124, 132, 134, 148–52, 155, 157, 158, 162, 169, 179–203

F
foreign direct investment (FDI), 93, 94, 124, 155, 157, 158, 160, 163, 181, 184, 189
France, 93, 98
free riding, 38, 39, 46
free trade area, 5, 22, 46, 66, 102, 109n1, 116, 122–4, 129, 180, 185, 186, 189, 198, 199, 228

G
Germany, 93, 98
globalisation, 10, 42, 180, 230
global market, 1, 2, 11, 14, 17, 34, 42, 43, 53, 54, 56, 57, 63, 67, 81, 82, 118, 120, 132, 139, 147, 149, 151, 156, 181, 187, 199, 216, 222, 229
Global South, 3, 116, 120, 182, 213, 214, 220, 221, 223–30
Gross Domestic Product (GDP), 18, 67, 69, 124, 151, 155,184

H
hegemon
  benevolent, 34, 35, 55, 72, 197
  regional, 17, 34, 55, 72, 98, 107, 109, 197
hub-and-spoke, 106, 184, 192
hypothesis, 54, 55, 71–3, 139, 140, 169, 170, 199, 200, 214, 216–18

I
implementation, 43, 47, 49, 57, 80, 82, 96, 105, 116, 123, 124, 131, 134, 136–8, 154, 159, 189, 190, 195, 197, 214, 216, 218, 225–7
import substitution, 11, 52, 67, 118, 120, 181, 230

incomplete contracting, 40
Indonesia, 20, 72, 93, 99, 100, 117, 119–21, 124, 126, 132, 133, 135, 140, 140n1, 214, 217
institution
  intergovernmental, 4, 8, 34, 35, 136
  regional, 4, 8–10, 13, 15, 16, 34, 36, 41–3, 48, 49, 51, 54, 57, 58, 78, 82, 116, 134–6, 213, 219, 221, 223–6
  supranational, 4, 5, 8, 9, 70, 136, 137, 154, 221, 223, 225
integration theory
  institutionalism, 34
  (liberal) intergovernmentalism, 2, 7, 8, 34, 35, 91
  neofunctionalism, 2, 6–9, 34, 35, 91
interest group, 7, 91
International Monetary Fund (IMF), 121, 125–8, 161
interpresidentialism, 49, 150
interregional
  negotiation, 12, 43, 53, 82, 130, 151, 152, 165, 166, 170, 173n48 193, 196, 212, 224, 228
  trade agreement, 21, 228, 229
interregionalism, 12, 228–9
intraregional
  economic interdependence, 2, 6–9, 12, 13, 18, 34, 35, 53, 63, 75, 76, 80, 91, 92, 99, 103, 105, 133, 150, 151, 153, 155, 185, 191, 192, 222, 223
  investment, 2, 5, 171, 184, 213, 220
  trade, 2, 5, 7, 9, 10, 12–16, 18–22, 24n3, 33–41, 44, 50–3, 55–7, 65, 69, 75, 76, 78, 81, 84, 84n4, 91, 92, 94–108, 117–19, 121–4, 126, 129, 131, 134, 138, 139, 141n10, 150–2, 156, 162, 181, 182, 186, 188–92, 199, 200, 201n9, 212, 215, 216, 221, 223, 224, 227, 229

trade share, 69, 150, 155, 156, 162, 189
investment
  extra-regional, 11, 12, 14–16, 20, 21, 34, 35, 37, 42–6, 48, 50, 51, 53, 54, 56, 57, 63, 67, 78, 80–3, 117–21, 124, 151, 156, 169, 170, 181, 182, 189, 214–16, 223, 227
  flow, 47, 170, 184
  intraregional, 171, 184, 213, 220
issue linkage, 15, 16, 54, 64, 82
iterated game, 36

J
Japan, 20, 21, 74, 99, 101, 103, 104, 116, 119, 124, 125, 127–34, 136, 139, 140, 147, 150, 183, 191, 192, 215, 217, 220, 222, 231

L
legalisation, 40, 49, 50
level of analysis
  macro, 75
  micro, 84
liberalisation, 7, 9–11, 14–16, 34, 36–9, 76, 121–3, 134, 181, 185, 187, 188, 194–7, 212, 214–16, 224, 225, 227
logic of regional integration
  extra-regional, 2, 18, 42–50, 63, 64, 67, 68, 71, 83, 170, 212, 213, 220, 222–4, 226, 227, 229
  intraregional, 35–41, 50, 212, 213, 222–4

M
macroeconomic stability, 14, 42
majority vote, 41, 136, 225

Malaysia, 20, 72, 93, 99–101, 117, 119–21, 124, 126, 130, 132, 133, 140, 140n1, 217
market access, 12, 14, 34, 44–7, 54, 55, 66, 82, 133, 139, 193, 230
member state, 211–30
Mercado Común del Sur (Common Market of South America, MERCOSUR), 2, 4–9, 11–23, 24n4, 33–5, 37–57, 64, 66–73, 75–8, 80–3, 84n4, 92–9, 101–9, 110n3, 115–39, 140n1, 148–59, 162–70, 179–200, 202n21, 202n24, 96
MERCOSUR Customs Union (MERCOSUR-CU), 74, 149, 215
monitoring bodies, 39, 40

N
Nash equilibrium, 39–41
negative externalities, 6, 7, 35, 127
negotiations, 8, 10–12, 14, 22, 23, 34, 35, 42–4, 49, 53, 81, 82, 117, 123, 130, 134, 136, 139, 151–3, 162, 164–7, 170, 173n48, 185–8, 190, 193–200, 212, 216, 218, 219, 224, 226–30
network
  analysis, 19, 20, 23, 65, 75–8, 80, 84, 91–110
  graph, 94–7, 104, 109
non-tariff trade barrier, 14, 52, 134, 166
North America, 2, 9, 119, 121, 211, 213, 230
Northeast Asia, 2, 9, 20, 21, 118, 125, 126, 129, 139, 211, 213, 215

O
observable implications, 74, 80–2, 84, 108

open policy window, 213
overlapping regionalism, 165, 226–8

P
package deal, 15, 16, 41, 48–50, 54, 56, 57, 64, 82, 225, 230
Pareto
  efficient, 39, 41
  inferior, 39
  superior, 15
path dependency, 213, 224
periphery, 95, 98
process tracing, 19, 65, 75, 78–84
protectionism, 15, 39, 117, 118
Protocol on Trade, 180, 186–9

R
Rambo
  behaviour, 21, 22, 81, 82, 93, 101, 166, 171
  situation, 16, 20, 46–51, 55, 57, 64, 80, 82, 92, 93, 104, 105, 107–9, 120, 148, 225
region
  developing, 1–4, 9–13, 16–18, 42, 50–8, 63–84, 92, 96, 104, 108, 131, 139, 140, 190, 200, 212, 214, 216, 217, 220–31
  well-developed, 2, 8, 9, 13, 16, 17, 23, 51–3, 55–7, 82, 83, 92, 99, 118, 182, 212, 221, 230
regional
  cooperation, 1, 3–8, 11, 13–17, 19–23, 35, 37, 39, 46, 48, 50, 51, 53–8, 64, 68, 74–5, 78–84, 105, 107, 115–42, 148, 151–6, 159, 162, 167, 169, 180, 181, 185, 189, 197, 199, 200, 211–31
  defection, 17, 35, 46, 47, 54, 55, 57, 74, 80, 82, 104

institution, 4, 8–10, 13, 15, 16, 34, 36, 41–3, 48, 49, 51, 54, 57, 58, 78, 82, 116, 134–6, 213, 219, 221, 223–6
institution-building, 9, 10, 13, 36, 51
integration, 2–8, 10–18, 21–4, 33–58, 63–4, 67–74, 76–8, 80–3, 91–7, 99, 102–8, 115–40, 147–71, 180, 181, 185, 188, 190, 191, 193, 197–200, 211–15, 217–24, 226–31
leadership, 17, 21, 55, 56, 58, 58n2, 128, 154, 161, 164, 169, 187, 194, 197, 199, 200, 212, 215–19
liquidity arrangement, 20, 116
market, 2, 7, 9, 11, 14–16, 22, 33, 34, 36–8, 40, 42, 43, 46, 53, 56, 63, 76, 78, 123, 124, 134, 151, 153, 156, 157, 159, 169, 180, 181, 184–6, 188–90, 212, 216, 222, 223
member state, 5, 11, 14, 15, 33–5, 42, 46–8, 54, 57, 64, 69, 75, 77, 78, 80, 82, 84n4, 95, 101, 104, 108, 109, 124, 200, 212, 216, 221, 227
neighbour, 14, 17, 21, 39, 48, 52, 54, 57, 67, 76, 82, 147, 148, 151, 152, 158, 159, 161, 164, 166, 189, 196, 199, 214, 215, 219
norms, 9, 40, 218
organisation, 1, 4–7, 11, 13, 15, 17, 18, 20, 21, 23, 34, 37, 38, 40, 41, 43–6, 48, 50, 55, 56, 64–74, 76, 78, 83, 92–4, 96, 102–5, 108, 109, 110n3, 115–17, 119, 123, 125, 126, 130, 131, 136–8, 183, 195, 198, 213, 219, 223, 224, 226, 227, 229, 231

power, 64, 65, 71, 72, 75–8, 80–4, 93, 101, 102, 107, 116, 119, 120, 127, 128, 130–3, 136, 137, 139, 140, 147, 148, 150–3, 157–9, 161, 162, 165, 166, 169, 170, 180, 182, 184–9, 191, 192, 194, 196, 197, 199, 200, 212, 214–19, 222, 231
Rambo, 16, 17, 19, 35, 49, 55–8, 64, 81–3, 107, 108, 156–61, 167, 170, 171, 197, 200, 212, 217, 225, 226, 229, 230
trade agreement, 10–12, 21, 66, 68, 84n1
trade network, 77, 81–3, 95, 104, 107, 108, 129, 147, 179
Regional Indicative Strategic Development Plan (RISDP), 180, 190, 198
regionalism
 comparative, 2–4, 65, 70, 92, 109, 221
 new, 1–24, 34, 42, 45, 50, 53, 66–8, 70, 78, 96, 117, 118, 120–2, 124, 138, 179, 180, 211, 215, 216, 224–9
 old, 11, 42, 67, 180
 open, 11, 67, 121, 149, 181, 186, 190
regulatory standard, 7, 15, 40
relational data, 77, 78, 93
research
 design, 23, 75, 96
 method, 63–84
rules of origin, 46, 186–8, 199, 216

S
sanction, 15, 16, 45, 47, 49, 50
security community, 99, 117
selection bias, 75
side payment, 48–50, 57, 64, 80, 82, 169, 225, 230

Singapore, 20, 67, 72, 93, 99–101, 117–22, 125, 130, 132, 133, 136, 140, 213, 214, 217
size and stability effect, 2, 14, 16, 43, 51–3, 57, 63, 78, 82, 120, 193
South Africa, 22, 23, 24n4, 71, 72, 77, 93, 105–9, 116, 137, 179–89, 191–4, 196, 197, 199, 200, 201n1, 201n15, 214, 216, 218, 219, 222, 229
South America, 1, 7, 68, 73, 93, 103–5, 116, 147–73, 211, 215–18, 220, 226
Southeast Asia, 20, 73, 99, 115, 116, 119–25, 128, 132, 134–6, 138–40, 215–17, 219
Southern Africa, 22, 73, 116, 180–4, 188–91, 194, 196, 199, 200, 216, 219, 220
Southern African Customs Union (SACU), 24n4, 109n1, 184, 187, 188, 197, 198, 201n15
Southern African Development Community (SADC)
 SADC Customs Union (SADC-CU), 22, 23, 24n4, 74, 180, 181, 190–200, 201n15 218, 219
 SADC Free Trade Area (SADC FTA), 22, 74, 105, 109n1, 180–94, 198–200, 216, 218, 222
Southern African Development Coordination Conference (SADCC), 105, 180, 181
spaghetti bowl, 10, 129, 198, 231
spillover, 6, 7, 9, 13, 35, 91, 220, 222, 223
stylised fact, 65, 76, 84, 92
supply of regional integration, 34, 51, 54–7
swap agreement, 20, 117, 126, 128, 140n3

T

tariff, 4, 14, 37, 40, 42, 46, 52, 67, 99, 118, 120, 122–4, 134–7, 153, 161, 181, 185–7, 194, 202n23 229

Thailand, 20, 72, 93, 99, 117, 119–21, 124–6, 128, 130, 132, 133, 135, 140, 140n1 183, 217

tit-for-tat, 39, 41, 47, 49, 56, 225

trade
- agreement, 10–12, 16, 21, 23, 44, 48, 54, 66–8, 84n1, 116, 117, 129, 130, 133, 139, 140, 151, 165, 166, 195, 198, 215, 218, 228, 229
- creation, 10
- data, 19, 65, 76–8, 93, 94, 183, 184, 192
- diversion, 10, 11
- flow, 21, 55, 80, 81, 93, 94, 126, 181, 183, 191
- negotiation, 10–12, 14, 34, 42–4, 53, 82, 123, 151, 165, 166, 170, 186–8, 193, 212, 216, 224, 227–30
- network, 19–22, 75, 77, 78, 80–3, 91–110, 119, 129, 132, 147, 179, 182, 184, 191, 217
- pattern, 65, 75–8, 84, 92, 93, 95, 96, 99, 100, 102, 105, 184

Trade, Development and Cooperation Agreement (TDCA), 23, 194, 196–8, 200, 218, 219, 228

Tripartite Free Trade Area (TFTA), 23, 198

U

unanimity, 7, 41, 136, 150, 154, 225

UN ComTrade database, 78, 94, 119, 132, 150, 157, 163, 183, 192

unilateral action, 65, 83, 169

Union of South American Nations (UNASUR), 148, 162, 165–7, 169, 170, 218, 226, 227

United Kingdom (UK), 93, 95

USA, 20, 96, 99, 101, 103, 104, 183

V

variable
- dependent, 51, 64, 66, 71, 74, 75
- independent, 65, 66, 70, 71, 75–7, 83, 220, 221

visone, 94

visualisation, 77, 94, 95

W

Washington Consensus, 127, 149

win-set, 133–5, 229

world region, 2–9, 11–14, 18, 19, 24n2, 34–6, 43–5, 48, 52, 53, 55–7, 63, 65, 70, 77, 109, 121, 127, 138, 213, 214, 221, 224, 226, 231

World Trade Organization (WTO), 10–12, 66, 68, 84n1, 134, 136, 164, 167, 186

GPSR Compliance
The European Union's (EU) General Product Safety Regulation (GPSR) is a set of rules that requires consumer products to be safe and our obligations to ensure this.

If you have any concerns about our products, you can contact us on

ProductSafety@springernature.com

In case Publisher is established outside the EU, the EU authorized representative is:

Springer Nature Customer Service Center GmbH
Europaplatz 3
69115 Heidelberg, Germany

www.ingramcontent.com/pod-product-compliance
Lightning Source LLC
LaVergne TN
LVHW020343260326
834688LV00045B/1505